The VP Advantage

MANCHESTER
1824

Manchester University Press

The VP Advantage

How running mates influence home state voting in presidential elections

Christopher J. Devine and Kyle C. Kopko

Manchester University Press

Published by Manchester University Press
Altrincham Street, Manchester M1 7JA
www.manchesteruniversitypress.co.uk

British Library Cataloguing-in-Publication Data
A catalogue record for this book is available from the British Library

Library of Congress Cataloging-in-Publication Data applied for

ISBN 978 1 7849 9337 5 hardback
ISBN 978 1 7849 9338 2 paperback

First published 2016

Typeset by Out of House Publishing
Printed in Great Britain by CPI Group (UK) Ltd, Croydon, CR0 4YY

To our running mates –
Trudy, Hayes David, and Miles Wilson Devine
CJD
Sarah and Mary Elizabeth Kopko
KCK

Contents

Figures

Tables

Acknowledgments

Many individuals deserve recognition for their help in bringing this book to the point of publication. First, we sincerely thank our families and our colleagues at Mount Vernon Nazarene University and Elizabethtown College, without whom this project would have been impossible. For their feedback on our early work on this topic, we thank Lawrence Baum, Jeffrey Budziak, Steven Nawara, and Herbert Weisberg. For their assistance in securing permissions to reprint online materials in this book, we thank Kyle Kondik of *Sabato's Crystal Ball*, Sarah Latimore of *Slate*, and the staff of *Presidential Studies Quarterly*. For their assistance in obtaining research material from presidential archives, we thank the staffs of the John F. Kennedy Presidential Library and Museum and the Lyndon B. Johnson Presidential Library. Finally, for their insight and professionalism in preparing this work for publication, we thank Matthew Koppel, Michelle Chen, Frances Pinter, Tony Mason, and the Manchester University Press staff.

Preface

Media speculation about the 2012 Republican "veepstakes" was already intense when on April 25 of that year the *Wall Street Journal* published an op-ed by Karl Rove – formerly the senior adviser to governor, presidential candidate, and two-term president, George W. Bush – provocatively titled: "I was wrong about Dick Cheney … and other lessons I learned from vetting vice presidential candidates."[1]

For a man known by admirers as "The Architect" of Bush's presidential victories, and by detractors as "Bush's Brain," the headline suggested a startling admission – that Rove regretted Bush's selection of Cheney for the Republican ticket in 2000, and that Rove was now publicly seeking absolution for this mistake. It was perhaps this impression that caused Rove's op-ed to attract enormous media and public attention in the immediate wake of its publication. "I can't tell you how many comments I got about the column," Rove noted two weeks later. "It was the most read piece in the *Wall Street Journal* that day and number one on Realclearpolitics.com for most of the week."[2] To the surprise (and perhaps disappointment) of many readers, though, Rove's op-ed turned out not to be a renunciation of Cheney's selection. It was, instead, a repudiation of his initial, electorally driven *opposition* to picking Cheney. George W. Bush made the right choice, Rove concluded; "Bush's Brain" got it wrong.

Cheney was, in fact, a surprising choice in 2000 – if only because he was the man Bush had actually tapped to *lead* his search for a vice presidential candidate. As that search neared completion, though, Bush found himself increasingly leaning toward selecting Cheney. Rove was uneasy with the idea and Bush, recognizing this, invited him to lay out in full detail the case against making the selection. The two arranged a meeting, and when Rove arrived, he was surprised to discover a second member in the audience: Dick Cheney – "sitting mute and expressionless, next to the governor." Undeterred, Rove presented eight "political objections" to Cheney's selection – that is, eight reasons why Cheney would not help, and might even hurt, Bush's chances of winning the presidency. One of the most significant objections was a matter of simple geography and math: "Cheney's presence on the ticket would add nothing to the electoral map, since Wyoming's three electoral votes were among the most reliably Republican in the country."

"The next day," Rove recalls, "Mr. Bush called to say I was right" about the political disadvantages of selecting Cheney – but that Bush was naming Cheney to the ticket anyway. Rove, not surprisingly, thought his candidate was making a big mistake. But a decade later, as detailed in his op-ed, Karl Rove's perspective had changed; he no longer considered the Cheney selection a mistake, and to that year's Republican nominee he offered this advice on choosing a running mate: "Choose the best person for the job [of vice president]. Leave the politics to the staff."

What caused Karl Rove to change his mind by 2012? Two factors, according to the op-ed, were decisive: experience and scientific research. In regard to the former, he believed that Cheney had served capably as vice president during his eight years in office and in doing so had fulfilled his primary function better than a more politically advantageous running mate might have done. Quite simply, "The country was better served by Mr. Bush's decision than by my advice." In regard to the latter, Rove cited political science research calling into question the electoral significance of vice presidential candidates. The first example was an article by Bernard Grofman and Reuben Kline (2010) measuring the net electoral impact of vice presidential candidates in 2008. The second example was an article of ours measuring vice presidential home state advantages across the 1884–2008 presidential elections (Devine and Kopko 2011). The evidence from both articles indicated that vice presidential candidates have a minimal effect on vote choice in presidential elections – far less than what conventional wisdom, and sometimes leading political strategists, might suggest.

The Rove op-ed is revealing in two respects that highlight major themes of this book. First, it attests to the enduring perception of a vice presidential home state advantage in American politics – a perception recognizable among citizens, journalists, historians, political elites, and even presidential candidates, and one that persists despite dramatic changes in presidential politics and contradictory impulses among those who express it. Indeed, as we demonstrate in this book, these actors' perception of a vice presidential home state advantage is more pronounced and consequential than most of them seem to realize, and often quite disconnected from their expressed conclusions and conscious knowledge about the subject. A major objective of this book is to document the pervasive perception of a vice presidential home state advantage, as well as its potential to influence the vice presidential selection process and campaign strategy more broadly.

Second, Rove's conversion on the electoral significance of vice presidential candidates – and the wisdom of picking Dick Cheney, specifically – powerfully illustrates the importance of exposing one's perceptions and experiences to scientific testing, and being open to unexpected results. We speak from experience in describing that process. Our research on this topic began unconsciously with the transmitted notion that geography *is* relevant to vice presidential selection and performance, and then consciously with a veepstakes-inspired conversation in the summer of 2008 that raised the question of whether, and how well, that notion had been subjected to scientific scrutiny. Valuable contributions – including, but not limited to, our own – have been made toward that end; but, in our judgment, they are not enough. Our central aim in this book is to provide a definitive analysis of the vice presidential home state advantage, comprehensive in its scope and sophisticated in its methodology, that will inform the perspectives of those who wish to know what the scientific evidence has to say about this topic and how any knowledge gained might be applied to improving public discourse and political decision-making in regard to the vice presidential selection process.

Our conclusion, based upon the research presented in this book, can be summarized as follows: there is so little chance of a vice presidential home state advantage making a meaningful electoral difference that presidential candidates are far wiser, and more responsible to their constituents, to discount such strategic considerations and – in Karl Rove's words – simply "Choose the best person for the job [of vice president]."

Notes

1 See: www.wsj.com/articles/SB10001424052702304811304577365870484193362. Accessed February 23, 2015.

2 Personal correspondence with the authors, May 7, 2012.

1

Origins and evolution of the vice presidential home state advantage

After being elected the first vice president of the United States, John Adams embarked upon a week-long journey from his home in Braintree, Massachusetts, to the nation's then-capital, New York City, on the picturesque spring day of April 13, 1789. The 54-year old Adams, who had contributed so greatly to the government of his state and the birth of a new nation, was treated to a "hero's send-off" by the people of his state and his region – punctuated by cannon salutes, municipal awards, and the gift of a locally manufactured brown broadcloth inaugural suit – as he traveled ceremoniously with a parade of cavalrymen and a forty-carriage caravan along the southwestern route. His neighbors' celebratory spirit bespoke pride and confidence not only in Adams and his achievements, but also in the knowledge that a leader from their own stock would now hold the second-highest office in the nation's new system of government. And so, "All through Massachusetts and Connecticut people lined the road to cheer Adams as one of their own, a New England man" (McCullough 2001, 394).

While surely gratified by such celebrations – he did, after all, have a reputation for inordinate vanity – Adams was considerably less enthusiastic than his fellow New Englanders about the vice presidency. "My country," he famously lamented, "has in its wisdom contrived for me the most insignificant office that ever the invention of man contrived or his imagination conceived."[1] Indeed, by measure of actual power, it was a rather hollow office. The United States Constitution, ratified by the requisite three-quarters of states the previous summer, invested the vice presidency with minimal formal duties. First, as "President of the Senate," he would cast a vote in the rare event of a tie among senators (Article II, Section 3),[2] and every four years he would open certificates containing the votes of the various states in the Electoral College (Article II, Section 1). Second, and most significantly, he would "exercise the Office of President of the United States" (Article II, Section 3) under conditions not specified in the Constitution until ratification of the Twenty-fifth Amendment in 1967[3] – but understood, at least in subsequent practice, to encompass presidential death or incapacity. The first set of duties demanded little of the vice president, while the second – invoked on eight occasions[4] to date, and not for the first time until 1841 – constituted his most significant governmental function. It was with the latter duty in mind that Adams most aptly described the nation's second office: "I am vice president. In this I am nothing, but I may be everything" (Milkis and Nelson 2011, 486).

Historical perspective

Whereas the president's power expanded – through evolving constitutional interpretation and executive assertion – from the Washington Administration to Franklin Roosevelt's establishment of "The Modern Presidency," the vice president's power(lessness) remained static and comically underwhelming until the mid- to late-twentieth century. In the meantime, its reputation as a dead-end job for politicians whose only prospect of relevance lay in presidential mortality made the vice presidency the butt of endless jokes – and not least among individuals who actually held the office. Most famous is the story of two brothers, variously attributed to Vice Presidents Thomas Marshall, Alben Barkley, and Hubert Humphrey[5]: "One became a sailor and went to sea; the other became vice president of the United States. Neither has been heard from since." The vice president, Marshall once mused, is like "a man in a cataleptic fit; he cannot speak; he cannot move; he suffers no pain; he is perfectly conscious of all that goes on, but has no part in it" (Milkis and Nelson 2011, 486); his chief activity was "to ring the White House bell every morning and ask what is the state of health of the president" (Milkis and Nelson 2011, 487). After being selected as Franklin Roosevelt's running mate in 1944, Harry Truman gave a similar, and ultimately ironic, assessment: "The Vice President simply presides over the Senate and sits around hoping for a funeral" (McCullough 1992, 298–299). Death, in fact, has been a recurring theme of vice presidential jokes. When Daniel Webster was offered the Whig Party's vice presidential nomination in 1848, he declined, explaining: "I do not propose to be buried until I am dead" (Milkis and Nelson 2011, 490).

Even in recent years, despite more than a half-century of expanding vice presidential power, the vice presidency is often described in similar terms. When asked about the possibility of becoming George W. Bush's running mate in 2000, John McCain scoffed: "The vice president has two duties. One is to enquire daily as to the health of the president, and the other is to attend the funerals of third world dictators. And neither of those do I find an enjoyable exercise."[6] Even Walter Mondale, who is widely credited with accelerating the expansion of vice presidential power while serving under Jimmy Carter, refused to be considered for the Democratic ticket in 1972 because, he said: "There is no way on earth people can take the vice president of the United States seriously."[7]

The well-known limitations of the office had a profound effect on vice presidential selection, from the earliest years of the republic. In short, the realization that vice presidents would play no consequential role in governing reduced the calculus for selecting a vice presidential candidate to one almost strictly based upon electoral considerations. A vice presidential candidate could appeal to the national electorate, as well as state and regional electorates, on any number of characteristics including experience, vocation, religion, ideology, and so forth. Yet, without doubt, geography was the most important consideration. Whether justified by a sense of shared identity, common interest, or the prospects of energizing state and local party machines, a perception emerged immediately and quite universally that vice presidential candidates' most effective service was to persuade their "friends and neighbors," through reputation or activity, to support the presidential ticket. Voters, it was assumed, would be more responsive to an appeal from "one of our own."[8] And so, by the early nineteenth century, "the parties had already begun to degrade the vice presidency into a device for geographically balancing the ticket in the election" (Milkis and Nelson 2011, 490). Even a century-and-a-half later, "Ticket balancing to unite the party and increase its appeal on election day continued to dominate the selection of vice-presidential candidates" (Milkis and Nelson 2011, 496).

The early republic

A review of vice presidential selections throughout history is instructive in demonstrating the significant, and in some cases seemingly determinative, role of geographic considerations. Even in the first presidential election of 1789, geography appears to have been a predominant factor: "Because Washington, a Virginian, was certain to become President, it was widely agreed that the vice presidency should go to a northerner, and Adams was the leading choice" (McCullough 2001, 392). Washington, who meddled little in the electoral process and did not have the responsibility of choosing a running mate, nonetheless acknowledged this reality. According to a biographer, "Washington remained studiously neutral" about a potential vice president, "saying only that he would probably come from the powerful state of Massachusetts" (Chernow 2010, 551).

Regional balance continued to be a major factor in subsequent vice presidential selections, according to historians. In 1800, with Virginia's Thomas Jefferson heading the Democratic-Republican ticket, a common assumption about the running mate was that "It would have to be a New Yorker, for regional balance." The only "serious question," according to Congressman Albert Gallatin, was which New Yorker it would be – "[Governor George] Clinton or [Senator Aaron] Burr" (Isenberg 2007, 201). Likewise, in 1804, "The selection of Governor George Clinton of New York [to run alongside Jefferson] … seemed a good maneuver, maintaining a North-South balance" (Ketcham 2000, 433). And in 1812 "[Virginia's James] Madison was glad to have on the ticket a famous patriot able to draw Northern votes," in Massachusetts's Elbridge Gerry (Ketcham 2000, 523).

Broad geographic considerations (e.g., North-South balance) in time gave way to the targeting of a specific battleground state through vice presidential selection. Supreme Court Justice John Catron, writing to fellow Tennessean Andrew Jackson in 1840 to argue for James Polk's selection as Martin Van Buren's Democratic running mate, explained: "Our state follows men … and to a certainty can only be carried by means of a local candidate" (Cole 2004, 357). Four years later, Polk himself made a similar argument to Van Buren, the man he presumed would be the nominee once more in 1844. "The implied message" of his letter to that effect, says biographer Walter R. Borneman (2009, 65), "was that Polk was still the vice presidential candidate Van Buren needed on his ticket if the Democrats were to capture Tennessee's electoral votes." After Polk, the "dark horse" candidate, instead won the presidential nomination at that year's Democratic Convention, some delegates urged their party brethren to target other key states with the vice presidential nomination. "Benjamin Butler suggested that in the interest of harmony – as well as strong Democratic turnout in New York state – the nomination should be offered to Silas Wright," a US senator from New York (Borneman 2009, 106). Wright declined the nomination, which then was offered to and accepted by the former senator from Pennsylvania, George M. Dallas. This seemed to be a good fit; "Dallas proved acceptable to both factions [of the Democratic Party], and Pennsylvania promised to be a proper geographic balance with Tennessee" (Borneman 2009, 107).

The emergent opposition party, the Whigs, followed suit. Part and parcel with its efforts in each election to balance the delicate North-South cleavage that would eventually ruin the party, Whigs targeted key states outside the presidential candidate's region through vice presidential selection. In 1852, for instance, Whigs chose former North Carolina Senator William A. Graham as the running mate for Pennsylvania's General Winfield Scott because, in contrast to a leading rival from Maryland, "Graham hailed from a state with ten, not just eight, electoral votes" that year; thus, "shoring up North Carolina seemed the top priority." Immediately after Graham's nomination, a delegate from that state declared the ticket now certain to carry North Carolina by at least 10,000 votes (Holt 1999, 724).

The Republican Party, which soon replaced the Whigs as chief rival to the Democratic Party, was sensitive to geographic concerns as well. Recognizing their limited appeal to southern states (aside from substantial successes in the Reconstruction era, made possible by suffrage limitations that stifled latent Democratic dominance), Republicans focused on balancing the party's eastern and western power bases while also targeting key electoral states. In 1860 the Republicans ran Hannibal Hamlin for vice president, a "nomination [that] balanced Lincoln, a former Whig from the West, with a former Democrat from the East" (White 2009, 331). Hamlin's candidacy was, reportedly, intended not only to provide East-West balance but also to enhance the party's performance in Maine. Because it held elections for Congress and state offices in September, Maine was "considered the 'finger-board' of victory or defeat in that presidential canvass" – with the assumption that a strong performance in the early elections would generate momentum for the presidential vote in November (Waugh 2001, 197).

Post-Reconstruction

Never did the targeting of key electoral states influence vice presidential (or, for that matter, presidential) selection more than in the post-Reconstruction era, when the combination of a solid Democratic South and a Republican-leaning North and West narrowed the electoral map to a small set of states from which both parties sought desperately to extract any conceivable advantage – most conveniently, by selecting a presidential or vice presidential candidate from one of those states. Between the elections of 1876 and 1920, in fact, seventeen of twenty-four major party presidential candidates and seventeen of twenty-four vice presidential candidates (70.8% in each case) came from *only three states*, which also happened to be the most significant electoral battlegrounds in the United States: New York, Ohio, and Indiana.

Historical accounts attest to the primacy of home state considerations in this period of vice presidential selection (and historians' assumptions of a home state advantage). For example:

- 1876 Republican (Hayes-OH/Wheeler-NY): "When the convention selected Congressman William A. Wheeler of New York as its vice-presidential nominee, it … achieved a balanced ticket that would run well in the crucial states of New York and Ohio" (Hoogenboom 1995, 265).
- 1876 Democratic (Tilden-NY/Hendricks-IN): "His running mate, Thomas A. Hendricks, was from an important, doubtful Midwestern state" (Hoogenboom 1995, 265).
- 1880 Republican (Garfield-OH/Arthur-NY): "It seemed obvious to a good many politicians that the vice-presidential nomination would go to a New Yorker, as it had in 1876, for the state was pivotal in a national election" (Reeves 1975, 178).
- 1880 Democratic (Hancock-PA/English-IN): "With the party's forces apparently united in New York and a native son from Indiana on the ticket, a great many Democrats were convinced they were in a superb position to gain revenge for 'the fraud of 1876'" (Reeves 1975, 187).
- 1888 Democratic (Cleveland-NY/Thurman-OH): "Governor Allen Thurman of Ohio … did, after all, come from a populous, needed-to-win state. On that basis alone, his being the unanimous choice [of the Convention, for vice president] was understandable" (Brodsky 2000, 223).

- 1892 Democratic (Cleveland-NY/Stevenson-IL): "[I]t was hoped that he [Stevenson] would help the party among the western silverites in general and in Illinois in particular" (Brodsky 2000, 274).
- 1900 Republican (McKinley-OH/Roosevelt-NY): "[Theodore Roosevelt] was popular in New York, which wanted the nomination and was always a hard state for the Republicans to carry in the national campaign" (Leech 1959, 529).
- 1920 Democratic (Cox-OH/Roosevelt-NY): "FDR's credentials would have placed him on any nominee's short list [for vice president] … Above all [he was] a Roosevelt from New York, by far the most populous state in the Union, with forty-five electoral votes, roughly one-fifth of the number required for election" (Smith 2008, 178).

Post-World War II

Prominent historians also have pointed to the assumed vice presidential home state advantage when recounting subsequent vice presidential selections. James MacGregor Burns, the celebrated biographer of Franklin Roosevelt, explains Harry Truman's selection in 1944 in part by saying: "He was from the Midwest, from a politically doubtful border state" (Burns 1970, 505). Lewis Gould, one of the foremost historians of the American presidency, likewise explains Richard Nixon's selection as Dwight Eisenhower's running mate in 1952 by noting: "California's electoral votes might be crucial in a close election, and Nixon had proved he could carry the state" by winning a US Senate seat there in 1950 (Gould 2003, 330).

In fact, Gould's (2003) history of the Republican Party, *Grand Old Party*, ridicules several presidential candidates of the later twentieth century for not giving sufficient weight to the vice presidential home state advantage when selecting their running mates. About Barry Goldwater's selection of New York's William E. Miller in 1964, Gould writes: "The nominee [Goldwater] would have been better advised to have selected a figure from a border state or the Middle West" (p. 364). As for Bob Dole's selection by Gerald Ford in 1976, "Dole added little to the Republican chances since Kansas was safely in the GOP column" (p. 410). George H. W. Bush's selection of Dan Quayle in 1988 was also ill-advised: "Much of the appeal of Quayle … was cosmetic since Bush was certain to carry Indiana anyway" (p. 443). And Jack Kemp's selection by Bob Dole in 1996 "brought little electoral appeal to the ticket since Dole had no chance of carrying New York against [President Bill] Clinton" (p. 470).

Over the course of American history, the expectation of a vice presidential home state advantage and its relevance to vice presidential selection had become so ingrained as to appear self-evident. Conventional wisdom dictated that vice presidential candidates should be selected primarily on the basis of electoral considerations, and that the most effective way to gain an electoral advantage through vice presidential selection was to choose a running mate from a key battleground state whose native appeal would attract otherwise-unsecured electoral votes. To challenge or disregard this perception when choosing a vice presidential candidate seemed rather foolish.

The modern era

The most famous example of a vice presidential home state advantage came in 1960 when Democratic presidential candidate John F. Kennedy selected Lyndon B. Johnson as his running mate. As a young senator from Massachusetts confronted by intra-party division over civil rights policy, doubts about his readiness to lead a nation engaged in the Cold War, and suspicions over his Catholic faith, Kennedy made a difficult and, by most historical judgments, brilliant decision in selecting Johnson – then the US Senate's majority leader and formerly Kennedy's rival for the presidential nomination.

Johnson's appeal to Kennedy was multifaceted, to be sure, but no factor attracted more attention then or now than LBJ's potential to secure electoral votes throughout the South and particularly in his home state of Texas, where opposition to the civil rights policies advanced by Kennedy and the national party threatened to disrupt decades-long Democratic regularity. The electoral opportunity was hardly lost on members of the Kennedy-Johnson campaign. Immediately after Kennedy decided to select Johnson, brother and campaign manager Robert Kennedy directed a campaign adviser "to add up the electoral votes in the states we're sure of and to add Texas" (Dallek 2003, 271). On the campaign trail and in the press, the candidates and their supporters prominently advertised their "Boston-Austin" alliance. Johnson, for his part, reportedly "was haunted by his fear that Texas would go Republican and that he, on the ticket primarily to ensure his state's twenty-four electoral votes, would be blamed" (Unger and Unger 1999, 251).

Kennedy's strategy seemed to work, as he won Texas by the slim but decisive margin of 46,257 votes, or two percentage points. The victory added twenty-four electoral votes to the Democratic column, not enough to decide the election (since Kennedy had a nine-vote electoral majority of 279 without Texas) but important because otherwise Nixon might have pressed vote fraud allegations in Illinois and perhaps challenged the election results. To the vice president-elect's credit, Democrats held on to a majority of the Old Confederacy states. Lyndon Johnson had done his job: he had delivered Texas, and the South. Such is the judgment of history – as well as Johnson himself. Never one to be accused of modesty, he relayed this update to Kennedy in an election night phone call: "*I* am carrying Texas and we are doing pretty well in Pennsylvania" (Unger and Unger 1999, 251, emphasis added).

A half-century later, the legacy of the Johnson selection is a curious one. Rather than invigorating the conviction that home state considerations are and should be relevant to vice presidential selection, most often political commentators cite it as a coda to a bygone era of presidential elections, a cautionary note to would-be strategists playing the quadrennial "veepstakes." Journalists, pundits, and campaign insiders regularly use the Johnson selection to frame a new conventional wisdom: vice presidential candidates used to deliver home states – but those days are over. Examples are so common as to defy exhaustive collection. Here is a sample:

- "Political historians maintain that vice presidential picks rarely matter, pointing to the 1960 election of John Kennedy as the last time the veep candidate – Sen. Lyndon Johnson of Texas – clearly helped pull in a crucial state" (*Christian Science Monitor*, June 21, 2004).[9]
- "From their war rooms, the political pros point out that the last running mate to have any real clout at the ballot box was Lyndon Johnson, who delivered Texas for John Kennedy back in 1960" (*The Economist*, July 8, 2004).[10]
- "Geography is not as important as it used to be. The last vice presidential candidate chosen mainly to deliver a state's electoral votes was Lyndon B. Johnson, and that campaign was in 1960, a year before [Barack] Obama was born" (*Los Angeles Times*, June 30, 2008).[11]
- "Vice-Presidential choices rarely tip the balance in an election. The last time a Veep played a pivotal role was 1960, when Lyndon Johnson delivered Texas for John F. Kennedy" (*Bloomberg Businessweek*, May 21, 2000).[12]
- "'1960 was the one year where the vice presidential choice was decisive; Johnson really helped in the south in a tight race,' says Charlie Cook of the Cook Political Report" (*Washington Monthly*, July/August 1999).[13]
- "Probably Lyndon Johnson was the last time a VP seriously helped carry a state" (Mike DuHaime, former presidential campaign manager for Rudy Giuliani, quoted in *Politico*, August 18, 2011).[14]

Bob Ellsworth, who headed Bob Dole's vice presidential search in 1996, articulated the lessons of the Johnson selection most perceptively. As summarized by Bob Woodward in his book, *The Choice*: "Ellsworth believed that a brilliant pick could be found occasionally, such as John Kennedy's decision in 1960 to select Senator Lyndon Johnson. Johnson helped carry some key southern states, including his home state of Texas. But such an opportunity for a politically adroit move was rare" (Woodward 1996, 426).

The emergent narrative about vice presidential selection, and the relevance of home state considerations in particular, is a counterintuitive response to the Johnson selection of 1960 and a dramatic departure from the conventional wisdom developed throughout the first century-and-a-half of American presidential politics. All of which begs two critical questions: (1) what changed?; and, (2) is the perception of a vice presidential home effect *really* dead?

What changed?

Two factors have contributed to increased skepticism about the vice presidential home state advantage and its relevance to vice presidential selection: (1) the expansion of vice presidential power; and, (2) the selection of running mates who did not contribute to the geographic balance of their ticket and/or came from small and non-competitive states.

First and most important is the expansion of vice presidential power since the mid-twentieth century. When and why this expansion took place is a matter of dispute. Some observers trace its starting point to the Eisenhower Administration, when – perhaps inspired by the exigencies of the Cold War and Harry Truman's sudden and dramatically consequential elevation from vice president to president in 1945 – Richard Nixon was allowed to assume a higher profile in domestic decision-making and international diplomacy as vice president. Reflecting on his role as vice president, Nixon – who, it must be noted, had an interest in portraying his contributions as significant – described his tenure as a turning point:

> The vice presidency had traditionally been a political dead end, and most Vice Presidents were old party wheelhorses or regional politicians added to balance the ticket .... Until Eisenhower completely changed the concept of the office, the Vice President was almost exclusively a ceremonial figure who went to the receptions and dedicated the dams the President didn't have time for. (Nixon 1978, 104)

Nixon most clearly contributed to the prestige of the vice presidency by earning his party's presidential nomination in 1960, making him the first sitting vice president to do so since Martin Van Buren in 1836. Hubert Humphrey, the next sitting vice president at the time of a presidential election, also earned his party's presidential nomination in 1968. Since that time, the only sitting vice president *not* to seek or win his party's presidential nomination when the incumbent president did not face reelection was Dick Cheney in 2008.[15] The vice presidency's new function as a stepping stone to the presidency, or at least a presidential nomination, has greatly increased its significance in the modern era.

Most scholars, however, credit Walter Mondale with institutionalizing an active and influential vice presidency. As described by Pika and Maltese (2013, 272), the office "emerged from the shadows during the Carter Administration." President Jimmy Carter granted Mondale unprecedented access and influence in his administration, providing Mondale with an office in the West Wing of the White House and allowing him daily intelligence briefings and weekly one-on-one lunch meetings. Mondale also played an active role as an administration liaison to Congress, contributing to the passage of national energy legislation and the Panama Canal treaties (see Gillon 1992). Indeed, whereas "many vice presidents" – including Mondale's immediate predecessors Lyndon Johnson, Hubert Humphrey, Spiro Agnew, and Gerald Ford – "had previously pursued a more substantial role in policy making, Mondale was unique in the fact that he actually achieved it."[16]

Today, the vice president's constitutional power remains meager and yet his influence has become significant. Recent presidents have continued to integrate vice presidents into the decision-making and legislative processes, while also using them as high-profile international ambassadors and campaign surrogates. The two most recent vice presidents, Dick Cheney and Joe Biden, bear witness to this expansion of power. Cheney exerted tremendous influence over Bush Administration policies on issues ranging from energy to national security and war strategy. Biden, for his part, has played a key role in shaping the Obama Administration's domestic policy, most notably on the 2011 debt limit negotiations; and foreign policy, most notably on the war in Afghanistan.[17]

The vice president's expanded role in governance does not, however, mean that running mates are selected on the exclusive or even primary basis of their capacity to govern. Michael Nelson, a preeminent scholar of the presidency, says flatly: "Candidates choose Vice-Presidents based on the sole criterion of how they can help win the election."[18] While perhaps hyperbolic, this argument is not the same as saying that selections continue, as in times past, to be primarily based upon geography and the healing of intra-party wounds; rather, electoral considerations may encompass a range of concerns among voters about the vice president's capacity to execute governing functions, advise the president, and succeed the president if necessary.

Milkis and Nelson (2011, 497–498) provide a more nuanced explanation of the vice presidential selection calculus in the modern era:

> To meet the new public expectations about vice-presidential competence, most modern presidential candidates have paid considerable attention to experience, ability, and political compatibility in selecting their running mates. Winning votes on election day is still as much the goal as in the days of old-style ticket-balancing. But presidential nominees realize that voters now care more about competence and loyalty – a vice-presidential candidate's ability to succeed to the presidency ably and to carry on the departed president's policies faithfully – than they do about having all regions of the country or factions of the party represented on the ticket.

Indeed, the two most recent presidents – George W. Bush and Barack Obama – selected running mates in Cheney and Biden, respectively, who utterly defied the rules of the past: both came from predictably partisan states with the minimum number of electoral votes. Instead of winning over home state voters, these picks seemed primarily designed to reassure voters *nationwide* about the relatively inexperienced candidates at the top of the ticket: Cheney was a veteran of Congress as well as a former White House chief of staff and secretary of defense, while Biden was a six-term US senator and chairman of the Senate Foreign Relations Committee. In short, the Cheney and Biden selections addressed major electoral concerns about the presidential candidates that, because of the vice president's expanded role in modern governance, were not and need not be geographic or factional in nature.

The preceding discussion dovetails with the second major change in the politics of vice presidential selection: a series of recent running mates who offered no obvious regional balance or valuable home state targets. Cheney and Biden are only the most recent examples of such selections, not the first ones. In 1992, Bill Clinton, then governor of Arkansas, became the first presidential candidate in more than four decades to select a running mate from a neighboring state – Tennessee's Senator Al Gore.[19] Against all conventional wisdom the Gore selection not only failed to balance the Democratic ticket geographically, but also in terms of age and ideology. Yet it worked; Clinton was elected president in 1992, and then reelected with Gore in 1996.

By breaking the traditional rules of vice presidential selection, and getting away with it, Clinton had set a precedent that could loosen the psychological constraints of ticket-balancing for future presidential candidates. Perhaps emboldened by the Clinton precedent, in 2000 Bush selected in Cheney not just a running mate from a small and safe home state but one who, at the time of Bush's decision, was a fellow legal resident of Texas.[20] While all other recent selections have provided geographic balance – aside from Clinton-Gore, only McCain-Palin represented the same US Census region and no running mates have come from the same regional division since 1948 – many have offered little hope of a consequential home state advantage. In 1996, Bob Dole selected Jack Kemp from solidly Democratic New York; in 2000, Gore selected Joe Lieberman from solidly Democratic Connecticut; in 2008, McCain selected Sarah Palin from seemingly-safe Alaska (see Chapter 3 for further discussion); and, again, Cheney in 2000 and Biden in 2008 represented small states sure to vote for the party ticket anyway.

The recent pattern of vice presidential selection does not mean that geography is now considered irrelevant to that process; as we discuss in the next two chapters, there is ample reason to believe that perceptions of a vice presidential home state advantage continue to influence the selection process and campaign strategy more broadly, even in some of the cases just listed. The immediate import of these cases, and particularly the Clinton-Gore ticket, is that they provided precedents for the questioning or outright repudiation of geographic considerations now prevalent in public discussions of the vice presidential selection process. For instance, in 2012 media critic and *Daily Beast* columnist Howard Kurtz wrote: "In the old days, geographic balance was practically a must. But ever since Bill Clinton of Arkansas picked Al Gore of neighboring Tennessee, that seems less important in the media age."[21] Likewise, in 2008, *Politico* reporter Jonathan Martin wrote: "Regional balance, it seems, no longer matters in a rapidly homogenizing country. Vice presidents are increasingly picked for reasons other than their ability to deliver their home state or region – as was the case with [John] Edwards, Kemp, and Cheney."[22]

In other words, geography used to be relevant to vice presidential selection, but the rules have changed. This is the new conventional wisdom. Or is it?

Is the perception of a vice presidential home state advantage really dead?

Stuart Rothenberg, author of the Rothenberg Political Report and a prominent political pundit during election seasons, published a provocative column on April 27, 2012, titled "Truth about Mitt Romney's running mate choice."[23] The truth referenced in this title was that, according to Rothenberg, vice presidential candidates exert so little influence on voting in presidential elections that then-rampant speculation over the 2012 veepstakes was essentially a waste of time. Citing Dick Cheney's recent comment that "it's pretty rare" for a vice presidential candidate to influence the outcome of a presidential election, Rothenberg says the former vice president "was reflecting the views of most serious students of American politics." Echoing the emergent conventional wisdom summarized in the preceding section of this chapter, Rothenberg explains:

> There are, of course, exceptions, including the 1960 presidential race when the selection of Lyndon Johnson probably allowed the Democratic ticket to carry Texas. But the homogenizing of American culture (via television and the Internet) and the increased polarization of the country and ideological purity of the two parties have made it less likely that a running mate can "deliver" his or her state.

In conclusion, Rothenberg ridicules the ongoing veepstakes obsession. "So go ahead and have fun if you enjoy listening to the speculation," he writes.

> Play the VP selection game at cocktail parties or around the kitchen table. Write your comments about the best pick for Romney, or the worst, at the end of articles on the Web. Just remember that the 2012 election is between President Barack Obama and former Massachusetts Gov. Mitt Romney.

Rothenberg's analysis is representative of the prevailing conventional wisdom among political journalists and pundits, not only because it echoes comments detailed earlier in this chapter about the irrelevance of the vice presidential home state advantage, but also because he does not consistently apply the lesson so confidently advanced by those comments. In March 2012, one month before the dismissive column just cited, the *Rothenberg Political Report* featured a column – written by Stuart Rothenberg – titled "Who else for vice president but Marco Rubio?"[24] As the then-presumptive nominee of the Republican Party, Rothenberg writes that Mitt Romney would "need to look for the right running mate to help him unify the party and breathe some excitement into the Republican ticket. In other words, he'll need Florida Sen. Marco Rubio." He goes on to note that "Rubio, of course, isn't the only Republican who could enhance a Romney ticket" – Virginia Governor Bob McDonnell and Louisiana Governor Bobby Jindal were promising alternatives. How to choose between them? Rothenberg begins with the home state advantage: "Like Jindal, McDonnell comes from a Southern state and should appeal to the party's conservative base. But Virginia is a swing state, unlike Louisiana, which gives the popular McDonnell some extra appeal as a running mate." Advantage McDonnell.

This was not the first time Rothenberg had played the veepstakes or focused on home state considerations in doing so. In 2008 he told CNN that Virginia Governor Tim Kaine "makes a lot of sense" as a running mate for Barack Obama. His explanation: "Virginia is going to be one of the two or three key states for Obama."[25]

Nor is Rothenberg alone in his contradiction. Chris Cillizza, founder and editor of the *Washington Post* blog "The Fix," authored a post on August 9, 2012, titled "The vice presidential pick is overrated. Here's why."[26] After observing that "The political world – up to and including this blog – is consumed at the moment with trying to divine the identity of Mitt Romney's vice presidential pick," Cillizza provides this stark cautionary note: "The simple reality is that the vice presidential pick – viewed through the lens of recent history – has almost no broad influence on the fate of the ticket and, to the extent the VP choice has mattered, it's been in a negative way." As for considerations of a home state or region advantage: "The most common argument for why the vice presidential pick matters is geography. But, there's scant evidence in recent VP picking that geography really matters." In fairness, Cillizza's focus here seems to be on the selection process more than voting behavior. Nonetheless, he labels the vice presidential pick as "overrated," describes the impact of running mates as neutral or negative, and the column includes a photo with the caption: "Lyndon B. Johnson (second from left), the last VP pick that really mattered" – from which a reader clearly draws the conclusion that vice presidential candidates do not deliver home states or regions.

Cillizza does, however, go on to credit Al Gore with delivering not only Tennessee but much of the South twenty years earlier:

> The last vice presidential pick who could make a real argument that he helped the presidential nominee win a swing state or one that leaned against his party was Al Gore in 1992. After the Democratic presidential nominee had lost the Volunteer State by 16 points in 1984 and 1988, Bill Clinton and Gore carried it – thanks in part to the popularity of the then Tennessee Senator (and his father) [former Tennessee Senator Al Gore, Sr.].

Indeed, Gore could "lay a solid claim to delivering a region for the presidential nominee," even though Clinton came from the neighboring southern state of Arkansas. This, in itself, is no contradiction to Cillizza's earlier arguments, for he explains that circumstances have changed dramatically in the subsequent two decades. The first change has been technological, says former George W. Bush campaign adviser and White House press secretary Ari Fleischer, "With communications reaching everywhere for the last two decades, the race is about the presidency, not the vice-presidency."[27] The second change concerns recent precedents in vice presidential selection, detailed earlier in this chapter; citing the selections of Cheney, Lieberman, Edwards, Biden, and Palin, Cillizza concludes that the presidential nominees – and their senior staffs – "grasp the declining importance of geography." Apparently, the author does as well.

Not so. In 2012, as in previous election years, Cillizza authored a "veepstakes" series for "The Fix" that evaluated and ranked top vice presidential contenders, with the first edition coming even before the Republican presidential nomination was decided. A look at any of these lists reveals Cillizza's substantial and recurring focus on geographic considerations. For instance, the inaugural edition of *Veepstakes 2012* discusses the strengths and weaknesses of ten potential running mates, usually in three to five sentences.[28] Home state considerations are mentioned as pros or cons for five candidates, and regional considerations are mentioned for one. Explaining the credentials of Marco Rubio, who heads the list, Cillizza writes: "He's from Florida, a major swing state." Of Bob McDonnell, ranked second: "McDonnell is the popular governor of perhaps the swingiest state, er, Commonwealth in the country." Meanwhile, Susana Martinez comes from New Mexico, "and the Land of Enchantment is regarded as a swing state this fall;" Paul Ryan "is from a swing state"; and, unfortunately for Chris Christie, "there's no way that Christie on the ticket delivers New Jersey."

A similar pattern is found in Cillizza's 2008 lists.[29] For example, Tim Kaine "is also the highest ranking elected official in an emerging battleground state and his popularity coupled with Obama's appeal to African American voters statewide and white voters in northern Virginia could make the contest for the Commonwealth a barnburner." Likewise, Tim Pawlenty "has been elected twice in a Democratic-leaning state that is almost certain to be a battleground in the fall."

An enduring perception

Rothenberg and Cillizza are not unique; rather, they exemplify a profound disconnect common if not pervasive among political commentators between how they characterize the vice presidential home state advantage, in general, and how they apply that knowledge to specific cases. This is not to say that they are dishonest or even wrong in doing so; rather, it is to say that, emphatic declarations to the contrary notwithstanding, the perception of a vice presidential home state advantage is not dead, after all.

In Chapter 2 we provide a more systematic analysis to justify this claim. We begin by analyzing the content of "veepstakes" candidates' profiles appearing in major media outlets, to gauge journalists' perception of a vice presidential home state advantage. Then, to determine whether this perception is shared by the individuals most directly affecting vice presidential selection, we turn our attention to the presidential campaign – specifically, to top campaign advisers and the presidential candidates themselves.

Notes

1 See: www.whitehouse.gov/about/presidents/johnadams. Accessed February 23, 2015.

2 As of 2013, the vice president had cast a tie-breaking vote in the Senate on 244 occasions (Pika and Maltese 2013, 272). Vice President Joe Biden cast no such votes during his first term in office.

3 Proposed and ratified in the wake of President Kennedy's assassination in 1963, the Twenty-fifth Amendment provides for vice presidential succession in cases of the president's death or removal from office (Section 1), and when the president is declared "unable to discharge the powers and duties of his office" (Section 3).

4 Or nine occasions, if one counts Gerald Ford's ascension to the presidency following the resignation of Richard Nixon.

5 Milkis and Nelson (2011, 486) attribute the quote to Marshall; Smith (2008, 177–178), to Barkley; and Unger and Unger (1999, 255), to Humphrey. The original source of the joke is uncertain.

6 "Meet the Press," March 3, 2000. Transcript accessed via the Lexis/Nexis database.

7 Neal, Steve. 1984. "And now, the race for second place." *Chicago Tribune*, June 10. Available at: http://archives.chicagotribune.com/1984/06/10/page/73/article/and-now-the-race-for-second-place. Accessed February 23, 2015.

8 Perhaps the most telling indicator of this assumption is found in the original draft of the US Constitution. Article II, Section 1 required electors to "vote by Ballot for two Persons, of whom one at least shall not be an Inhabitant of the same state with themselves." This same requirement was later incorporated into the Twelfth Amendment, which altered the manner in which members of the Electoral College cast ballots for president and vice president. It would seem that even the framers of the Constitution sensed that electors were more inclined to vote for candidates from their home state. To that point, note that the original language of Article II, Section 1, and the Twelfth Amendment, does not prohibit electors in general from voting for presidential and vice presidential candidates from the same state; rather, it prohibits this only when the elector comes from the same state as both candidates.

9 See: www.csmonitor.com/2004/0621/p01s01-uspo.html/(page)/3. Accessed February 23, 2015.

10 See: www.economist.com/node/2900114. Accessed February 23, 2015.

11 See: http://articles.latimes.com/2008/jun/30/nation/na-veepstakes30. Accessed February 23, 2015.

12 See: www.businessweek.com/stories/2000-05-21/despite-all-the-name-dropping-the-veep-short-list-is-short-indeed. Accessed February 23, 2015.

13 See: www.washingtonmonthly.com/features/1999/9907.starr.campaign.html. Accessed February 23, 2013.

14 See: www.politico.com/news/stories/0811/61616_Page3.html. Accessed February 23, 2015.

15 Vice President Joe Biden would become the second example since 1968 if he does not seek or win his party's nomination in 2016, as appears likely at the time of this writing.

16 University of Virginia's Miller Center, "American President: A reference resource." See: http://millercenter.org/president/carter/essays/vicepresident/1829. Accessed February 23, 2015.

17 For insight into Biden's role in the former, see Bob Woodward's *The Price of Politics* (2012); for his role in the latter, see Woodward's *Obama's Wars* (2010).

18 See: www.businessweek.com/stories/2004-03-03/the-strategy-behind-kerrys-veepstakes. Accessed February 23, 2015.

19 The last pair of running mates to come from bordering states prior to 1992 was Harry Truman (Missouri) and Alben Barkley (Kentucky), in 1948. Theirs was the first such pairing since 1868, when Ulysses Grant (Ohio) ran with Schuyler Colfax (Indiana).

20 Although Cheney mostly grew up in Wyoming and represented that state in the US House of Representatives, by 2000 he was living in Texas and serving as CEO of the Halliburton corporation. The day before he was announced as Bush's running mate, Cheney flew to Wyoming to change his voter registration, thus avoiding a constitutional obstacle that would have prevented Texas electors from voting for both candidates in the Electoral College. An enterprising reporter caught wind of the residency change and broke the news, thus spoiling what Bush had intended to be a surprise announcement.

21 See: www.thedailybeast.com/articles/2012/01/11/mitt-romney-s-dilemma-picking-a-running-mate-if-he-s-the-gop-nominee.html. Accessed February 23, 2015.

22 See: www.politico.com/news/stories/0508/10652_Page2.html. Accessed February 23, 2015.

23 See: http://rothenbergpoliticalreport.com/news/article/truth-about-mitt-romneys-running-mate-choice. Accessed February 23, 2015.

24 See: http://rothenbergpoliticalreport.com/news/article/who-else-for-vice-president-but-marco-rubio. Accessed February 23, 2015.

25 See: www.cnn.com/2008/POLITICS/07/30/dem.veepstakes/. Accessed February 23, 2015.

26 See: www.washingtonpost.com/blogs/the-fix/post/the-vice-presidential-pick-is-overrated-heres-why/2012/08/09/ac6942b8-e23d-11e1-a25e-15067bb31849_blog.html. Accessed February 23, 2015.

27 See: www.washingtonpost.com/blogs/the-fix/post/the-vice-presidential-pick-isoverrated-heres-why/2012/08/09/ac6942b8-e23d-11e1-a25e-15067bb31849_blog.html. Accessed February 23, 2015.

28 See: www.washingtonpost.com/blogs/the-fix/post/veepstakes-2012-the-inaugural-edition/2012/03/22/gIQAAAbKUS_blog.html. Accessed February 23, 2015.

29 See: http://voices.washingtonpost.com/thefix/the-line/the-friday-line-veepstakes-1.html. Accessed February 23, 2015.

2

The home state advantage is dead ... long live the home state advantage!

The perception of a vice presidential home state advantage remains widespread among a range of important actors – including journalists, campaign insiders, and presidential candidates – who influence or potentially influence the vice presidential selection process. How do we know this is the case? In this chapter, we present content analysis of public commentary from each set of actors that demonstrates the significant role home state considerations play in their evaluations of vice presidential contenders – even among individuals who, like Stuart Rothenberg and Chris Cillizza in the previous chapter, purport to discount the relevance of such considerations. In presenting evidence that the perception of a vice presidential home state advantage endures today, we do not argue that this perception is well-founded or that it is determinative of vice presidential selection; our goal in this chapter is simply to document its prevalence and thus its potential impact on the selection process and presidential campaign strategy. A concrete analysis of its actual impact is reserved for Chapter 3.

Media coverage

"Veepstakes" is an appropriate term for the media's treatment of the vice presidential selection process as a parlor game for political junkies fascinated by electoral strategizing. Indeed, the first known use of the term – in the May 13, 1952, edition of the Omaha, Nebraska, *Evening World-Herald* – captures the game-like quality of the exercise: "Veepstakes provide laughs even in serious campaign." Beginning weeks and even years before the presidential nomination is decided,[1] media outlets devote extraordinary attention to the veepstakes. For example, in mid-August 2008, as Barack Obama and John McCain prepared to announce their running mates, a study by the Pew Research Center's Project for Excellence in Journalism found that 41% of media coverage of the 2008 presidential campaign focused on the veepstakes, with 27% devoted to Obama's selection process, 5% devoted to McCain's selection process, and 9% devoted to the Biden announcement. These figures represent a large share of total news content: campaign coverage accounted for 35% of total news content during the same period, including 60% of cable television news and 46% of radio news.[2]

The media's extensive coverage of vice presidential selection, during the veepstakes and during the general election campaign, often focuses on the running mate's ability to influence voting in his or her home state. For instance, in 2012 numerous news items focused upon Paul Ryan's ability to "deliver" his home state of Wisconsin, a presumed battleground in that year's election despite the fact that the Badger State voted for Democratic candidates in each of the five preceding presidential elections. Headlines included the following: "Can Paul Ryan deliver Wisconsin for Romney?" (*Washington Post*, August 11); "Ryan could move Wisconsin into the toss-up column" (*The New Republic*, August 11); "With Paul Ryan, Romney brings Wisconsin into Play. But it's no sure bet" (*Christian Science Monitor*, August 13); "Can Paul Ryan win Wisconsin for Mitt Romney" (*The Week*, August 14); "Will Paul Ryan help Romney win Wisconsin?" (Fox News Channel, October 9); "Paul Ryan hasn't delivered Wisconsin to GOP ticket" (McClatchy Newspapers, October 9); "Will Ryan help Romney turn Wisconsin red?" (CBS News, October 12); "Ryan tries to break through Obama's Midwestern firewall, deliver Wisconsin" (*The Hill*, October 17).

A series of "word clouds" published on *Slate* magazine's website in April 2012 furthers the point. To characterize eleven of the leading contenders in that year's Republican veepstakes, or at least media coverage of them, *Slate* collected articles about the veepstakes from a range of prominent news sources – including ABC News, CBS News, NBC News, MSNBC, CNN, Fox News, *Time*, *Newsweek*, the *Daily Beast*, the *New York Times*, the *Washington Post*, *National Journal*, the *Atlantic*, and *Politico* – published over the previous month. The resulting word clouds graphically illustrate the frequency with which various terms were used to describe those contenders; the larger the word or phrase, the more often it appeared in the individual's media profiles. In the interest of space, we present in Figure 2.1 three of the eleven word clouds – one for each of Romney's eventual vice presidential finalists: Paul Ryan, Rob Portman, and Tim Pawlenty.

The *Slate* word clouds provide an initial indication that media coverage of the veepstakes does, in fact, heavily emphasize geographic – especially home state – considerations. Indeed, "swing state" was one of the terms most commonly used in discussions of Paul Ryan and Rob Portman. In Portman's case, only one term was used more frequently than "swing state," and the identity of that state – Ohio – also figured prominently. However, no geographic terms appear in Pawlenty's word cloud. Among the eight word clouds not featured in Figure 2.1, three included the term "swing state" – for Marco Rubio, Bob McDonnell, and Chris Christie – while Christie's also included the term "northeasterner" and Kelly Ayotte's included "New England." In total, six of the eleven word clouds included home state references and one included only a regional

2.1 2012 veepstakes word clouds (from *Slate*)

reference. Indeed, it would seem that geographic considerations play a leading role in media coverage of the vice presidential selection process.

Nonetheless, one might reasonably argue that these data are inconclusive. After all, not every article that uses geographic terms can be assumed to express the perception of a vice presidential home state, or region, advantage; a journalist, for instance, could write an article explaining why it is irrelevant that Rob Portman comes from a "swing state." Moreover, the word cloud data cover only an early portion of a single veepstakes; perhaps media coverage becomes more focused on substantive considerations as the selection process matures, or perhaps the 2012 election was somehow atypical. These are valid concerns that require a more systematic analysis of media veepstakes coverage.

Content analysis: Data and methodology

An excellent opportunity for systematic analysis is found in the news articles and blog posts devoted to handicapping the veepstakes that have become fixtures of recent elections across a range of prominent mainstream and niche news sources. Typically, these articles are organized in list form or in ranked order, with short blurbs dissecting the strengths and weaknesses or pros and cons associated with top vice presidential contenders. Other items communicate similar information in the format of a traditional news article. In most cases these articles are presented as guides to readers interested in assessing the merits of the various vice presidential contenders and their likelihood of selection. Others are news reports describing the presidential candidate's progress toward making a selection.

A representative example is the "Election guide 2008" featured on the *New York Times* website, titled "Potential running mates."[3] Authors Adam Nagourney and Jeff Zeleny analyze the cases for nine potential Democratic vice presidential candidates and eleven potential Republican vice presidential candidates, with each individual inhabiting a designated section of the page accompanied by his or her picture and a paragraph-long discussion of credentials and likely electoral impact. Geographic considerations figure prominently in these descriptions. Among their comments about Republican vice presidential contenders are the following:

- Charlie Crist: "Mr. Crist's appeal can be summed up in three words: Florida, Florida, Florida. He is popular there, and could help John McCain carry the battleground state that has been at the heart of the past two presidential elections."
- Tim Pawlenty: "He is young – he will be 48 in November – and telegenic, and he comes from a battleground state. That said, it is hardly clear that Mr. Pawlenty could deliver Minnesota for Mr. McCain; he was re-elected there by one percentage point in 2006."
- Tom Ridge: "In many ways, Mr. Ridge might be an ideal choice for Mr. McCain. He is a former governor of Pennsylvania, a state Mr. McCain would love to put in play."
- Mitt Romney: "His Michigan roots might help Mr. McCain pick off a key state."
- Mark Sanford: "One thing that Mr. Sanford would not bring with him is a state; if Mr. McCain has to worry about South Carolina in November, he probably is in a whole world of hurt."
- Rob Portman: "[H]e is a former congressman from Ohio, a position he held for 12 years – making him an attractive choice geographically."

The authors raise no geographic considerations in their discussion of the four other Republican contenders: Lindsey Graham, Mike Huckabee, Bobby Jindal, and Joe Lieberman. Home state or region references are included in four of the nine treatments of Democratic contenders.

To provide a systematic analysis of media veepstakes coverage, we conducted a content analysis – much like the one presented above – of ten veepstakes articles from prominent news and opinion sources published prior to the selection of the last six non-incumbent vice presidential candidates: 2012 (Republican); 2008 (Democrat); 2008 (Republican); 2004 (Democrat); 2000 (Democrat); 2000 (Republican). Articles were identified through Internet searches[4] and selected, in cases of abundance, with a preference for those that came from reputable news or opinion sources; included a large number of vice presidential contenders; and provided organized, substantive discussions of the contenders' credentials.[5] The article's congruence with our characterization of media coverage played no role in article selection; in several cases, we chose a less supportive article because it better met the criteria just described.

As a first step in the content analysis, we identified each vice presidential contender discussed in each article. Next, we determined whether his or her appeal to a home state or region was referenced in the article. In most cases this was a straightforward determination; in other cases it was more complex. If the article referenced the contender's appeal to a particular state that was not his or her current state but one in which (s)he was born or spent a significant part of his/her life (for example, the preceding quote about Mitt Romney), we counted this as a home state reference. If, however, the article referenced a contender's appeal to a particular state or region based on demographic considerations such as religion, ethnicity, or socioeconomic background alone – with no reference to coming from that state or region – we did not count this as a home state reference. For instance, if an article said that Marco Rubio might help win states with large Hispanic populations like Florida, Nevada, and Colorado, this would not count as a home state reference even though Rubio is from Florida – because his appeal is framed in terms of *ethnicity* rather than geography.

Content analysis: Results

The results of our content analysis, presented in Table 2.1, indicate that geographic considerations indeed figure prominently in media coverage of the vice presidential selection process.[6] The sixty articles used in this analysis, spanning the 2000–2012 veepstakes, include 635 cases in which a vice presidential contender was substantively discussed or characterized (including multiple profiles of the same candidate, across separate articles). In 285 of these cases, journalists reference the contender's potential to influence the presidential vote in his or her state, while in forty-six additional cases journalists reference the potential to influence voting in a home region. As a percentage of total cases, presented in the second column of Table 2.1, 44.9% include home state references and 52.1% include home state/region references.

Table 2.1: Home state or region references in media coverage of veepstakes contenders, 2000–2012

	(1)	(2)	(3)
2000 Democrat (N=77)			
	References	Total case %	Avg. article %
Home state	37	48.1	46.1
State + region	40	51.9	49.5
2000 Republican (N=85)			
	References	Total case %	Avg. article %
Home state	26	30.6	31.8
State + region	30	35.3	37.8
2004 Democrat (N=156)			
	References	Total case %	Avg. article %
Home state	75	48.1	51.2
State + region	96	61.5	69.0
2008 Democrat (N=99)			
	References	Total case %	Avg. article %
Home state	51	51.5	54.5
State + region	58	58.6	60.4
2008 Republican (N=116)			
	References	Total case %	Avg. article %
Home state	46	39.7	42.8
State + region	53	45.7	47.7
2012 Republican (N=102)			
	References	Total case %	Avg. article %
Home state	50	49.0	49.1
State + region	54	52.9	52.4
TOTAL 2000–2012 (N=635)			
	References	Total case %	Avg. article %
Home state	285	44.9	45.9
State + region	331	52.1	52.8

The data in this table represent cases (N=635, including non-unique cases across separate articles) in which a vice presidential contender was substantively featured in one of ten veepstakes articles in a given election year, between 2000–2012 (see Appendix A). The numbers and percentages in this table represent how often such cases included a reference to the featured contenders' home state or region. For example, if Paul Ryan was featured in an article on the 2012 veepstakes and that article mentioned Wisconsin in explaining why Mitt Romney should or should not pick Ryan, this would count as a "reference." And if the same type of reference were made in six of ten articles about the 2012 veepstakes, this would constitute six total references. Column 1 lists the number of contenders for whom such references were made, in a given election year or in total; Column 2 lists the percentage of contenders in a given year or set of years for which such references were made; Column 3 lists the percentage of contenders within individual articles for which such "references" were made, averaged across a given year or set of years.

Of course, some journalists are more likely to emphasize geographic considerations than others. To account for potential skews in our data, in the third column of Table 2.1 we treat each article about a given veepstakes – rather than individual discussions of each vice presidential contender, including multiple discussions within one article – as our unit of analysis and present for *each designated set of articles* (e.g., 2008 Republican) its average percentage of home state and home state/region references.[7] The average percentage of home state references across all sixty articles is slightly higher, at 45.9%, than in the initial analysis, as is the percentage of home state/region references, at 52.8%. Across either measurement, we find that home state and region references appear in approximately half of all media discussions of potential vice presidential candidates.

A deeper analysis of the data reveals two interesting trends. First, references to home state and regional appeal are more common for Democrats than for Republicans. Across the three Democratic veepstakes, home state references appear in 49.1% of the total cases, in comparison to 40.1% for the three Republican veepstakes. The explanation for this discrepancy is not immediately apparent; perhaps it reflects the belief that Democratic voters are more likely to be mobilized by a home state candidacy than Republicans, since Democrats historically vote at a lower rate and are therefore more responsive to exceptional motivating factors (see Dudley and Rapoport 1989 for more on this argument).

Second, disaggregating the data by party shows that references to the home state and region have actually *increased* over time. As a percentage of total cases in each year, home state references in the Republican veepstakes have increased linearly and dramatically, from 30.6% in 2000 to 39.7% in 2008 to 49.0% in 2012. Incorporating regional references or using the average article percentage from Column 3 only reinforces this trend. Meanwhile, home state references in the Democratic veepstakes have increased slightly over time, from 48.1% in both 2000 and 2004 to 51.5% in 2008. However, apparently due to some outliers in the 2000 or 2004 data, the increase becomes substantial and linear for Democrats when using the average article percentage of home state references for a given veepstakes: 46.1% in 2000; 51.2% in 2004; 54.5% in 2008. Incorporating regional references – when using either method of calculation – also reveals a substantial, albeit non-linear, increase over time for Democrats.

Far from discarding the old rules of vice presidential selection, journalists in general advance the notion that the vice presidential home state advantage is real, and that it is and should be relevant to the selection process. To better appreciate this fact, consider a few additional points.

Content analysis: Discussion

First, it is common for journalists to not only reference a vice presidential home state or region advantage, but to present it as a matter of obvious fact – as seen in the following sample:

- Marco Rubio, 2012 – *National Journal*: "On paper, this is a no-brainer. He's from a must-win battleground state."[8]
- Bob McDonnell, 2012 – *National Journal*: "There is no Republican path to victory that doesn't include Virginia, and putting a governor with a 62 percent approval rating in the Commonwealth on the ticket would work wonders."[9]
- Bill Richardson, 2008 – *Newsweek*: "[T]he governor of New Mexico would almost surely bring along his own state, which also narrowly went to Bush in 2004, if he joined the Democratic ticket" (Fineman 2007).
- Tim Kaine, 2008 – *New York Times*: "The selection would undoubtedly put Virginia into play" (Nagourney and Zeleny 2008).
- Bob Graham, 2004 – National Public Radio: "Had he been the VP nominee in 2000, it would be President Gore today" (Rudin 2004).
- Jay Rockefeller, 2004 – CNN: "The case for Rockefeller is a simple one: if Gore had won West Virginia four years ago, he would not have needed Florida's electoral votes to win the White House" (Holland 2004).
- Evan Bayh, 2004 – CNN: "Technically, Indiana isn't a toss-up state – the last Democratic presidential candidate to win there was Lyndon Johnson in 1964 – but if Sen. Evan Bayh were on the ticket, the Hoosier state would definitely be in play" (Holland 2004).
- Gray Davis/Tom Ridge, 2000 – *New York Daily News*: "If Gore picks California Gov. Gray Davis or Bush taps Pennsylvania Gov. Tom Ridge, those states become electoral locks for the candidates" (DeFrank 2000).

In fairness, it is also common for journalists to note that a particular vice presidential contender has no chance of delivering his or her home state. Yet even a negative assessment of home state effects only reinforces the notion that another vice presidential contender *could* deliver a home state and, more generally, that geographic considerations are relevant to the discussion.

Second, journalists' belief in the vice presidential home state advantage is so strong, in general, that it sometimes leads them to posit far-fetched advantages in states to which a vice presidential contender has more tenuous connections. In 2004 and 2008, several of the articles included in our content analysis suggested that Kansas Governor Kathleen Sebelius might boost the Democratic ticket in Ohio because her father had been governor of that state. A *Time* article in 2008, for instance, noted: "Sebelius is popular in Kansas ... and even offers a family connection in the key swing state of Ohio, where her father John Gilligan served as governor in the '70s" (Calabresi 2008).[10] Being born in a swing state, or attending college in one, might also help: "Demographically and geographically, [Virginia Governor] Tim Kaine is the full package ... Kaine was also born in Minnesota and went to college in Missouri, two swing states in the Midwest" (Malveaux *et al.* 2008); likewise, from the *Washington Post* in 2004, "New Hampshire is expected to be one of the key swing states in play during the fall campaign, and [former governor] Jeanne Shaheen's experience

Final Five			
Candidate		Key Advantages	Key Disadvantages
	Tim Pawlenty Fmr. Governor, MN	-Safe -Gov. experience -Vetted -Vanilla ticket	-Probably can't carry home state -Bombed as POTUS candidate
	Rob Portman Senator, OH	-Reinforces economic message -Vanilla ticket -From key swing state	-Bush connection -Held responsible for budget problems
	Marco Rubio Senator, FL	-Hispanic -From most valuable swing state -Rising star -Charismatic	-Vetting issues regarding family -Romney needs to carry Florida on own to win race -Too fresh a fresh face?
	Bobby Jindal Governor, LA	-Sterling gubernatorial resume -Diversity for GOP ticket -State/fed. experience	-Not nationally vetted -Unremarkable SOTU response -LA not competitive
	Paul Ryan Rep., WI	-Articulate -Young and energetic -Fiscal focus -Swing state	-House member – has never even run statewide -Has touched 3rd rail of politics too many times

2.2 Republican vice presidential possibilities, 2012 (from *Sabato's Crystal Ball*)

there could be helpful. In addition, she was born in Missouri and attended college in Pennsylvania, two other states expected to be presidential battlegrounds" (*Washington Post* 2004).[11] *National Journal*'s Chuck Todd in 2000 even suggested that Al Gore might improve his chances of winning Pennsylvania if he selected John Kerry, the US senator from Massachusetts, as his running mate (see Todd 2000). Why? Because Kerry's wife, Teresa Heinz-Kerry, had been married to a former US senator from Pennsylvania, John Heinz, and after his death became heiress to the Pennsylvania-based Heinz Corporation ketchup fortune. One wonders whether the journalists who posit these advantages would consider *themselves* more likely to vote for a presidential ticket because the running mate attended college in their home state, or is married to someone who was married to someone who used to hold office in that state.

Third, the perception of a vice presidential home state advantage is not exclusive to the journalists who report on news and politics. As evidenced by our discussion of Stuart Rothenberg, the experts that journalists turn to for sophisticated analysis of campaign politics also frequently advance the notion of a home state and region advantage. In some cases these experts, like Rothenberg, are political scientists. For instance, Larry Sabato, perhaps the most visible political scientist in American media, on many occasions has emphasized geographic considerations in his analysis of the vice presidential selection process. Figure 2.2, borrowed from *Sabato's Crystal Ball*, on the website of the

University of Virginia Center for Politics, presents Sabato's handicapping of the 2012 Republican veepstakes.[12] For *each* of the five designated contenders, home state considerations are listed as a key advantage or a key disadvantage: representing a swing state is a key advantage to selecting Portman, Rubio, or Ryan; meanwhile, a key disadvantage to selecting Pawlenty is that he "Probably can't carry [his] home state" and, for Bobby Jindal, Louisiana is "not competitive." The accompanying commentary furthers these points: "What would Pawlenty add? Probably not a great deal in the Electoral College, though he could have an impact in his home region"; "On the other hand, the *Crystal Ball* has long believed Portman can add a point or two to Romney in a state any Republican almost certainly must have to win." The basis for estimating Portman's home state advantage is not specified. To be sure, Rothenberg and Sabato are not unique among media experts in attesting to the relevance of the vice presidential home state advantage. And it is understandable, given the status of such experts, that journalists value – and in many cases accept – their conclusions about vice presidential selection.

Finally, when evaluating this evidence of journalistic faith in the vice presidential home state advantage, it is important to consider that our analysis is based upon content from much of the nation's most reputable and/or influential media outlets. Moreover, many of the journalists who produced that content are among the most reputable and/or influential practitioners in their field. Take, for example, the "Election guide 2008" cited above (Nagourney and Zeleny 2008); this feature, which referenced a home state or region advantage for half of the Democratic and Republican veepstakes contenders, appeared in the national "newspaper of record," the *New York Times*, and it was authored by two of the most respected journalists in the business. Therefore, while it is easy – and not altogether inaccurate – to characterize veepstakes speculation as mindless pontificating in the lazy summer months preceding the full-scale presidential campaign – designed to entertain media consumers and fill empty print or web space – in general the media outlets and journalists who advance the notion of a vice presidential home state advantage are ones that we should expect to highly value and carefully guard their reputation for keen analysis and political expertise. Their vested interest in being right should discourage them from willfully courting ill-founded embarrassments out of laziness or insincerity.

In short, it is hard to believe that the journalists whose reporting we use to conduct our analysis would so prominently emphasize geography in their coverage of the vice presidential selection process if they did not genuinely believe its impact on campaign strategy and voting behavior in presidential elections to be real. And yet their analysis often contradicts itself on this point, since so many journalists dismiss the vice presidential home state advantage in the abstract (see Chapter 1). The apparent disconnect between journalists' assessment of the vice presidential home state advantage, in a broad sense, and their application of it in the particular is profound and, we suspect, reflective of the tension inherent in integrating learned lessons of the past with contrasting evidence in the present.

Presidential campaigns

Does the perception of a vice presidential home state advantage extend to campaign insiders and even presidential candidates? This question is more significant than the one involving media perception, because it focuses upon actual participants in the vice presidential selection process. Yet it is also more difficult to answer, since presidential campaigns carefully limit access to internal deliberations and, when making public statements, downplay the role of electoral motivations to avoid being seen as nakedly political rather than principled in their decision-making processes. It would follow, then, that campaign insiders and presidential candidates are less transparent than journalists about the strategic elements of vice presidential selection. Moreover, the incentive for obfuscation is greatest during a presidential campaign, when unflattering disclosures about the selection process might lead to negative press coverage and perhaps a loss of electoral support. Evaluating perceptions of the vice presidential home state advantage within a presidential campaign therefore requires careful analysis of insights provided inside and outside of the immediate electoral context. Our analysis first focuses upon campaign advisers and then upon actual presidential candidates.

Campaign advisers

Top advisers to presidential campaigns past and present, much like journalists, tend to downplay geographic considerations when discussing the vice presidential selection process in general. Kevin Madden, spokesman and senior adviser to the 2012 Mitt Romney campaign, offered this skeptical assessment of geography's role in the selection process:

> A name will make the media's list, even if that name is not really on the candidate's list if that person has been elected statewide from a swing state or could bring gender or ethnic diversity to the ticket. But the vetting process tends to put more of a premium on the personal rapport with the presidential nominee, the ability to endure the rigors of a campaign and ultimately the question of whether or not they are ready to serve on Day One.[13]

In 2008, Obama campaign manager David Plouffe said of geography's role in the selection process, "I don't think that's going to be a factor." Emphasizing the running mate's qualifications to be president and to serve as a "partner in governing" instead, Plouffe went on to cite the Clinton-Gore and Bush-Cheney tickets as evidence that geography-based appeal is not vital to electoral success.[14]

If at all relevant to the selection process, top campaign advisers depict geographic considerations as minor. Mary Matalin – George H. W. Bush's deputy campaign manager for political operations in 1992, whose husband James Carville also served as a senior strategist on Bill Clinton's presidential campaigns – in 2012 emphasized the primary importance of a working relationship between running mates. She then added, "All the rest: geography, demography, political profile, etc. is gravy if it's good, but largely irrelevant in the end, because no one votes FOR the VP."[15] Chris Lehane, press secretary and top adviser to Al Gore's 2000 presidential campaign, echoed that assessment almost exactly in 2012: "All else – geographic balance, message synergy, electoral college math, campaign skill – are important, but secondary."[16]

Yet, as previously demonstrated for journalists, there is evidence of a disconnect between campaign advisers' broad assessments of geographic considerations in the vice presidential selection process and their application of that lesson to specific cases. Moreover, this disconnect is most apparent when the adviser is not actively involved in a presidential campaign and thus least constrained by transparency concerns. Consider David Axelrod, a top campaign adviser to Barack Obama in 2008 and 2012. In 2000, Axelrod – then a prominent Democratic campaign consultant based in Chicago – was asked about the possibility of Al Gore selecting Chicago's Bill Daley as his running mate. Axelrod responded, "I think there is some logic to it, because Bill is a Catholic, *he is from a swing state* and has an impeccable reputation from his various tenures in Washington but especially as a commerce secretary [emphasis added]."[17]

Also in a 2000 interview,[18] James Johnson – Walter Mondale's 1984 presidential campaign manager and in 2004 the head of John Kerry's vice presidential search process – had this to say when describing the criteria for choosing a running mate: "And in many cases, you're trying to do some geographical balance." Later, Johnson reiterated, "You look at the geography of it," but also noted noncommittally, "There may be no geography. There may be some geography." Qualifications notwithstanding, the fact that Johnson included geography in his selection calculus is telling.

Two other examples come from top Republican advisers to previous presidential campaigns. The first is Scott Reed, who served as Bob Dole's presidential campaign manager in 1996. In a 2000 interview,[19] Reed heavily emphasized geography when discussing the ongoing veepstakes: Tom Ridge, Republican governor of Pennsylvania, "does something nobody else does: He nails down a battleground state. He gets you 23 electoral votes." Meanwhile, Senator Fred Thompson, "obviously, being from Tennessee, causes [Gore] to have to look over his shoulder and worry about spending time and spending money in [his home state of] Tennessee." As for a potential Democratic running mate, "I'd be worried about [Florida Senator Bob] Graham. I think Florida is a state that the polls are very close right now, tighter than everybody seems to think." By implication, Graham would help to tip the balance toward Democrats if selected.

Next consider Mark McKinnon, chief media adviser to the 2000 and 2004 George W. Bush presidential campaigns, who was asked in a 2012 interview on National Public Radio: "Who would be a good fit for a Romney GOP [vice] presidential nominee?" Without being prompted to discuss geography, McKinnon responded: "Well, you know, Marco Rubio is interesting because he checks so many boxes when you think about what a Republican nominee needs. *He brings Florida*, he's young, he's Hispanic, the Tea Party likes him." Also,

> *He* [Romney] *could balance the ticket by going to somebody from Ohio* – like a Rob Portman, for example – or somewhere in the Rust Belt ... *Rob Portman is from Ohio* and very well-liked by senior members of the campaign and Mitt Romney himself ... *So, he's very strong – Ohio,* and he's got a good jobs message [emphases added].[20]

This evidence indicates that senior advisers to presidential campaigns spanning the past two decades – including campaign managers and the head of a vice presidential search process – incorporate geographic considerations into their evaluation of potential vice presidential candidates, and sometimes rather emphatically. It stands to reason that this perception of a vice presidential home state or region advantage – expressed before and after service on a presidential campaign – also operates *during* the adviser's campaign service, quite possibly influencing actual campaign advice. Moreover, it is likely that other top advisers share the same perception and express it internally. The fact that we find no such expressions from an *active* campaign adviser is, in our judgment, hardly dispositive; we assume that these individuals fear their transparency would reflect poorly on the campaign, suggesting that the vice presidential selection process is being guided by electoral strategy rather than principle and professional credentials.

Still, one might wonder whether there is any *direct* evidence of a top campaign adviser recommending for or against a vice presidential selection at least partly on the basis of geographic considerations. In fact, as discussed in our preface, senior George W. Bush campaign adviser Karl Rove made just such a case against Dick Cheney in 2000. In a private meeting with Bush and Cheney just before the selection was finalized, Rove argued: "Cheney's presence on the ticket would add nothing to the electoral map, since Wyoming's three electoral votes were among the most reliably Republican in the country" (Bush 2010, 69). Perhaps Rove is unique in making such a recommendation. Given the evidence just cited, actually we suspect that Rove is unique for *admitting* it. After all, there are many reasons for campaign advisers not to make such an admission even after the fact, including confidentiality concerns and an interest in avoiding embarrassment if the recommendation was rejected, if it led to the selection of a vice presidential candidate who did not deliver his or her home state, or if it led to the selection of a generally disappointing candidate. Moreover, campaign advisers, like campaigns in general, might fear being seen as cravenly political rather than principled, despite the obvious nature of their work.

Presidential candidates

Presidential candidates also disclaim or downplay interest in geographic considerations when publicly discussing their choice of a running mate. For instance,

Jimmy Carter told voters during the 1976 Democratic primaries that he "would pick a vice-presidential running mate who was, in order of priority – someone qualified to become president, someone with whom he felt politically and personally compatible, and, least important, someone from outside the South who would give the traditional balance to the ticket" (Bourne 1997, 331). More than three decades later, John McCain cited recent precedent in eschewing geographic considerations: "Former president Clinton and former vice president Gore showed that you don't have to be regionally different," McCain told reporters during the 2008 Republican primaries. "I think that America is such now that regional differences doesn't [sic] play the role that maybe they did in earlier times."[21]

Perhaps these comments reflect the actual thinking of presidential candidates, who, unlike journalists and campaign advisers, must weigh the strategic considerations of vice presidential selection against the prospects of governing together with the vice president for four or eight years to come. Moreover, selecting a running mate in the modern era often means establishing an heir apparent to carry on the president's political agenda after leaving office. In short, the presidential candidate has far more riding on this choice than anyone else. And yet, unfortunately, evaluating a presidential candidate's selection calculus is exceptionally difficult. Many of his public comments about vice presidential selection – like those from Carter and McCain above – are made during the presidential campaign when, again, there is the least incentive for transparency. Even after the campaign, presidential candidates have a legacy to protect, one that might be tarnished by admitting to politicization of a major campaign decision. What's more, the club of ex-presidential candidates is small and access to their inner thoughts is limited.

Personal memoirs provide the best opportunity for gaining first-hand access to a presidential candidate's selection criteria. While prone to self-serving edits of history, the personal memoir is promising because it allows the candidate to discuss aspects of the campaign in great detail and to frame the selection process, if at all, on his own terms – free of suggestive prodding about any particular factor such as geography. Of course, many presidential candidates do not write memoirs, and those who do so do not always discuss the vice presidential selection process in detail. Nonetheless, we find evidence in three memoirs, all from ex-presidents, that presidential candidates at least sometimes allow the perception of a home state or region advantage to influence their evaluation of potential running mates.

The first example comes from Richard Nixon, who experienced both sides of the vice presidential selection process: being selected as a running mate in 1952 and 1956, and selecting a running mate in 1960, 1968, and 1972. About his selection by Dwight Eisenhower, Nixon wrote: "There was undoubtedly a geographic element in [Eisenhower's] choice – the recognition of the postwar influence of the western United States and particularly of California" (Nixon 1978, 108). Nixon goes on to explain, rather candidly, the political calculations behind his selection of Maryland Governor Spiro Agnew in 1968:

> From a strictly political standpoint, Agnew fit perfectly with the strategy we had devised for the November election. With George Wallace in the race, I could not hope to sweep the South. It was absolutely necessary, therefore, to win the entire rimland of the South – the border states – as well as the major states of the Midwest and West. Agnew fit the bill geographically. (Nixon 1978, 386)

The next two examples come from the most unlikely of sources: Bill Clinton and George W. Bush. Clinton, whose selection of Al Gore and subsequent electoral victory set a precedent cited by journalists, campaign advisers, and presidential candidates, for years to come, wrote in *My Life* that Gore's "selection defied the conventional wisdom that the vice-presidential candidate should provide political and geographic balance." After all, "We were from neighboring states" (Clinton 2004, 414). However, this does not mean that Clinton dismissed geographic considerations or rejected the vice presidential home state/region advantage as inoperative or irrelevant. He went on to say of Gore: "I also thought his selection would be good politics in Tennessee, the South, and other swing states." Clinton's perception of a vice presidential home state advantage is even clearer when discussing Florida Senator Bob Graham: "[H]e would almost certainly bring Florida into the Democratic column for the first time since 1976" (Clinton 2004, 413).

Bush, in *Decision Points*, writes of selecting Cheney: "His lack of impact on the electoral map did not concern me either. I believe voters base their decision on the presidential candidate, not the VP" (Bush 2010, 67). Yet his discussion of other potential running mates suggests otherwise, stressing in particular their potential to deliver a home state. "Lamar Alexander, Bill Frist, and Fred Thompson were fine men," Bush wrote, "and they might help me pull off an upset in Tennessee, the home state of the Democratic nominee, Vice President Al Gore" (Bush 2010, 67). John Danforth, runner-up to Cheney in the selection process, had this selling point: "As a dividend, he might help carry Missouri, which would be a key battleground state" (Bush 2010, 68). And in reference to the advice of a top campaign adviser, Bush wrote: "Karen [Hughes] recommended Tom Ridge, a Vietnam veteran from a key swing state" (Bush 2010, 67). The potential to deliver a home state clearly factored into Bush's evaluation of potential vice presidential candidates, even if he ultimately decided upon a running mate with little geographic appeal. Under different circumstances, geography might have made the difference.

Conclusion

Our argument throughout this chapter has been that the perception of a vice presidential home state advantage endures in American politics, and with these examples we see that it is operative *even among presidential candidates*. Moreover, these examples point to a now-familiar disconnect between broad assessments of the vice presidential home state advantage and its application to specific cases: while dismissing geography, in word and deed, as irrelevant to the selection process in general, Clinton and Bush nonetheless regarded the home state advantage as actual and relevant when discussing the merits of potential running mates. The perception of a vice presidential home state advantage is not dead, it appears, even among the men who allegedly killed it. In fact, as detailed in the next chapter, we find signs of life where it matters most of all: on the campaign trail.

Notes

1 A column titled "Let the veepstakes begin" was published on the liberal blog "Daily Kos" on June 8, 2006 – more than two years before Barack Obama secured the Democratic Party's presidential nomination. See: www.dailykos.com/story/2006/6/8/153143/5397/586/217062#. Accessed February 23, 2015.

2 See: www.journalism.org/node/12514. Accessed February 23, 2015.

3 See: http://politics.nytimes.com/election-guide/2008/candidates/vp/index.html. Accessed February 23, 2015.

4 Internet searches were conducted through Google, and common search terms included "veepstakes 2012," "Romney running mate 2012," "Obama running mate 2008," or appropriate variations thereof, depending on the election year. As necessary, particularly in the earlier years when qualifying articles were more difficult to locate, we adapted the search terms to include, for instance, specific news sources or the names of prominent vice presidential contenders. At no point did we use geographic references as search terms (e.g., "geography," "home state," "Ohio").

5 Of course, online news sources have grown in presence and scope since 2000 and archived news articles from a decade ago often are no longer accessible. Qualifying articles were therefore more difficult to find for the earlier years of analysis, and less-than-ideal ones were included more often in those years. For example, we use the transcript of a CNN Crossfire taping in 2004 because an ideal CNN list was not available; and in 2000 we use news reports about the Republican veepstakes that include a limited number of contenders and discuss the credentials of some in brief detail. These, however, are the exceptions. In most cases, even in 2000 and 2004, the articles meet or closely approximate our ideal criteria.

6 See Appendix A for a complete list of articles used in this analysis.

7 For instance, consider a set of three articles: Article 1 includes home state references for 25% of candidates mentioned, Article 2 also includes home state references for 25% of candidates, and Article 3 includes home state references for 100% of the candidates mentioned therein. The average percentage of home state references across all articles would therefore be 50% [(0.25 + 0.25 + 1.00)/3 = 0.5].

8 See: "Your favorite vice: Hotline's veepstakes power rankings." *National Journal*, February 1, 2012. www.nationaljournal.com/politics/your-favorite-vice-hotline-s-veepstakes-power-rankings-20120201. Accessed July 15, 2014.

9 See: "Your favorite vice: Hotline's veepstakes power rankings." *National Journal*, February 1, 2012. www.nationaljournal.com/politics/your-favorite-vice-hotline-sveepstakes-power-rankings-20120201. Accessed July 15, 2014.

10 Speaking of far-fetched, a 2008 CNN article said of Sebelius: "The popular two-term governor of Kansas could help Obama carry the state for the first time since 1964." (Malveaux, Schneider, Yoon, Silverleib, and Homick 2008). Obama, who went on to win the national popular vote by seven percentage points, lost Kansas by fifteen.

11 See: www.washingtonpost.com/wp-srv/politics/elections/2004/veepomatic_bios.htm. Accessed July 15, 2014.

12 See: www.centerforpolitics.org/crystalball/articles/final-veepstakes-ratings-pawlenty-portman-continue-to-top-list/. Accessed February 23, 2015.

13 See: www.politico.com/news/stories/0811/61616.html. Accessed February 23, 2015.

14 See: http://nymag.com/daily/intelligencer/2008/06/heilemann_on_obamas_vp_conundrum.html. Accessed February 23, 2015.

15 See: ww.politico.com/news/stories/0412/74896.html. Accessed February 23, 2015.

16 See: www.politico.com/news/stories/0811/61616.html. Accessed February 23, 2015.

17 See: http://articles.chicagotribune.com/2000-05-03/news/0005030219_1_gore-and-texas-gov-nominees-political-parlor-game. Accessed February 23, 2015.

18 See "The NewsHour with Jim Lehrer," July 24, 2000. Transcript accessed via the Lexis/Nexis database.

19 See: http://transcripts.cnn.com/TRANSCRIPTS/0007/18/cf.00.html. Accessed February 23, 2015.

20 See: http://m.npr.org/news/Politics/150230254. Accessed February 23, 2015.

21 See: http://abcnews.go.com/blogs/politics/2008/02/let-the-veepsta/. Accessed February 23, 2015.

3

When perception becomes campaign reality

Demonstrating that the perception of a vice presidential home state advantage (HSA) is pervasive in American politics, as we do in the previous chapter, is not the same as demonstrating that it *matters* in terms of influencing actual campaign decisions. Does the perception of a vice presidential HSA, in fact, influence campaign behavior? Or is it merely a curiosity, the remnant of what was once – and is no longer – a topic relevant to understanding presidential politics? To answer these all-important "so what?" questions, in this chapter we present systematic analyses of: (1) the vice presidential selection process; and, (2) general election campaign strategy. The purpose of our analyses is to determine whether the *perception* of a vice presidential HSA has a discernible impact on actual campaign *behavior*. Discernment is the key word here, since campaigns rarely announce the strategic motivations behind their decisions. Our inferential task, in that case, is to identify a pattern of behavior that a campaign would follow if it *were* acting upon perceptions of a vice presidential HSA, then to test our expectations against actual campaign behavior to see if the patterns align.

Vice presidential selection

If the perception of a HSA influences the vice presidential selection process, we would expect to find that vice presidential finalists disproportionately come from competitive, or "battleground," states. In light of the evidence from Chapter 2, we hypothesize that this is indeed the case.

Data and methodology

To test our hypothesis through systematic analysis, we begin by updating Goldstein's (1982) and Sigelman and Wahlbeck's (1997) lists of vice presidential finalists since 1940, when Franklin Roosevelt became the first presidential candidate in American history to select his running mate.[1] We have adopted these lists in their entirety, as well as Hiller and Kriner's (2008) list of Democratic finalists in 2004, and Baumgartner's (2008) list of Democratic and Republican finalists in 2008. To identify Democratic and Republican finalists in 2000, as well as Republican finalists in 2012, we apply the methodology established by Goldstein and Sigelman and Wahlbeck.[2]

Next, we measure the competitiveness of each state at the time of each selection process by computing the average difference between two-party vote shares in the three previous presidential elections,[3] and ranking them in ascending order from most competitive (smallest difference in average two-party vote share) to least competitive (largest difference in average two-party vote share).[4] This is, we conclude, a valid measure of state competitiveness, as indicated by its ranking of the top ten battleground states for 2012: Ohio (1); Florida (2); Colorado (3); Nevada (4); Iowa (5); New Hampshire (6); Virginia (7); Missouri (8); New Mexico (9); Wisconsin (10).

Finally, we calculate a neutral, or "expected," proportion of vice presidential finalists that should come from a designated set of states *if competitiveness were not a factor in vice presidential selection.* At first blush, this seems straightforward: *ceteris paribus*, 10% of finalists in any given selection process should come from the top five battleground states, since there are fifty total states (5/50 = 0.1). However, nine of the twenty-eight selection processes took place when only forty-eight states existed and had previous voting records.[5] Weighting the data accordingly, we arrive at 1,382 total states [(9 x 48) + (19 x 50)]. Of this total, 140 states represent the five most competitive in various selection processes (28 selections x 5 states). Thus, as a proportion of all vice presidential finalists, we should expect 0.1013 (140/1328), or in percentage terms 10.13%, to have come from the five most competitive states in a given selection process. This expected proportion provides a baseline against which to judge the proportion of states within a designated range of competitiveness *actually* represented by vice presidential finalists. If the expected and actual proportions align, state competitiveness would seem to have no bearing on who gets selected as a vice presidential finalist; essentially, the finalists' states would be randomly distributed in terms of competitiveness. If, on the other hand, battleground states are disproportionately represented among actual finalists, this would suggest that presidential candidates give weight to home state considerations when narrowing their selection field. Also, to provide a summary judgment of the data, we can compare the expected mean level of state competitiveness to the actual mean level among vice presidential finalists. With 1,382 states in the data and twenty-eight selection processes, the average number of states in a given selection year is 49.357. Dividing by two yields an expected state competitiveness mean of 24.679, against which we compare the actual mean for vice presidential finalists.[6]

Empirical results

Table 3.1 presents a complete list of the 158 vice presidential finalists in the 1940–2012 selection processes, ranked according to the competitiveness of

Table 3.1: Vice presidential finalists and home state competitiveness

Year	Finalist	Home state	Battleground #	Year	Finalist	Home state	Battleground #
1960-D	Orville Freeman	Minnesota	1	1944-D	Harry Truman	Missouri	23
1960-D	Hubert Humphrey	Minnesota	1	1948-R	Harold Stassen	Minnesota	23
1960-R	Walter Judd	Minnesota	1	1952-R	William Knowland	California	23
1988-D	Al Gore	Tennessee	1	1952-R	Richard Nixon	California	23
1988-R	Lamar Alexander	Tennessee	1	1960-R	Nelson Rockefeller	New York	23
2012-R	Rob Portman	Ohio	1	1964-R	William Miller	New York	23
1940-D	Henry Wallace	Iowa	2	1980-R	George H.W. Bush	Texas	23
1948-R	Charles Halleck	Indiana	2	1948-D	Alben Barkley	Kentucky	24
1976-D	John Glenn	Ohio	2	1968-D	Fred Harris	Oklahoma	24
1992-D	Jay Rockefeller	West Virginia	2	1984-D	Tom Bradley	California	24
1952-D	Oscar L. Chapman	Colorado	3	1984-D	Dianne Feinstein	California	24
1952-R	Daniel Thornton	Colorado	3	1988-D	John Glenn	Ohio	25
1980-R	Jack Kemp	New York	3	2008-D	Joe Biden	Delaware	25
2004-D	Bob Graham	Florida	3	1964-D	Mike Mansfield	Montana	26
1968-D	Richard Hughes	New Jersey	4	1996-R	Ben Campbell	Colorado	27
1960-R	Thruston Morton	Kentucky	5	1968-D	Terry Sanford	North Carolina	28
1964-D	Robert Kennedy	Massachusetts	5	1968-D	Sargent Shriver	Maryland	28
1976-D	Adlai Stevenson	Illinois	5	1968-R	Rogers Morton	Maryland	28
1960-D	Henry Jackson	Washington	6	1968-R	Spiro Agnew	Maryland	28
1968-R	Howard Baker	Tennessee	6	1976-D	Edmund Muskie	Maine	28
2000-R	Lamar Alexander	Tennessee	6	1968-D	Edmund Muskie	Maine	29
2000-R	Fred Thompson	Tennessee	6	1988-R	George Deukmejian	California	29
2000-R	Bill Frist	Tennessee	6	1952-D	Alben Barkley	Kentucky	30
1980-R	Gerald Ford	Michigan	7	1976-R	William Ruckelshaus	Indiana	30

1980-R	Guy Vander Jagt	Michigan	7
1984-D	Geraldine Ferrarro	New York	7
1944-D	Henry Wallace	Iowa	9
1976-D	Peter Rodino	New Jersey	9
1976-R	Anne Armstrong	Texas	9
1992-D	Harris Wofford	Pennsylvania	9
2000-D	Jeanne Shaheen	New Hampshire	9
1960-D	Stuart Symington	Missouri	10
2012-R	Paul Ryan	Wisconsin	10
1968-R	Robert Finch	California	11
1976-D	Henry Jackson	Washington	11
2012-R	Tim Pawlenty	Minnesota	11
1944-R	John Bricker	Ohio	12
1952-R	Charles Halleck	Indiana	12
1960-R	Henry Cabot Lodge	Massachusetts	12
1964-R	William Scranton	Pennsylvania	12
1980-R	Bill Simon	California	12
1984-D	Martha L. Collins	Kentucky	12
2000-D	Evan Bayh	Indiana	12
2000-R	John Engler	Michigan	12
2004-D	Dick Gephardt	Missouri	12
1948-R	John Bricker	Ohio	13
1964-D	Hubert Humphrey	Minnesota	13
1964-D	Eugene McCarthy	Minnesota	13
1984-D	Michael Dukakis	Massachusetts	13
1996-R	Jack Kemp	New York	13

1980-R	Howard Baker	Tennessee	30
1944-R	Earl Warren	California	31
1952-D	Warren Magnuson	Washington	31
1952-R	Arthur Langlie	Washington	31
1972-D	Thomas Eagleton	Missouri	31
1976-D	Walter Mondale	Minnesota	31
1984-D	Lloyd Bentsen	Texas	31
1984-D	Henry Cisneros	Texas	31
2008-D	Evan Bayh	Indiana	31
1948-R	Earl Warren	California	32
1976-R	Howard Baker	Tennessee	32
1980-R	Paul Laxalt	Nevada	32
1988-D	Lloyd Bentsen	Texas	32
1940-D	Cordell Hull	Tennessee	33
1944-D	William O. Douglas	Washington	33
1948-D	William O. Douglas	Washington	33
1968-D	Nelson Rockefeller	New York	33
1960-R	James Mitchell	New Jersey	34
1988-R	Pete Domenici	New Mexico	34
1952-D	Robert Kerr	Oklahoma	35
1952-D	Mike Monroney	Oklahoma	35
1988-D	Bob Graham	Florida	35
2008-R	Joe Lieberman	Connecticut	35
1988-D	Lee Hamilton	Indiana	36
1988-R	Dan Quayle	Indiana	36
1992-D	Lee Hamilton	Indiana	36

Year	Finalist	Home state	Battleground #	Year	Finalist	Home state	Battleground #
2000-D	Dick Gephardt	Missouri	13	2000-R	Frank Keating	Oklahoma	36
2000-R	John Danforth	Missouri	13	2008-D	Chet Edwards	Texas	36
1940-D	Alben Barkley	Kentucky	14	1976-R	Bob Dole	Kansas	37
1984-D	Wilson Goode	Pennsylvania	14	1972-D	Frank Church	Idaho	38
2004-D	John Edwards	North Carolina	15	1952-D	Estes Kefauver	Tennessee	39
1964-R	Gerald Ford	Michigan	16	1992-D	Bob Graham	Florida	39
1972-D	Reubin Askew	Florida	16	1960-R	Fred Seaton	Nebraska	41
1996-R	John Engler	Michigan	16	1972-D	Sargent Shriver	Maryland	41
2000-R	Tom Ridge	Pennsylvania	16	1988-R	Bob Dole	Kansas	41
2004-D	Tom Vilsack	Iowa	16	1952-D	William Fulbright	Arkansas	42
2008-R	Tom Ridge	Pennsylvania	16	1972-D	Walter Mondale	Minnesota	42
1960-R	Gerald Ford	Michigan	17	1980-R	Richard Lugar	Indiana	42
1964-D	Sargent Shriver	Maryland	17	2000-R	Dick Cheney	Wyoming	42
1992-D	Al Gore	Tennessee	17	2008-D	Kathleen Sebelius	Kansas	42
2008-D	Tim Kaine	Virginia	17	1952-D	Richard Russell	Georgia	44
1964-D	Robert McNamara	California	18	2008-R	Sarah Palin	Alaska	44
1960-D	Lyndon Johnson	Texas	19	1952-D	John Sparkman	Alabama	45
1960-R	Robert Anderson	Texas	19	1976-D	Frank Church	Idaho	45
2000-R	Jon Kyl	Arizona	19	2000-R	Chuck Hagel	Nebraska	46
2008-R	Tim Pawlenty	Minnesota	19	1988-R	Alan Simpson	Wyoming	47
1980-R	Donald Rumsfeld	Illinois	20	2008-R	Mitt Romney	Massachusetts	47
1988-D	Dick Gephardt	Missouri	20	1940-D	Jimmy Byrnes	South Carolina	48
2000-D	John Edwards	North Carolina	20	1944-D	Jimmy Byrnes	South Carolina	48
1940-D	William O. Douglas	Washington	21	1968-R	John Volpe	Massachusetts	48

1952-R	Walter Judd	Minnesota	21	1992-D	Bob Kerrey	Nebraska	48
1972-D	Gaylord Nelson	Wisconsin	21	2000-D	John Kerry	Massachusetts	48
1988-R	James Thompson	Illinois	21	1972-D	Lawrence O'Brien	Massachusetts	49
1944-D	Alben Barkley	Kentucky	22	1972-D	Kevin White	Massachusetts	49
2000-D	Joe Lieberman	Connecticut	22	1972-D	Ted Kennedy	Massachusetts	49

Note: Battleground rankings (in Columns 4 and 8) are based upon the average difference between two-party vote shares in the three presidential elections preceding a given year in a given state. For each year, states are ranked from most (1) to least (48 or 50) competitive.

the home state at the time of a given selection process. The data indicate that vice presidential finalists disproportionately come from competitive states, as we hypothesized. First, the mean home state battleground ranking for actual finalists is 22.892, as compared to an expected mean of 24.679 – suggesting that vice presidential finalists typically come from states more competitive than the average. The difference between actual and expected mean falls slightly below the conventional level of statistical significance, $p = 0.053$, according to a one-sample t-test. Further analysis also indicates that our finding is not an artifact of the past; the mean battleground ranking for finalists in the 1992–2012 veepstakes is 21.738, as compared to a modern expected mean of 25.

Second, the actual percentage of vice presidential finalists coming from the most competitive states exceeds the expected percentage across several points of comparison, including: the most competitive state (3.8% actual to 2.03% expected); the two most competitive states (6.33% actual to 4.05% expected); the three most competitive states (8.86% actual to 6.08% expected); the four most competitive states (9.49% actual to 8.1% expected); the five most competitive states (11.39% actual to 10.13% expected). Widening our scope to the ten most competitive states nearly brings the actual and expected percentages into alignment – 20.89% actual to 20.26% expected – but only temporarily; the percentage of actual finalists from the fifteen most competitive states is four-and-a-half points higher than the expected percentage (34.81% actual to 30.39% expected); as is the case for the twenty most competitive states (44.94% actual to 40.52% expected).

Discussion

In terms of selecting vice presidential finalists, presidential campaigns act as if motivated in part by the perception of a HSA. In short, individuals are more likely to make the final list if they come from a more competitive state. The tendency toward choosing finalists from battleground states admittedly is far from overwhelming; this we readily attribute to the fact that geography is but one of many factors relevant to vice presidential selection. In fact, we do not argue that geography is determinative of selection – only that it is a real factor in the process, as our analysis suggests. As a factor, geographic considerations could therefore have significant consequences; under the right circumstances, coming from an electoral battleground state (or not) could tip the balance in favor of (or against) a candidate's advancement to the status of vice presidential finalist or even running mate.

Campaign strategy

If the perception of a vice presidential HSA influences campaign behavior, the most telling indicator would be compensatory adjustments to campaign strategy in the running mate's home state after his or her selection. In particular, we would expect both campaigns to more vigorously contest a state for which the vice presidential HSA figures to increase competitiveness, and to less vigorously contest or even abandon a state for which the vice presidential HSA figures to decrease competitiveness. If, on the other hand, the perception of an HSA is irrelevant to campaign strategy, we would expect to see no change in campaign strategy within a vice presidential candidate's home state pre- versus post-selection. To evaluate the effect of geographic considerations on presidential campaign strategy, next we present a series of case studies followed by systematic analyses of campaign visits and spending on campaign advertisements in the 2012 election.

Case study: John Edwards, 2004

By way of illustrative example, first consider the 2004 presidential election. On July 6 of that year, Senator John Kerry of Massachusetts selected Senator John Edwards of North Carolina as his running mate on the Democratic ticket. To that point, the Kerry campaign had made no serious efforts to contest North Carolina, a state that incumbent President George W. Bush had won by 12.8% in 2000, yet some observers regarded as potentially competitive in 2004. (Four years later, North Carolina would become one of three southern states – along with Florida and Virginia – to vote for Democrat Barack Obama.) That strategy seemed to change immediately after Kerry picked Edwards.

On July 7, the day after Edwards's selection, the Kerry campaign began airing its first television advertisement in North Carolina. The ad – which was reportedly scheduled to "saturat[e] the airwaves in North Carolina for at least a week and also ... air in other states and nationally on cable"[7] – featured Kerry and Edwards, describing the latter as "the son of a mill worker who all his life has stood up for ordinary people against powerful interests." Campaign officials described the ad buy as part of an effort to begin targeting states made more competitive by the Edwards selection; according to senior campaign adviser Tad Devine, "the advertisements in North Carolina reflected the campaign's calculation that the presence of Mr. Edwards on the ticket would allow Mr. Kerry to compete in Southern states like North Carolina, Arkansas, and Louisiana."[8]

Three days later, on July 10, the Kerry-Edwards team wrapped up a four-day post-announcement tour of battleground states with a rally in North Carolina. The candidates apparently tailored their remarks to appeal to southern voters, "lacing their down-home message with increased references to faith, God and the small North Carolina town where the newcomer to the ticket grew up." Edwards, for his part, "talked about religion more than usual." The event, which attracted 25,000 spectators, appeared a major boon to the Kerry campaign. As described by the *New York Times*, "the huge turnout – Mr. Edwards' aides said it was the largest political rally ever in North Carolina – increased the Democrats' long-shot hopes of contesting a state that President Bush carried by 13 percent in 2000."[9]

The response from Kerry's opponent was immediate. On July 8 the Bush campaign announced that it would begin airing advertisements on North Carolina television as well. That same day, President Bush visited North Carolina for a fundraiser that campaign aides insisted had been scheduled weeks in advance. Organizational efforts in North Carolina also increased, or rather began taking shape; according to the *Washington Post*, "The Bush-Cheney campaign had not appointed a state leadership or begun developing a grass-roots organization in North Carolina, but it now plans to do so."[10] Bush, of course, went on to win North Carolina in 2004 by 12.4%. Nonetheless, in the immediate aftermath of the Edwards selection both campaigns clearly reacted as if it had become a more competitive state, by devoting time and money there.

Case study: Sarah Palin, 2008

Four years later, the campaign dynamics were inverted. Buoyed by an impressive organizational effort in the state's 2008 Democratic caucus, and polling that showed its candidate within four or five percentage points of Republican nominee John McCain,[11] the Barack Obama campaign announced that it was planning to contest Alaska. Deputy campaign manager Pete Rouse explained: "We've taken a look at the political dynamic of Alaska and, as a result, have made Alaska one of our 18 battleground states. We believe we can win Alaska and we're making it a priority" (cited in Cockerham 2008). Most observers assumed the announcement was a bluff; Alaska only once had voted for a Democratic presidential candidate, and that was in the Johnson landslide of 1964.

To the skeptics' surprise, however, the Obama campaign actually devoted resources to Alaska. In late June it began airing television advertisements there and in several other traditionally Republican states. The state campaign boasted several paid staffers, including a state director, field director, a general election director, and a press secretary who was a "fixture on local news" (Quinn 2008). By one media account, "hardly a day went by" (Quinn 2008) that summer without the Obama campaign issuing a press release or contacting reporters. The campaign's state director even announced that Obama was planning to visit Alaska "sometime before November."[12] "That is the plan," she assured journalists; "we are pretty sure he's going to come at the end of the summer."[13]

Democrats were not alone in viewing Alaska as competitive; the state's top Republican official agreed. In late August 2008, just days before McCain announced his selection of a running mate, Governor Sarah Palin observed in an interview with the *New Yorker*:

> Something's kind of changing here in Alaska, too, for being such a red state on the Presidential level. Obama's doing just fine in polls up here, which is kind of wigging people out, because they're saying, "This hasn't happened for decades

that in polls the D[emocrat] is doing just fine." To me, that's indicative, too. It's the no-more-status-quo, it's *change*.

Later in the interview, Palin described Alaska as "more independent" and "Turning maybe purple" due to voters' frustration with "obsessive partisanship" (Gourevitch 2008).

Then, on August 29, McCain announced his running mate: Sarah Palin. Journalists declared her selection "a blow to Obama's slim hopes of capturing Alaska" (Quinn 2008) and a move that "has taken Alaska away from Mr. Obama."[14] The Obama campaign responded as if it believed that to be the case. Within three weeks the campaign had cut spending in Alaska dramatically, pulled all state television advertisements, consolidated two of its existing state campaign offices into one, canceled the scheduled opening of an additional state office, and reassigned a press secretary to a different state. Campaign officials also announced that Obama would not visit Alaska, after all. "Initially, yeah, we thought [we] might see him," said a Democratic spokesperson. "But when your governor is running for vice president, it makes it more difficult for the opposing candidate to do well in that state" (Quinn 2008).

Case study: Joe Biden, 2008

Barack Obama's running mate in 2008, on the other hand, seemed to have no bearing on the electoral map; Delaware Senator Joe Biden came from a solidly Democratic state with only three electoral votes, which Republicans apparently had no intention of contesting. Electorally speaking, he was the Democratic Dick Cheney. Nonetheless, Obama campaign strategy suggests the perception of a geographic advantage in Biden's selection – that is, in Pennsylvania. Biden was born and raised in this battleground state, and the Obama campaign heavily emphasized his roots there. In a speech introducing his running mate, Obama repeated three times that Biden came from Scranton, Pennsylvania. Later that month, in one of many campaign stops in Pennsylvania, Biden echoed his running mate's introduction: "My name is Joe Biden," he told the exuberant crowd. "And I'm from Scranton, Pennsylvania!" Biden went on to announce the campaign's commitment of "an inordinate amount of resources, hundreds of permanent staff, significant office openings" in the state, seemingly linking these developments to his candidacy. Pennsylvanians, he noted immediately afterward, would also see a great deal of him during the campaign "because I'm coming home."[15] The appeal to state voters was not subtle; in fact, references to Biden's roots were so heavy-handed that they became something of a running joke among campaign observers. One Pennsylvania-based blogger for the *Guardian* wrote: "I know that he was born in Scranton. After all, he hasn't let anyone forget. But

I hadn't realised that we had annexed the small state to our south and gained a third (but not a fourth) senator."[16]

Admittedly, this illustration is not as strong as the two preceding. Pennsylvania, after all, was not Biden's home state, and the incessant references to his Scranton roots surely reflected, in part, a strategic effort to build rapport with working class voters nationwide. Yet, given the heavy geographic overtones of its campaign rhetoric and Obama's well-publicized difficulties in connecting with Pennsylvania voters during that year's Democratic primaries, there is good reason to believe that the perception of a vice presidential home (or in this case native) state advantage influenced the Obama campaign's strategy in Pennsylvania. If so, the Biden case is all the more striking because at first glance the selection of a Democratic running mate from Delaware seems to utterly disprove geographic motivations.

Case study: Paul Ryan, 2012

Finally, we consider Paul Ryan's vice presidential candidacy in 2012. Anecdotally, the Ryan pick was seen as a boon to Republican prospects in Wisconsin, a state that had voted for Democratic candidates in each of the five preceding presidential elections. "Until Ryan was selected as Romney's running mate, it was unclear whether Wisconsin was in play at all," *The Hill* noted in an article that October.

> Neither campaign targeted it early with ads, partly to give voters a break after the emotional June recall election of Wisconsin Gov. Scott Walker (R). But Ryan's pick helped the Republican faithful shake off their post-recall hangover, a number of GOP activists in the state told *The Hill*: Those worn out from the hard-fought recall race and those who had been less than enthusiastic about Romney rallied to the ticket once Ryan was added.[17]

An ABC News report from September echoes the theme of a HSA:

> Republicans credit the attention [from the recall election] and Romney's selection of Janesville native Rep. Paul Ryan for vice presidential running mate with boosting Romney in the polls here, and prompting Democrats to rethink their strategy. The Obama campaign began running TV ads in the state for the first time this campaign ten days ago [on September 12] and has stepped up appearances by Obama surrogates across the state.
>
> Vice President Joe Biden's two visits this year – to Eau Claire and Green Bay – have come in the past three weeks. First Lady Michelle Obama held her single Wisconsin rally of the campaign in Milwaukee in late August.[18]

Together, these reports give a sense of the change in campaign conditions and campaign strategy in Wisconsin following Mitt Romney's selection of Paul

Ryan on August 11. Their clear implication is that Ryan's selection increased Republican hopes of winning the Badger State and, based on the perception of a HSA and reported improvements in Republican performance, forced the Obama campaign to more vigorously contest that state. In other words, the perceived strength of a home state candidate caused a significant change in presidential campaign strategy, particularly in terms of candidate visits and campaign advertising.

Is this true, though? Based on media reports alone, we cannot be sure. What we need is a more systematic analysis of campaign behavior designed to measure changes occurring within the home state of the vice presidential candidate before and after his selection. To the extent that such changes occur, and in accordance with the expectation that the running mate in question will increase or decrease home state competitiveness, this analysis would provide the strongest evidence yet that: (1) presidential campaigns perceive the vice presidential HSA to be actual; and, (2) the perception of a vice presidential HSA influences the conduct of presidential campaigns.

We propose the following hypothesis: presidential campaign activity will increase in a state following the selection of a native candidate whose party does not hold the advantage in that state prior to his or her selection. Applying this hypothesis to the 2012 vice presidential candidacy of Paul Ryan, we expect campaign activity in Wisconsin to have increased among both campaigns following the announcement of Ryan's selection on August 11.[19] To measure campaign activity we use two indicators: campaign visits and spending on campaign advertisements.

Empirical analysis: Campaign visits to Wisconsin, 2012

The data for campaign visits come from an interactive graphic on the website of the *Washington Post*, titled "Presidential campaign stops: Who's going where."[20] Included in these data are records of each campaign visit made by one of the two major party presidential candidates, their running mates, or any of the four candidates' spouses, between May 29, 2012, and November 6, 2012.[21] Multiple visits within or across states on a given day are counted separately, as are joint appearances by multiple campaign personnel. For instance, a joint appearance by Barack and Michelle Obama at a campaign rally would count as two visits, and three of their joint appearances in a day would count as six visits. Recognizing that campaign activity, in general, increases as Election Day nears, we divide the number of campaign visits to Wisconsin before and after August 11 by the number of campaign visits throughout the United States before and after August 11, respectively, to derive the percentage of total campaign visits that occurred within that state.

Table 3.2 presents the results of our campaign visits analysis. The differences are dramatic, and consistent with our hypothesis. Prior to August 11, Mitt Romney was the only member of either presidential campaign to visit

Table 3.2: Presidential campaign visits to Wisconsin, June–November 2012

Pre-Ryan selection (June 1–August 10)		
	Democratic campaign	Republican campaign
June 18	–	Mitt Romney (1)
Total Visits – WI	**0**	**1**
Total Visits – US	**150**	**101**
% Wisconsin	**0%**	**0.99%**
Post-Ryan selection (August 11–November 6)		
	Democratic campaign	Republican campaign
August 12	–	Mitt Romney (1)
	–	Paul Ryan (1)
August 23	Michelle Obama (2)	–
August 27	–	Paul Ryan (1)
September 1	Joe Biden (1)	–
September 12	–	Paul Ryan (1)
September 13	Joe Biden (1)	–
September 20	–	Ann Romney (1)
September 22	Barack Obama (4)	–
September 28	Michelle Obama (1)	–
October 4	Barack Obama (1)	–
October 12	Joe Biden (2)	–
	Jill Biden (1)	–
October 15	–	Paul Ryan (1)
October 19	Michelle Obama (2)	–
October 20	Jill Biden (1)	–
October 21	Jill Biden (3)	–
October 22	Jill Biden (1)	–
October 26	Joe Biden (2)	–
October 29	–	Mitt Romney (1)
October 30	–	Paul Ryan (2)
	–	Ann Romney (1)
October 31	–	Paul Ryan (3)
November 1	Barack Obama (1)	–
November 2	Joe Biden (3)	Mitt Romney (1)
November 3	Barack Obama (1)	–
November 5	Barack Obama (1)	Paul Ryan (1)
Total Visits – WI	**28**	**15**
Total Visits – US	**375**	**364**
% Wisconsin	**7.47%**	**4.12%**

Source: *Washington Post*, "Presidential campaign stops: Who's going where." November 7, 2012. Available at: www.washingtonpost.com/wp-srv/special/politics/2012-presidential-campaign-visits. Accessed August 1, 2014.

Wisconsin, on June 18. As a percentage of Romney's 101 total campaign visits in the pre-selection period, Wisconsin constitutes 0.99%. The Obama ticket made 150 campaign visits prior to August 11, and none to Wisconsin (0%). The combined percentage for both campaigns is 0.4%.

The Republican ticket made the next visit to Wisconsin on August 12, the day after the Ryan announcement, for a joint appearance in Waukesha. Eleven days later, Michelle Obama visited Wisconsin for the first time, to speak at a campaign event and to meet with victims of a recent Sikh temple shooting. From there, campaign visits to Wisconsin steadily increased. In total, during the post-August 11 period, Barack Obama visited the state eight times; Mitt Romney, three times; Joe Biden, nine times; Paul Ryan, ten times; Michelle Obama, five times; Ann Romney, two times; Jill Biden, six times; Janna Ryan, zero times. The total number of Democratic campaign visits to Wisconsin, post-August 11, is twenty-eight, and the total number of Republican campaign visits is fifteen, for a combined total of forty-three. As a percentage of total campaign visits during this period, Wisconsin hosted 7.47% of all Democratic events, 4.12% of all Republican events, and 5.82% combined.

A close analysis of the data reveals some interesting patterns. First, the Democratic ticket visited Wisconsin nearly twice as often as the Republican ticket. Had the opposite been true, we might conclude that Republicans overplayed their hand in Wisconsin due to false hope in the vice presidential HSA, or as a strategy to lure Democrats into contesting a state they knew to be secure. The fact that Democrats played defense so aggressively in Wisconsin suggests that they had real concerns about the state, almost certainly due in part to Ryan's presence on the ticket. Of course, one might also argue that Democrats had reason to be concerned about Wisconsin following its movement toward the Republican Party in the 2010 elections and Governor Walker's victory in the June 5 recall election. True, but then why did the Democratic ticket avoid Wisconsin until after Ryan's selection in mid-August? The more plausible conclusion is that Democrats sensed growing Republican momentum in Wisconsin, particularly after the Ryan selection, and increased their campaign activity there to avoid losing a state previously thought secure.

A second pattern concerns the distribution of visits between the presidential and vice presidential candidates. After August 11, Obama and Biden made almost the same number of visits to Wisconsin (eight and nine, respectively), while Romney made many fewer than Ryan (three and ten, respectively). These disparities suggest two conclusions. First, the campaigns did not merely consign their vice presidential candidates to Wisconsin, believing that it was a second-tier battleground unworthy of a visit by the presidential candidate. If that were the case, Obama and Biden would not have visited in nearly equal measure. Second, the fact that Ryan visited Wisconsin much more often than Romney suggests a different motivation: the Republican ticket calculated, presumably on the basis of a perceived vice presidential HSA, that Ryan would be more effective at appealing to Wisconsin voters than Romney. If the

Republican ticket did not believe that Ryan had exceptional appeal in his home state, it would have sent Romney and Ryan there in equal measure, as did their Democratic counterparts.

Finally, as noted above, the presidential campaigns devoted 5.8% of their total campaign visits to Wisconsin after Ryan's selection on August 11. To put this figure in perspective, only four states hosted a higher percentage of presidential campaign visits between June 1 and November 6, 2012: Ohio (17.05%); Florida (12.72%); Virginia (11.23%); and Iowa (7.71%). Putting the vice presidential HSA aside, it is difficult to argue that Wisconsin was the fifth most competitive state in the 2012 election. In fact, the Romney-Ryan ticket ended up losing Wisconsin by nearly seven percentage points: 52.9%-46%. Ten states were decided by smaller margins than Wisconsin: Florida (0.9%); North Carolina (2%); Ohio (3%); Virginia (3.9%); Colorado (5.4%); Pennsylvania (5.4%); New Hampshire (5.5%); Iowa (5.8%); and Nevada (6.7%). What's more, the outcome in Wisconsin was entirely consistent with recent electoral history; the battleground ranking used in our analysis of vice presidential finalists ranks Wisconsin as the tenth most competitive state in 2012, based on the average difference between two-party vote shares in the previous three presidential elections.

Of course, no one can know in advance which states will be the most competitive in a given election year. Campaigns do, however, have access to polling data that can be used to measure not only the competitiveness of the race in a given state but to determine whether that state is becoming increasingly competitive over the course of the campaign. Perhaps, then, the increase in campaign visits to Wisconsin following the Ryan selection is not attributable to the perception of a HSA, but rather to polling data indicating that Obama's lead had narrowed in that state in the late summer and early fall.

To test this alternative explanation, we conducted an analysis of polling data for each of the ten most competitive states in the 2012 presidential election (judging by our battleground ranking system), to determine whether the race in Wisconsin had tightened significantly – in comparison to the other states – after the Ryan selection in August. Specifically, we begin by calculating Obama's advantage (or deficit) in each state on the first of each month from June through November 2012, using polling averages obtained from RealClearPolitics.[22] Next, we calculate the average gap between Obama and Romney at the beginning of each of the three months prior to Ryan's selection (June, July, August) and at the beginning of each of the three months following Ryan's selection (September, October, November). Finally, we subtract the pre-Ryan average from the post-Ryan average in each state to determine the degree to which the race in that state had tightened between the two periods. If, in fact, the increase in campaign visits to Wisconsin was a response to polling data indicating increasing competitiveness in that state, we should find that the gap between Obama and Romney narrowed significantly, and to a greater degree in Wisconsin than in other battleground states.

Our analysis provides no evidence to support this alternative explanation. Obama's average lead over Romney in Wisconsin was 4.57% in the three months prior to Ryan's selection, and it grew slightly to 4.7% in the three months following. Quite simply, Wisconsin did not become more competitive as the campaign progressed (and candidate visits increased). In fact, of the ten states included in our analysis, only Missouri experienced a greater decrease in competitiveness than Wisconsin. The gap between Obama and Romney's polling averages narrowed in each of the eight remaining battleground states in the period following Ryan's selection, and in seven states the post-Ryan gap was smaller than in Wisconsin. Why, then, did the presidential campaigns seemingly overestimate Wisconsin's competitiveness in 2012, by devoting a disproportionate number of visits to that state? The obvious culprit for their misjudgment is the perception of a vice presidential HSA.

Empirical analysis: Campaign advertisements in Wisconsin, 2012

To further test the impact of the perceived vice presidential HSA on campaign strategy, we analyze spending on campaign advertisements in Wisconsin before and after the Paul Ryan selection on August 11, 2012. Data for this analysis again come from an interactive graphic on the website of the *Washington Post*, this one titled "Tracking TV ads in the presidential campaign."[23] Originally collected by Kantar Media/CMAG, the data included in this graphic track the amount of money spent on television advertisements – by media market – on behalf of the Obama and Romney campaigns, between the weeks of October 31–November 6, 2011, and September 17–23, 2012. Ad spending includes expenditures made by the campaigns themselves and by supporting political action committees or interest groups. Unfortunately, the data cannot be disaggregated on the basis of source or candidate preference, thereby precluding comparisons on either basis. They do, however, represent an unusually sophisticated public resource for evaluating campaign spending patterns between, and even within, states.

For our analysis, we compare campaign ad spending in Wisconsin, as a percentage of national ad spending, before and after the Ryan announcement. Since the weekly total nearest August 11 begins with August 13–19, and the latest available weekly total comes from September 17–23, our periods of comparison are July 2–August 12 (pre-Ryan selection) and August 13–September 23 (post-Ryan selection) – forty-one and forty-two days in length, respectively. The Wisconsin media markets included in our analysis are: Milwaukee; Madison; Green Bay-Appleton; Wausau-Rhinelander; La Crosse-Eau Claire; Minneapolis-St Paul; Duluth-Superior. We do not include the Marquette (Michigan) media market in our analysis because it incorporates an extremely small portion of Wisconsin. The Minnesota-based media markets (Minneapolis-St Paul and Duluth-Superior) are included because they cover a large area within Wisconsin. Recognizing that some of the ad spending

Table 3.3: Total spending on presidential campaign advertisements in US and Wisconsin media markets, July–September 2012

Pre-Ryan selection

Dates	*National*	*Milwaukee*	*Madison*	*Green Bay*	*Wausau*	*La Crosse*	*Minneapolis*	*Duluth*
July 2–8	$12,200,000	$69,010	$51,080	$20,720	$3,740	$25,290	$91,810	$21,060
July 9–15	$16,400,000	$56,320	$38,930	$17,620	$17,000	$24,940	$76,750	$17,000
July 16–22	$19,100,000	$0	$0	$0	$0	$0	$0	$0
July 23–29	$23,400,000	$3,600	$1,770	$1,020	$0	$0	$0	$0
July 30 – August 5	$36,000,000	$42,440	$25,910	$11,010	$8,870	$20,570	$0	$0
August 6–12	$23,100,000	$94,200	$29,470	$30,540	$19,930	$51,630	$101,590	$20,140
TOTAL	**$130,200,000**	**$265,570**	**$147,160**	**$80,910**	**$49,540**	**$122,430**	**$270,150**	**$58,200**

Post-Ryan selection

Dates	*National*	*Milwaukee*	*Madison*	*Green Bay*	*Wausau*	*La Crosse*	*Minneapolis*	*Duluth*
August 13–19	$33,900,000	$300,750	$96,480	$109,610	$85,880	$104,290	$254,010	$41,170
August 20–26	$34,700,000	$374,100	$126,570	$128,810	$90,090	$127,840	$247,050	$51,410
August 27–31	$21,700,000	$155,930	$35,340	$53,490	$42,940	$65,370	$148,850	$38,410
September 1–9	$14,300,000	$143,320	$6,570	$47,400	$30,400	$55,450	$208,130	$5,970
September 10–16	$19,600,000	$296,690	$150,620	$118,090	$37,970	$47,570	$73,610	$0
September 17–23	$31,800,000	$761,830	$398,690	$251,680	$93,980	$211,880	$69,860	$17,460
TOTAL	**$156,000,000**	**$2,032,620**	**$814,270**	**$709,080**	**$381,260**	**$612,400**	**$1,001,510**	**$154,420**

Source: *Washington Post*, "Tracking TV ads in the presidential campaign." September 25, 2012. Available at: www.washingtonpost.com/wp-srv/special/politics/track-presidential-campaign-ads-2012/v1/. Accessed February 23, 2015. The data presented on this website were originally collected by Kantar Media/CMAG.

in these markets might have been principally directed toward Minnesotans, though, we also conduct separate analyses excluding one or both. However, as some journalists noted during the 2012 presidential campaign, ads aired in these markets often were primarily intended for the more competitive state of Wisconsin.[24]

Table 3.3 and Table 3.4 present the results of our ad spending analysis – first, by total spending across Wisconsin media markets, and then as percentages of national spending. Including all Wisconsin media markets, the percentage of national ad spending in Wisconsin in the pre-Ryan selection period was only 0.76%. In the post-Ryan selection period, that percentage rose to 3.66% (a 381.58% increase over the first period's percentage). Excluding the Minnesota-based media markets only strengthens the relationship. Including all media markets except Minneapolis-St Paul, the pre- and post-Ryan selection percentages are 0.56% and 3.02%, respectively (a 439.29% increase). Including all media markets except Minneapolis-St Paul and Duluth-Superior, the pre- and post-Ryan selection percentages are 0.51% and 2.92%, respectively (a 472.55% increase). Finally, we isolate the Madison media market, which includes Paul Ryan's hometown of Janesville, Wisconsin. There, campaign ad spending represented 0.11% of national ad spending prior to the Ryan selection and 0.52% afterward (a 372.73% increase). In short, campaign ad spending in Wisconsin, as a percentage of all national ad spending, increased dramatically – quadrupling or nearly quintupling – after Ryan's selection as the Republican vice presidential candidate.

Comparing across weeks within each period (not all of which are properly divided into seven-day periods), the differences remain stark. Prior to Ryan's selection, the percentage of national ad spending in all Wisconsin media markets ranged between 0% and 2.32%, with the latter figure coming in early July. After Ryan's selection, the percentage of national ad spending in all Wisconsin media markets ranged between 2.49% and 5.68%, with the latter figure coming in the last week of analysis: September 17–23. In fact, in that last week ad spending in Ryan's home media market of Madison alone accounted for 1.25% of all national ad spending. Restricting the data to exclude Minnesota-based media markets does nothing to alter these trends.

In summary, Wisconsin's weekly share of national campaign ad spending was always higher in the post-selection period than in the pre-selection period, and its total share of national campaign ad spending in the post-selection period represented an approximately 400% increase over the pre-selection spending. These conclusions hold even when excluding Minnesota-based media markets and when isolating Ryan's home media market – which during one week in mid-September attracted $1 out of every $80 spent on presidential campaign ads in the United States. This evidence, combined with the preceding analysis of campaign visits, provides strong support for our stated hypothesis.

Table 3.4: Percentage of national spending on presidential campaign advertisements in Wisconsin media markets, July–September 2012

Pre-Ryan selection

Dates	*All Wisconsin markets*	*Excluding Minneapolis*	*Excluding Minneapolis and Duluth*	*Ryan home market (Madison) only*
July 2–8	2.32%	1.56%	1.39%	0.42%
July 9–15	1.52%	1.05%	0.94%	0.24%
July 16–22	0%	0%	0%	0%
July 23–29	0.03%	0.03%	0.03%	0.01%
July 30–August 5	0.3%	0.3%	0.3%	0.07%
August 6–12	1.5%	1.06%	0.98%	0.13%
TOTAL	**0.76%**	**0.56%**	**0.51%**	**0.11%**

Post-Ryan selection

Dates	*All Wisconsin markets*	*Excluding Minneapolis*	*Excluding Minneapolis and Duluth*	*Ryan home market (Madison) only*
August 13–19	2.93%	2.18%	2.06%	0.28%
August 20–26	3.3%	2.59%	2.44%	0.36%
August 27–31	2.49%	1.8%	1.63%	0.16%
September 1–9	3.48%	2.02%	1.98%	0.05%
September 10–16	3.7%	3.32%	3.32%	0.77%
September 17–23	5.68%	5.46%	5.4%	1.25%
TOTAL	**3.66%**	**3.02%**	**2.92%**	**0.52%**
Increase (pre- to post-)	**381.58%**	**439.29%**	**472.55%**	**372.73%**

Source: *Washington Post*, "Tracking TV ads in the presidential campaign." September 25, 2012. Available at: www.washingtonpost.com/wp-srv/special/politics/track-presidential-campaign-ads-2012/v1/. Accessed February 23, 2015. The data presented on this website were originally collected by Kantar Media/CMAG.

Conclusion

From the wealth of data presented here and in the previous chapter, we conclude: (1) the perception of a vice presidential HSA endures in American politics; and, (2) this perception has a discernible impact on actual campaign behavior. Indeed, it is neither a historical artifact nor an irrelevant curiosity. The perception is widespread and it has real-world consequences relevant to understanding presidential politics.

But is the perception a reality? Do vice presidential candidates actually strengthen a presidential ticket in their home state? And under what circumstances is a vice presidential HSA most likely to occur, or to be maximized? The answers to these questions are not just academically relevant; given the results of our analysis thus far, campaign strategists and even presidential candidates – not to mention journalists and the public at large – would be wise to test their perceptions of a vice presidential HSA against the empirical evidence. What they'll find in the chapters that follow may be surprising.

Notes

1 Prior to 1940, vice presidential nominations were decided by delegates to the Party Convention. The Republican Party did not allow its presidential candidate to select a running mate in 1940, however, and in 1956 Democratic presidential nominee Adlai Stevenson allowed his running mate to be chosen by vote of the Convention. Following Sigelman and Wahlbeck (1997), we exclude these two cases from our analysis.

2 Sigelman and Wahlbeck (1997, 857) explain:

> determining who is seriously considered for the vice presidential slot in a given year can be difficult, for there is no definitive, "official" source of such information. Goldstein (1982) compiled such lists from 1952 through 1980. Our search of source materials upheld the validity of those lists, so we adopted them here. Our remaining task was to extend the lists back to the beginning of the modern era, 1940, and forward to the most recent election year, 1996. We drew heavily on contemporary media reports (especially in *Newsweek, Time,* and the *New York Times*, for June, July, and August of each presidential election year); political biographies, memoirs, and oral histories (e.g., Martin 1977, Nixon 1978, Smith 1982); and numerous other sources (most notably Witcover's [1992] history of vice presidential selection and performance).

In applying this methodology, we arrive at a different list of vice-presidential finalists in 2000 than Hiller and Kriner (2008). First, with regard to Democrats, presidential nominee Al Gore took the unusual step of releasing his list of six vice-presidential finalists to the media shortly before selecting Joe Lieberman (see, for example: http://community.seattletimes.nwsource.com/archive/?date=20000804&slug=4035135. Accessed February 23, 2015). Two names on this list, Richard Gephardt and Jeanne Shaheen, are not included in Hiller and Kriner's list of finalists. While it is possible that Gephardt or Shaheen were included for public relations purposes and not seriously considered, we have seen no convincing evidence that this is the case and therefore include them as finalists. Second, with regard to Republicans, a new and more authoritative source has emerged since the publication of Hiller and Kriner's article. George W. Bush's 2010 memoir, *Decision Points*, reports that he considered ten vice-presidential finalists: Tom Ridge, Frank Keating, John Engler, Lamar Alexander, John Danforth, Chuck Hagel, Jon Kyl, Fred Thompson, Bill Frist, and Dick Cheney. Hiller and Kriner included two names not on Bush's list (John Kasich and Connie Mack), and did not include five of Bush's reported finalists (Engler, Kyl, Alexander, Thompson, and Frist).

3 Two-party vote shares are computed using 1928–2012 presidential election returns obtained from the online CQ Press Voting and Elections Collection. See: http://library.cqpress.com/elections/index.php. Accessed February 23, 2015.

4 Alaska and Hawaii are excluded from analysis of the 1940–1956 selections because they were not yet states, and from analysis in 1960 because they had no past voting record by which to measure competitiveness. They are, however, included in the 1964 and 1968 data by using one- and two-election voting trends, respectively.

5 Following the practice of Goldstein (1982) and Sigelman and Wahlbeck's (1997), we do not include incumbent vice presidents in our calculation, since there is only one case in which they have not been retained as running mates in the modern era (Nelson Rockefeller, 1976).

6 Differences in state population also could plausibly affect whether a given state is represented among the list of vice presidential finalists; quite simply, more populous states have more residents available for selection and thus may have an advantage that is not factored into this analysis. However, most vice presidential finalists come from the ranks of governors and US senators, which are equally distributed among states. (Of the 158 vice presidential finalists included in our sample, ninety-eight, or 62%, were currently serving as governors or senators, and an additional thirteen, or 8.2%, had previously served as governors or senators.) And since there is no reason to believe that state population is related to a state's competitiveness in presidential elections, population differences would not explain systematic overrepresentation of competitive states among vice presidential finalists.

7 See: www.foxnews.com/story/2004/07/07/kerry-camp-begins-airing-new-ads-in-nc/#ixzz2ZGvYF0EW. Accessed February 23, 2015.

8 See: www.nytimes.com/2004/07/09/us/2004-campaign-democratic-ticket-kerry-camp-sees-edwards-helping-with-rural-vote.html?pagewanted=all&src=pm. Accessed February 23, 2015.

9 See: www.nytimes.com/2004/07/09/us/2004-campaign-democratic-ticket-kerry-camp-sees-edwards-helping-with-rural-vote.html?pagewanted=all&src=pm. Accessed February 23, 2015.

10 See: www.washingtonpost.com/wp-dyn/articles/A34832-2004Jul7.html. Accessed February 23, 2015.

11 Obama trailed McCain by four percentage points in a June 16 poll conducted by Rasmussen Reports, a firm notorious among some Democrats for an alleged Republican bias; and by five percentage points in a June 25 poll conducted by David Dittman, a local pollster then employed by Alaska's Republican Senator Ted Stevens. Given these sources, it is unlikely that Obama's impressive performance was attributable to a pro-Obama bias among the pollsters.

12 See: www.huffingtonpost.com/amanda-coyne/obama-going-north-to-alas_b_109216.html. Accessed July 31, 2013.

13 See: http://latimesblogs.latimes.com/washington/2008/07/alaska-beckons.html. Accessed February 23, 2015.

14 See: www.telegraph.co.uk/news/worldnews/barackobama/2712605/Barack-Obama-lowers-expectations-as-John-McCains-popularity-surges.html. Accessed February 23, 2015.

15 See: http://abcnews.go.com/blogs/politics/2008/08/biden-calls-pa/. Accessed February 23, 2015.

16 See: www.theguardian.com/commentisfree/2008/aug/30/joebiden.democrats2008. Accessed February 23, 2015.

17 See here: http://thehill.com/homenews/campaign/262393-ryan-tries-to-break-through-obamas-midwestern-firewall. Accessed February 23, 2015.

18 See here: http://abcnews.go.com/blogs/politics/2012/09/obama-campaign-shifts-gears-in-wisconsin-strategy/. Accessed February 23, 2015.

19 As previously noted, Republicans had not won a presidential election in Wisconsin since 1984. Moreover, nearly all polls showed Mitt Romney trailing in Wisconsin prior to August 11, 2012. See: www.realclearpolitics.com/epolls/2012/president/wi/wisconsin_romney_vs_obama-1871.html#polls. Accessed February 23, 2015.

20 See: www.washingtonpost.com/wp-srv/special/politics/2012-presidential-campaign-visits/. Accessed February 23, 2015.

21 To simplify the time frame, we begin our analysis with data from June 1. Excluding the three previous days has no bearing on our conclusions, since neither campaign visited Wisconsin during that time.

22 See: www.realclearpolitics.com/epolls/2012/president/2012_elections_electoral_college_map.html. Accessed May 20, 2015.

23 See: www.washingtonpost.com/wp-srv/special/politics/track-presidential-campaign-ads-2012/v1/. Accessed February 23, 2015.

24 Consider, for example, this comment from a news report in the *Huffington Post*: "On Friday, the Romney campaign announced it would begin airing ads on broadcast television in Minneapolis – not to test the waters in Minnesota, though they welcomed speculation that that's what they were doing – but to filter into media markets in western Wisconsin." See: www.huffingtonpost.com/2012/10/26/mitt-romney-2012-campaign_n_2026484.html. Accessed February 23, 2015.

4

An empirical analysis of the vice presidential home state advantage (state-level data)

The perception of a vice presidential home state advantage (HSA) is alive and well in contemporary American politics. But is it a reality? *Do* vice presidential candidates enjoy an electoral advantage in their home state, after all? How does one measure the vice presidential HSA, anyway? How big (or small) is it, on average? And does the advantage apply to all vice presidential candidates in equal measure, or does it vary depending on candidate and state characteristics? If the latter, then which characteristics matter (most)? Our objective in this chapter is to answer these vital research questions, on an empirical – rather than a speculative – basis. To do so, we present a first-of-its-kind, multi-method analysis of the vice presidential home state advantage.

There is, in fact, no single empirical method for measuring home state advantages. Scholars have used multiple methods to do so, but only in independent analyses; no systematic comparison of methods exists to guide us toward preferring one method over another. In this chapter we compare and contrast the two leading methods of measuring the vice presidential HSA, to provide an empirical basis for judging their relative merits and identifying potential differences in the results they produce. The first method is the formal equation developed by Lewis-Beck and Rice (1983), which we use to estimate vice presidential HSAs in the 1884–2012 elections. The second method is a state-level, fixed effects regression model, which we also use to estimate vice presidential HSAs within the 1884–2012 period. To the extent that we discover meaningful differences between these two methods, our research may help future HSA scholars choose the most appropriate one for their analysis. Moreover, with respect to the present analysis, if both methods of operationalization yield similar results in terms of the statistical significance and magnitude of vice presidential HSAs, our substantive conclusions will not be attributable to the use of a particular empirical method but rather confirmed across multiple methods. It is also worth noting that we use aggregate (that is, state- and national-level) data for both methods of analysis in this chapter. Later in this chapter, we explain why the use of such data may be problematic, and in Chapter 5 we address this issue by using individual-level data (as well as dependent variables other than vote choice) to evaluate the vice presidential HSA.

Before we begin this analysis, it is important to answer a more fundamental question: is there any reason to expect a vice presidential candidate to provide an electoral advantage in his or her home state, in the first place? In other words, is there any *theoretical* basis for expecting a vice presidential HSA to occur? Answering this question is critical not only to understanding the subject of this book, but also to identifying the appropriate empirical method for measuring the HSA (if one exists) and the dynamics that shape it. To that end, in the following section we build on our discussion from Chapter 1 regarding the expectation that voters are more likely to support local candidates because such candidates are viewed as "one of our own." This is what V. O. Key famously referred to as the "friends and neighbors" hypothesis, and its theoretical implications for understanding the vice presidential home state advantage are profound.

The friends and neighbors hypothesis

V. O. Key first proposed the "friends and neighbors" hypothesis in his classic 1949 work, *Southern Politics in State and Nation*. According to Key, candidates for elected office should perform best among voters living in close geographic proximity to them. Key provided four reasons for expecting such an advantage; local voters are most likely to: (1) be familiar with the candidate and his/her political qualifications and stances; (2) come into personal contact with the candidate's staff, associates, or even the candidate him/herself; (3) view the candidate as knowledgeable about local concerns and inclined to direct government resources toward addressing them; and, (4) share a common sense of geographic identity and therefore see the candidate as "one of our own."

Empirical evidence

There is much evidence to support Key's four reasons for expecting a friends and neighbors effect. Let us consider examples for each of them, in order. First, to the point of voter familiarity with local candidates, research indicates that voters who reside outside of a candidate's media market are less likely to receive information about the candidate, and as a result, are less likely to vote for the candidate than voters in the candidate's home media market (Bowler, Donovan, and Snipp 1993). Second, we know that elected officials – such as members of Congress – make substantial efforts to maintain direct contact with constituents by spending time in their district, holding town hall meetings, and operating local offices that provide constituent services (see Fenno 1978). Moreover, some studies indicate that the electoral effects of such efforts, including direct contact with voters and casework on behalf of constituents, are significant and positive

(Kenny and McBurnett 1997; Serra and Moon 1994; Yiannakis 1981; but see Weisberg, Heberlig and Campoli 1999, 75). Third, "pork-barrel spending" – or legislators' efforts to direct budgetary resources toward localized projects and services – often by introducing amendments to unrelated bills – is an indisputable fact of legislative politics that has been shown to yield at least some electoral benefits for the responsible officeholder (see, for example, Alvarez and Saving 1997).[1] Fourth, the notion that voters are more likely to view a local candidate as "one of our own" is strongly supported by social identity theory. The social identity literature holds that individuals view the groups with which they identify as extensions of the self and therefore they favor fellow in-group members (see, for example, Tajfel and Turner 1979; Tajfel 1981; Turner *et al.* 1987). To the extent that individuals identify as members of their state, then, they should be expected to favor other members of that in-group, including home state candidates. Indeed, research indicates that geography can and does serve as a basis for meaningful social identities and their attendant attitudinal and behavioral consequences (e.g., Cuba and Hummon 1993; Paasi 1986, 2003, 2009).

Not only are Key's four motivational factors well-supported in the scholarly literature, but there is also robust evidence in the political science, economics, and geography literatures to support the friends and neighbors hypothesis in a variety of electoral contexts. Besides Key's (1949) original finding of a friends and neighbors effect in southern Democratic gubernatorial primaries, scholars have found similar effects when analyzing support for George Wallace among Alabama voters in the 1968 presidential election (Black and Black 1973); Congressional elections in Alabama (Kjar and Laband 2002); statewide elections in Mississippi (Tatalovich 1975); US Senate elections in Mississippi (Van Wingen and Parker 1979); statewide and state legislative elections in Mississippi, Montana, and Vermont (Bryan 1981); statewide elections in California (Rice and Macht 1987a); gubernatorial elections held in 1982 (Rice and Macht 1987b); gubernatorial elections held between 1998 and 2006 (Gimpel *et al.* 2008); voting for Franklin Roosevelt in communities surrounding Warm Springs, Georgia, in the 1940 and 1944 presidential elections (Mixon 2013); voting for state appellate court judges (Aspin and Hall 1989); and campaign donations to Texas Supreme Court candidates (Thielemann 1993). Nor is the friends and neighbors effect an exclusively American phenomenon; evidence of similar effects is found in nations as diverse as the United Kingdom (Arzheimer and Evans 2014), New Zealand (Johnston 1974), and the Czech Republic (Malcová 2012).

Applicability to presidential elections

While the friends and neighbors effect has been documented in state and local elections, there is some reason to question its general applicability to *presidential* elections. After all, state and local officials represent a much smaller constituency and address issues that can differ greatly – in type and in scale – from those that a president or vice president confronts. Is it reasonable, then, to expect that friends and neighbors effects found among home town, county, or district voters in state-level elections would extend to statewide electorates in presidential elections? To put it another way: are we safe to assume that the friends and neighbors hypothesis *scales up* to the highest level of American elections?

Key's conception of the friends and neighbors hypothesis was exclusive to elections at the state and sub-state level. In fact, he believed that the nationalization of politics by the mid-twentieth century rendered the friends and neighbors hypothesis irrelevant to presidential elections. Key explained:

> In recent decades the issues and forces of national politics have tended to wear down sectional groupings. The new issues push people, wherever they live, towards divisions different from the traditional sectional cleavages and the states gradually have become more alike in the manner of their presidential voting. (Key 1956, 26–27)

Lewis-Beck and Rice (1983), for their part, rejected Key's line of argument while adopting his theory in their groundbreaking study of the presidential HSA. Loyalty to a home state presidential candidate, they argued, "is not wholly unreasonable" because in such situations "We are offered the psychological satisfaction of identification with a president who is more like our 'friends and neighbors.' Further, we might hope that as president he would remember the 'folks back home' when distributing federal largess." At a more sentimental level, "It gives us a chance to show 'pride in our own' by voting for a native son" (Lewis-Beck and Rice 1983, 552; see also Brogan 1954, 197). Lewis-Beck and Rice's empirical analysis indicates they were right; presidential candidates receive, on average, a statistically significant and positive HSA. In other words, presidential candidates win a significantly higher percentage of the vote in their home state than what would be expected otherwise based upon state and national voting trends. And in subsequent studies, as we discuss later in this chapter, other scholars have confirmed this finding of a presidential HSA using various research methodologies.[2]

Dudley and Rapoport (1989) took the logical next step by studying whether – as so many observers of American politics have long assumed – friends and neighbors voting benefits *vice presidential* candidates in their home state. While Lewis-Beck and Rice find that presidential candidates receive, on average, a statistically significant and positive HSA, Dudley and Rapoport – using a variation of the Lewis-Beck and Rice formal equation, which we describe later in this chapter – find no such advantage among vice presidential candidates, in general (see also Garand 1988; Holbrook 1991; Rosenstone 1983). Instead, Dudley and Rapoport find that the vice presidential HSA is conditional; it depends on the population of the candidate's home state. Specifically, vice presidential candidates hailing from relatively less-populous states are most likely to receive an electoral advantage. Devine and Kopko (2011, 2013) later clarified the effect of home state population on the vice presidential HSA by demonstrating the presence of an interactive effect; candidates not only need to come from a relatively less-populous state to earn a statistically significant advantage, but they also must have substantial experience in elected office within that state. In other words, the vice presidential HSA is not generally applicable, but exclusive to candidates who have served at length, and presumably with some success, in a relatively intimate political environment. Vice presidential candidates who come from more populous states or lack extensive experience in state politics will not clearly meet these criteria, and thus are not expected to earn a significant HSA.

HSAs in presidential elections therefore vary systematically between presidential and vice presidential candidates; the effect of a home state candidacy is statistically significant for the former, in general; while it is conditional for the latter. And perhaps it is not surprising that such systematic differences exist. After all, there are many differences between presidential and vice presidential candidates. Presidential candidates generally receive far more media attention throughout the course of a campaign (see, for example, Ulbig 2010, 2013), and presidents exercise much more power in office than vice presidents. That these differences would influence how voters weight the relevance of a home state presidential versus vice presidential candidacy is not only unsurprising, it may be entirely reasonable.

Taking stock of the evidence provided thus far, we find strong empirical support for the assumptions and general applicability of Key's friends and neighbors hypothesis. The hypothesis even applies to presidential elections, despite Key's strong doubts, but differentially with respect to presidential versus vice presidential candidacies – the former being generally significant and the latter being conditionally so. To meaningfully evaluate these conclusions, however, requires that we answer a fundamental – and deceptively complex – question: what is the best way to measure a HSA? In other words, how do we know if, and by how much, a presidential ticket performs *better* in a vice presidential candidate's home state than it would have if that candidate had not been on the ticket? It is our objective in the next section to answer this question.

Measuring the HSA

Determining whether a vice presidential candidate delivers an electoral advantage in his or her home state is more complicated than one might initially expect. In fact, there are many ways to measure, or operationalize, the HSA in a presidential election. Although our focus in this chapter will be on the two most common methods used by scholars – the Lewis-Beck and Rice (1983) formal equation and regression models – it is useful to illustrate the merits of these methodological approaches by first considering the strengths and weaknesses of several simpler, alternative measures.

Descriptive measures

Perhaps the simplest way to descriptively measure[3] a vice presidential home state advantage is to calculate the percentage of running mates that have won their home state in a presidential election. Excluding uncontested elections (1789, 1792, 1820), or those in which both leading candidates had the same running mate (1824), there have been 106 major-party vice presidential candidacies since 1789. In sixty of those cases (56.6%) the vice presidential candidate's ticket has won his or her home state. Results vary slightly when excluding vice presidential candidates who shared a home state with an opposing vice presidential candidate (57%), and when excluding those who shared a home state with an opposing vice presidential candidate *or* presidential candidate (59.8%). In the modern era of vice presidential selection, the percentage is even higher; among running mates chosen directly by a presidential candidate, all since 1940, 75% have carried their home state.

Based upon this evidence it would appear that there is, in fact, a significant HSA; vice presidential candidates typically win in their home state, and their success rate has increased dramatically in recent years. Yet this descriptive method of evaluating the HSA has obvious deficiencies. Most notably, it does not account for a state's predisposition to vote for or against a given party. Take, for example, Wyoming in 2000 and 2004. The Bush-Cheney ticket won the state decisively in both elections, yet there is every reason to believe it would have done so even without Cheney on the ticket; Wyoming, after all, has voted Republican in every presidential election since 1968. In fact, the 75% success rate of modern vice presidential candidates in their home state, noted above, is much less impressive when considering that in 69% of those cases the state had also voted for that candidate's party in the previous election. To evaluate the vice presidential HSA, then, we must do more than tally wins and losses; we must determine whether the running mate's presence on the ticket led to an *improvement* in party performance, relative to past elections.

The starkest measure of improvement, in this context, is "flipping" a state – in other words, winning a vice presidential candidate's home state after the same party lost it in the previous election. After excluding cases in which the vice presidential candidate's party won his or her home state in the previous election, as well as those in which the vice presidential candidate came from the same state as an opposing presidential or vice presidential candidate, we are left with forty-nine cases to analyze. Of those forty-nine cases, the running mate's party flipped the home state only eighteen times, for a success rate of 36.7%. Clearly, vice presidential candidates are not guaranteed to "deliver" the home state; more often than not, they *fail* to reverse a party loss in the previous election. Even so, this measure is hardly equipped to capture the concept of a vice presidential HSA. Suppose, for example, that state i votes 60%–40% in favor of the Democratic Party in election t, without a home state running mate on either national ticket. Then, in election $t+1$, the Republican Party nominates a vice presidential candidate from state *i* and the state votes 51%-49% in favor of the Democratic Party. For the purpose of this illustration, let us assume that this reduction in the Democratic Party's margin of victory was due to the popularity of the vice presidential candidate in state *i*. Although the Republican running mate has failed to "flip" the home state in his party's favor, there is good reason to believe that he provided the ticket with a significant electoral advantage that, under more favorable conditions, could have provided the margin of victory. By the same token, a vice presidential candidate could provide an HSA by turning what would have been a narrow victory into a decisive one.

To provide a more nuanced measure of HSA, then, we ought to focus on *changes in party vote share* rather than electoral outcomes. The most obvious way of doing so is to subtract the vote percentage won by the vice presidential candidate's party in his or her home state in the previous election from the vote percentage won by the same party in the current election, when the home state vice presidential candidate appears on the ballot. More specifically, we calculate the difference in *two-party vote share* – i.e., the proportion of votes cast for the two major parties in that election – won by the vice presidential candidate's party, across the two elections, so as to account for the idiosyncratic effects of third-party candidacies on raw party vote percentages. After excluding candidacies for which reliable state vote percentages are not available in either or both elections,[4] as well as candidacies in which multiple home state candidates appeared on the ballot, we are left with seventy-eight cases to analyze. Across those cases, the average improvement in home state two-party vote share for the vice presidential candidate's party is 1.3%, and in forty cases (51.3%) the change in two-party vote share is positive. However, in ten of these cases the vice presidential candidate in question had also appeared on the ballot in the previous election; after eliminating those cases, we find that the average improvement in home state two-party vote share for the vice presidential candidate's party increases to 2.2%, with thirty-nine cases (57.4%) showing a positive change in two-party vote share.

While certainly an improvement over the preceding measures, this method of estimating the vice presidential HSA suffers from two major flaws: first, it fails to account for the concomitant influence of national electoral factors; second, the baseline for comparison is limited to a single preceding election. To illustrate the significance of these flaws, consider the case of John Nance Garner, Franklin Roosevelt's running mate in the 1932 presidential election. In 1932 the Democratic ticket won 88.6% of the two-party vote share in Garner's home state of Texas, after winning only 48.2% in the 1928 presidential election. Based solely upon the difference in two-party vote share between these two elections, Garner would be credited with an astounding 40.4% vice presidential HSA! The absurdity of this estimate becomes clear, however, when factoring in national voting patterns. In 1928 Republican presidential candidate Herbert Hoover won 58.2% of the national vote and forty-one of forty-eight states – including southern states, such as Texas, that had not voted Republican since

Reconstruction, if ever – owing largely to economic prosperity under the incumbent Republican administration and the Democratic Party's nomination of Al Smith, a Catholic and a "wet" on Prohibition. Following the stock market crash of 1929 and the onset of the Great Depression, the Democratic Party's electoral fortunes reversed almost completely; in 1932, the Roosevelt-Garner ticket won 59.1% of the national two-party vote share and forty-two of forty-eight states – including Texas and every other southern state.

To attribute changes in Texas's two-party vote share between these two elections to the introduction of a home state vice presidential candidate in 1932 is to ignore the idiosyncratic national forces at play in both elections. In 1928 and 1932, Texas's vote reflected the preferences of the nation at large, albeit skewing more toward the Democratic Party given the state's pronounced partisan leanings. Indeed, the 1928 election was clearly an aberration for Texas – given that it had never before voted for a Republican candidate – and thus serves as a misleading baseline for comparing the 1932 vote to past state voting trends. To accurately measure Garner's vice presidential HSA – or any other such advantage, since landslide elections are not unique to this time period and national forces shift to some degree in every election – therefore requires: (1) a more extensive baseline for comparison to previous elections; and, (2) a means of anchoring the home state's vote to the national vote. These two insights were central to the formulation of the political science literature's standard measure of the HSA: the Lewis-Beck and Rice equation.

The Lewis-Beck and Rice equation

For more than thirty years, Lewis-Beck and Rice's (1983) formal equation has served as the primary method of estimating the presidential HSA (Devine and Kopko 2013; Disarro, Barber, and Rice 2007; Garand 1988), vice presidential HSA (Devine and Kopko 2011, 2013; Dudley and Rapoport 1989), and home county advantage in state elections (Rice and Macht 1987a). Accounting for the deficiencies of alternatives measures, noted in the preceding discussion, Lewis-Beck and Rice operationalized the HSA as the difference between a home state's deviation from its past partisan voting trends and the nation's deviation from its past partisan voting trends. The formal equation accounting for these deviations is:

$$H = (S_a - S_e) - (N_a - N_e)$$

where H is the presidential candidate's estimated HSA in a given election; S_a is the vote percentage won by the presidential candidate in his or her home state in a given election; S_e is the average vote percentage won by the presidential candidate's party in his or her home state over the five most recent presidential elections; N_a is the vote percentage won by the presidential candidate nationally in a given election; and N_e is the average vote percentage won by the presidential candidate's party nationally over the five most recent elections.[5]

Undoubtedly, the Lewis-Beck and Rice equation's face validity has contributed to its endurance in the HSA literature. This equation essentially accounts for *deviations* in state voting trends over time relative to deviations in the national vote over time. The assumption underlying this equation is that the deviations in a state's vote can be attributed to the introduction of a home state candidate.[6] The five-election average of state and national voting trends helps to isolate any outlier elections that may have occurred in recent history. Also, by incorporating both state and national deviations, the equation should account for shocks that uniquely affect state and/or national voting. Since the equation simply focuses on deviations in aggregate voting trends – measurable through state and national election returns – it can be used to estimate HSAs across a wide range of elections throughout history. As conceived by Lewis-Beck and Rice, the equation is applicable to all elections since 1884.[7]

Using this equation, Lewis-Beck and Rice estimated the average *presidential* HSA in the 1884–1980 elections to be 4%, and statistically distinguishable from zero. More recent studies corroborate these findings. For example, Devine and Kopko's (2013) analysis of the 1884–2008 presidential elections estimated the average presidential HSA to be 3.61%, and statistically distinguishable from zero.

The Lewis-Beck and Rice equation is equally applicable to estimating the *vice presidential* HSA. "Such an extension," Dudley and Rapoport (1989, 537) have argued, "seems particularly warranted since the vice-presidential candidate is one political nomination still made by party elites who can purposely take regional appeals into account."[8] Using the Lewis-Beck and Rice equation, Dudley and Rapoport (1989) estimated the vice presidential HSA to be 0.3% in the1884–1984 presidential elections. However, unlike the presidential HSA, this estimate of the vice presidential HSA *was not* statistically distinguishable from zero.

These estimates are, of course, dependent upon the Lewis-Beck and Rice equation – and that equation is subject to methodological critique. For example, some scholars, including Tom Rice, have suggested that it makes more sense to use N_a–N_e as an independent variable in a regression model to predict S_a–S_e (see Disarro, Barber, and Rice 2007). Furthermore, Heersink and Peterson (2014) have argued that the Lewis-Beck and Rice equation violates the assumptions of the pre-post difference-in-difference research design, because state and national voting trends over time are not always parallel, resulting in biased HSA estimates in some cases.[9] An additional limitation is the fact that the Lewis-Beck and Rice equation does not produce reliable HSA scores for elections in which the two major party vice presidential candidates or a vice presidential candidate and a presidential candidate share the same home state – a limitation most commonly addressed by excluding such cases from analysis. When candidates share the same home state it is impossible to disentangle their electoral effects.[10]

Another potential criticism of the Lewis-Beck and Rice equation is that it uses a five-election trend to produce its estimates of the HSA. Why should current state and national vote projections be based in part on election results from sixteen or twenty years earlier? The reason, of course, is that longer lags help to flatten out the effects of idiosyncratic elections, in comparison to shorter lags that are more heavily biased by such elections. Certainly, using a two- or three-election trend for S_e and N_e may produce skewed estimates in response to a series of outlier elections. Take the 1988 presidential election, for example. Republicans won all but Minnesota and the District of Columbia in 1984, and all but six states plus the District of Columbia in 1980. If we were to calculate home state voting trends in 1988 based on the two most recent elections (maximizing our sensitivity to realignment trends), we would project Michael Dukakis's Massachusetts to vote Republican, and – since he won the state by eight percentage points – our calculations would then credit him with a very large presidential HSA. This would be a mischaracterization, though, since Massachusetts was still a strongly Democratic state, although it had voted for Ronald Reagan in two lopsided presidential elections won by his Republican ticket. Indeed, the state had not voted for a Republican since 1956 and has not voted for one since 1984. Such a skewed result would also occur, but to a lesser extent, using a three-election lag.

One could argue, however, that a four-election average more appropriately balances sensitivity to recent state trends and outlier elections than a five-election lag. That may be a fair criticism. To evaluate this alternative measurement strategy we estimate the Lewis-Beck and Rice formal equation using a four-election lag of two-party vote share and then compare it with results from the five-election lag to determine whether, and to what extent, substantial differences are discernible between the two estimates. No such systematic comparison exists elsewhere in the HSA literature.

Why stop there, though? What about a six- or seven-election lag? Frankly, we see no compelling reason to prefer a six- or seven-election lag. A five-election lag is sufficient to smooth over the effects of outlier elections, and extending the lags further only increases the risk of skewing our estimates in a different direction by including more of what political scientists call "critical elections," in which a sudden and lasting shift in party power and/or party constituencies takes place. Critical elections, after all, have typically occurred at thirty-six-year intervals, by the most common scholarly estimates. A twenty-four- or twenty-eight-year lag therefore brings us perilously close to guaranteeing the inclusion of a largely outdated, irrelevant election in many HSA estimates. What's more, using a six- or seven-election lag would limit the number of observations used to calculate HSA over time, by excluding some early elections from our analysis, while also unnecessarily distorting estimates for elections immediately following the now-excluded cases. In short, we see little benefit and significant cost in lengthening the lag any further. Comparing four- and five-election lags is worthwhile because both lags reasonably balance concerns over (recent) outlier and (distant) critical elections.

Table 4.1: VP home state advantage scores – Lewis-Beck and Rice equation

Party/year	Four-election lag HSA	Five-election lag HSA	Party/year	Four-election lag HSA	Five-election lag HSA
R2012	−0.04	−0.47	R1948	5.67	3.68
D2012	1.4	2.26	D1948	5.02	5.18
R2008	0.89	2	R1944	−0.72	−0.97
D2008	4.67	6	D1944	−3.49	−5.7
R2004	7	6.97	R1940	0.66	0.64
D2004	0.54	0.01	D1940	−1.78	−0.93
R2000	11.44	10.64	R1936	−0.81	−1.3
D2000	7.54	7.89	D1936	−3.78	−3.97
R1996	−6.04	−6.85	R1932	−1.21	0.18
D1996	−3.69	−4.76	D1932	0.52	1.49
R1992	2.66	2.64	R1928	12.15	12.39
D1992	−2.69	−0.81	D1928	−1.56	−0.4
R1988	1.98	1.52	R1924	0.9	0.82
D1988	–	–	D1924	1.26	4.23
R1984	3.39	4.03	R1920	1.02	0.83
D1984	2.3	1.43	D1920	−4.56	−4.66
R1980	1.6	1.84	R1912	–	–
D1980	1.52	2.59	D1912	−1.48	−0.84
R1976	−4.16	−3.92	R1908	1.01	1.03
D1976	0.83	0.99	D1908	2.72	3.05
R1972	–	–	R1904	−2.51	−2.47
D1972	–	–	D1904	3.79	3.41
R1968	−0.15	−1.04	R1900	−0.44	−0.22
D1968	12.53	13.32	D1900	0.9	1.17
R1964	−8.35	−8.37	R1896	10.22	10.36
D1964	−0.22	0.51	D1896	−9.78	−9.59
R1960	–	–	R1892	–	–
D1960	−12.11	−14.71	D1892	2.65	2.26
R1956	−1.58	−0.62	R1888	–	–
D1956	0.14	0.28	D1888	−0.56	−0.56
R1952	3.78	3.67	R1884	−0.25	−0.25
D1952	−7.59	−7.16	D1884	−0.06	−0.06

Empirical results

Table 4.1 presents vice presidential HSA estimates for each election between 1884 and 2012 in which the presidential and vice presidential candidates did not share a home state (N=55). These estimates can be used to answer our most fundamental question: do presidential tickets, in general, perform better than otherwise expected in a vice presidential candidate's home state? The evidence from Table 4.1 indicates that they do not. To be sure, the average vice presidential HSA is positive: 0.58% when using the four-election lag and 0.68% when using the five-election lag.[11] However, these scores are meaningless unless we can reject the null hypothesis that the actual effect of a home state candidacy is zero. To evaluate statistical significance, we use a one-sample t-test. The resulting p-values (0.38 and 0.31 for the four-election and five-election lags, respectively) fall well short of the conventional $p < .05$ significance level required to reject the null hypothesis. The average effect of a vice presidential candidacy on home state voting therefore is zero, statistically speaking. That is to say, in general, there is no vice presidential HSA.

Although there is no *general* vice presidential HSA, the individual estimates found in Table 4.1 suggest that some candidates do, in fact, provide such an advantage – even substantially so. For example, our estimates indicate that in 2000 Dick Cheney received a double-digit advantage in Wyoming. This is the case when using either version of the Lewis-Beck and Rice equation. The same is true for Edmund Muskie in 1968 (Maine), Charles Curtis in 1928 (Kansas), and Garret Hobart in 1896 (New Jersey). These are, in fact, the only examples of candidates earning a double-digit vice presidential HSA; most advantages are relatively modest or non-existent.[12] All of this begs the question of why some candidates receive a positive HSA score, while others do not. To provide answers, in the next section we analyze the determinants of the vice presidential HSA.

Causes of the vice presidential home state advantage

In their analysis of the 1884–1980 presidential elections, Lewis-Beck and Rice (1983) tested three predictors of the presidential HSA: (1) home state population, measured as a percentage of the national population; (2) the candidate's party identification; and, (3) whether the candidate was an incumbent president. State population's effect on presidential HSA scores was statistically significant and negatively signed. In fact, it was the strongest predictor in the model; for every one percentage point increase in a state's population (as a percentage of the national population), the presidential HSA was found to decrease by 0.97 percentage points. The "dominant influence" of population to Lewis-Beck and Rice "seem[ed] obvious." They explained:

> [The] conditions for strong local bonds are maximized in small states. The citizens of these states are more likely to know the candidate's home town, his friends, even the candidate himself .... Moreover ... locals are more affectively tied to the candidate, in part because he is one of their "group." Beyond these cognitive and affective links, self-interested voting has plausibility, since the president can more easily reward all the folks back home when they are few in number. (Lewis-Beck and Rice 1983, 252–254)

Six years after the publication of Lewis-Beck and Rice's article, Dudley and Rapoport applied their predecessors' framework to vice presidential candidates using 1884–1984 presidential election data. Their model of vice presidential HSA differed only slightly from the Lewis-Beck and Rice model. In addition to state population, candidate party identification, and presidential incumbency, Dudley and Rapoport included dichotomous variables representing vice presidential incumbency and a running mate's previous service as a governor or US senator in the home state. These authors, too, found that state population was the most important predictor of a HSA. The relationship between home state population and vice presidential HSA was statistically significant, and negative; for every one percentage point increase in a state's proportion of the national population, a vice presidential candidate's HSA decreased by 0.86%.

Interactive effect: Population x experience

As Lewis-Beck and Rice's discussion indicates, the relationship between state population and HSA makes intuitive sense. Presumably, it is easier for a candidate to meet home state voters, gain name recognition, and foster the connections necessary to induce friends and neighbors voting if the candidate hails from a less populous state – there are simply more opportunities to connect with a greater percentage of the state's electorate if the population is relatively small.[13]

But in our past research we have questioned whether state population should be assumed to have a direct effect on the vice presidential HSA. Considering the theoretical bases for friends and neighbors voting, we find no reason to expect that a vice presidential candidate will be able to capitalize upon the experiences, opportunities, and relationships necessary to achieve a HSA *simply because he or she comes from a small state*. Rather, such advantages seem likely to come with *experience* in serving the people of the state as an elected representative at the local, state, or federal level. More experienced elected officials are more familiar to voters, more knowledgeable about their concerns, more likely to engage in direct interaction, and more likely to be seen as "one of us." In short, experience reinforces the advantages of living in a small state as it pertains to friends and neighbors voting; merely living in the state guarantees nothing of the sort.

Take Vice President Joe Biden as an example. At the time of the 2008 presidential election, Biden's home state of Delaware accounted for approximately 0.29% of the US population – a very small state, relatively speaking. Had a political novice from Delaware been chosen as Barack Obama's running mate, it seems unlikely that he or she would have earned a significant HSA based on Delaware's small population alone. Joe Biden, however, was anything but a novice; by 2008 he was what one might call an "institution" of Delaware politics. First elected in 1970 as a member of the New Castle County Council, Biden was elected to the United States Senate in 1972 and reelected six times thereafter, giving him a total of thirty-eight years serving the people of Delaware prior to becoming vice president. If anyone has the opportunity to cultivate the advantages associated with friends and neighbors voting, it is someone like Biden – a veteran of state politics operating in a relatively intimate political setting. In fact, we are not surprised to find that Biden performs strongly in the data from Table 4.1 – in 2008 he delivered an estimated HSA of approximately five to six percentage points.

These considerations lead us to believe that previous HSA models, although establishing population as a statistically significant and negatively signed predictor in direct tests, suffer from omitted variable bias. That is, the models presented in earlier studies did not account for the influence of state population *and* political experience. We hypothesize that the interactive effect of state population and elected political experience within that state – at the local, state, or national level – determines the size of a vice presidential candidate's HSA; specifically, vice presidential HSAs are limited to instances in which the running mate comes from a relatively less-populous state and has extensive experience in elected office within that state.

Data and methodology

We test our hypothesis using data from the 1884–2012 presidential elections, constituting the most expansive model of the vice presidential HSA to date. As a means of comparison, we test the determinants of vice presidential HSA in Table 4.2 using the model proposed by Dudley and Rapoport, with both four-election and five-election lags, and then we estimate a model that accounts for the interactive effect of state population and political experience. The variables included in our HSA models, using four-election and five-election lags, are:

- β_1 Party identification (0=Democrat; 1=Republican)
- β_2 Incumbent vice president (0=No; 1=Yes)
- β_3 Incumbent president (0=No; 1=Yes)
- β_4 Service as senator or governor (0=No; 1=Yes)
- β_5 State population (as a percentage of national population)
- β_6 Political experience (number of years in elected office)[14]
- β_7 State population x political experience

All four of the models presented in Table 4.2 use robust standard errors, clustered by year, because the observations are not independent and identically distributed (see Primo, Jacobsmeier, and Milyo 2007, 447–54).[15] Many of the observations in the regression model include two observations from a given election year (a vice presidential candidate from the Democratic and Republican Parties). The strength of the Democratic presidential ticket has implications for the electoral performance of the Republican presidential ticket, and vice versa, and so it is necessary to use robust standard errors clustered by election year.

Table 4.2: Models of Lewis-Beck and Rice VP home state advantage scores, 1884–2012

Variables	(Model 1) Dudley and Rapoport model, four-election lag	(Model 2) Dudley and Rapoport model, five-election lag	(Model 3) Devine and Kopko model, four-election lag	(Model 4) Devine and Kopko model, five-election lag
Party ID	2.37⁺ (1.31)	2.18 (1.35)	2.49⁺ (1.34)	2.3 (1.2)
Incumbent vice president	0.33 (1.33)	0.69 (1.44)	–0.41 (1.65)	–0.12 (1.72)
Incumbent president	–1.38 (1.15)	–1.45 (1.24)	–1.22 (1.27)	–1.3 (1.6)
Service as senator or governor	–0.78 (1.15)	–0.78 (1.17)	–1.38 (1.07)	–1.44 (1.72)
State population as % of national population	–0.61* (0.26)	–0.69* (0.26)	–0.1 (0.3)	–0.09 (0.32)
Political experience	–	–	0.17⁺ (0.09)	0.19* (0.09)
Population x political experience	–	–	–0.04⁺ (0.02)	–0.05* (0.02)
Constant	2.54 (1.77)	2.98⁺ (1.72)	0.35 (2.19)	0.5 (2.3)
N	57	57	57	57
R^2	0.1463	0.1551	0.2067	0.23
Adj. R^2	0.0626	0.0722	0.0934	0.1201

Robust standard errors are clustered by year in parentheses.
"* denotes p < .05; + denotes p < .10, two-tailed test.

Empirical results

Table 4.2 presents the results from each of our regression models. In Columns 1 and 2 – respectively, estimating the Dudley and Rapoport models with four- or five-election lags – we find that home state population is the only variable to reach conventional significance levels, and it is negatively signed as expected. Depending on the number of lags used to calculate HSA scores, a 1% increase in a state's population results in a 0.61% (four-election lag) or 0.69% (five-election lag) decrease in the vice presidential HSA. These findings confirm the effect of population documented by Dudley and Rapoport, in updated data. However, we are yet to account for the effects of political experience – an omitted variable that may bias the results from Columns 1 and 2.

Columns 3 and 4 present estimates from the Devine and Kopko models (using four- and five-election lags, respectively), which test the interactive effect

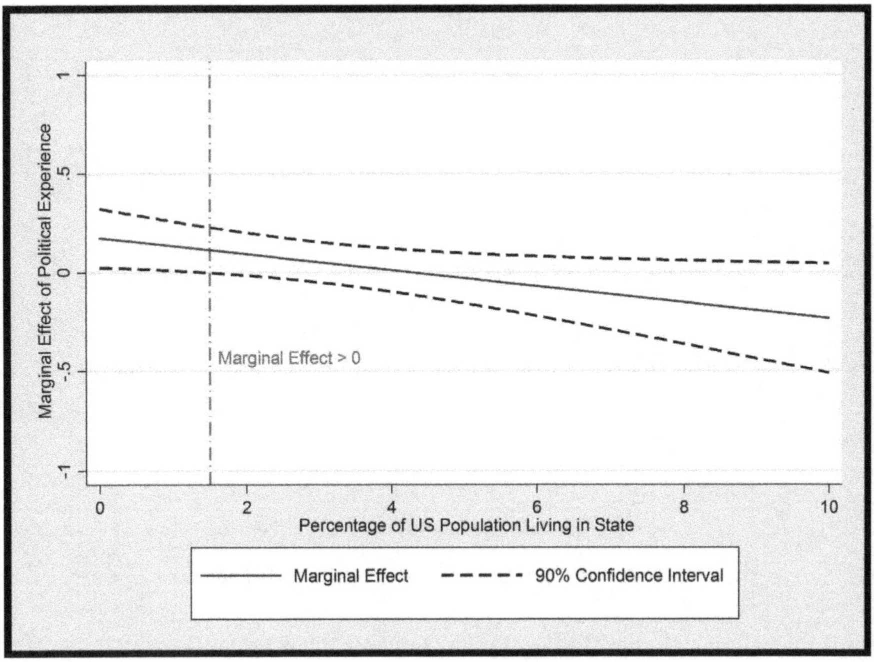

4.1 The marginal effect of political experience on VP home state advantage, four-election lag

of home state population and political experience on vice presidential HSA. The only variables to reach conventional significance levels in either model are political experience and its interaction with home state population. However, following conventional methodological precedent, we do not substantively interpret the significance levels and coefficients of the lower-order interaction variables or the interaction term since it comprises two continuous variables (see Brambor, Clark, and Golder 2006; Braumoeller 2004). Instead, we use graphs to evaluate the marginal effect of political experience on HSA as state population varies.

Figure 4.1 and Figure 4.2 depict the marginal effect of political experience on vice presidential HSA, at various levels of home state population, when using four-election lags and five-election lags, respectively. The horizontal dashed lines in each figure represent 90% confidence intervals for the projected effect of political experience on vice presidential HSA;[16] and for comparison purposes, the vertical dashed line represents the point at which the lower confidence interval no longer includes a value of zero. In other words, to the left of the vertical line we can say with 90% certainty that the marginal effect of political experience is positive.

The graphs in Figure 4.1 and Figure 4.2 are virtually identical in their projections. Both figures show that the marginal effect of political experience on HSA scores is statistically significant and positive only among the least populous states in our analysis. Among the most populous states, experience's marginal effect is

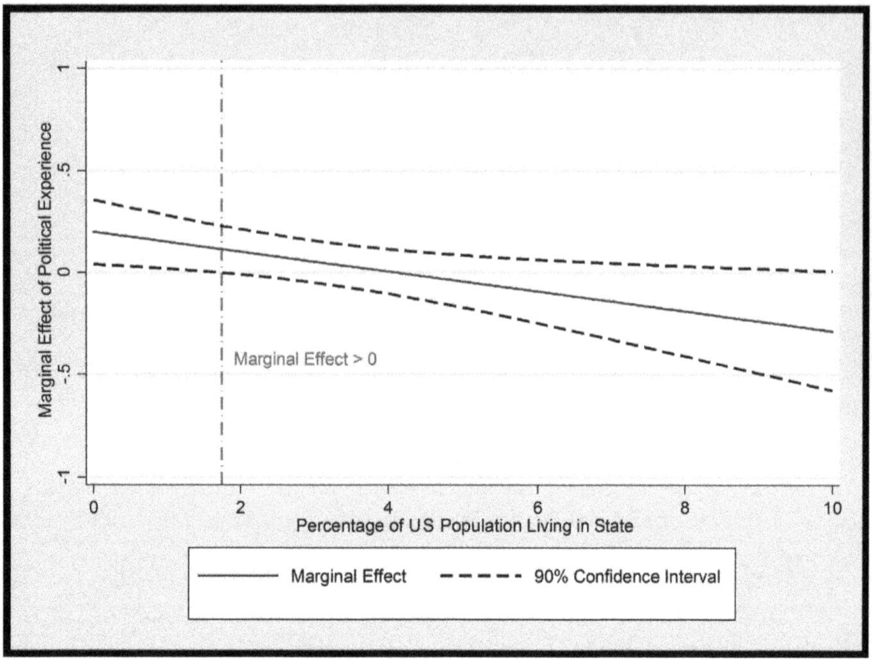

4.2 The marginal effect of political experience on VP home state advantage, five-election lag

essentially zero. In Figure 4.1 we see that the four-election lag model produces a statistically significant marginal effect when state population represents 1.5% of the national population or less. In Figure 4.2 we see that the five-election lag model produces a statistically significant marginal effect when state population represents 1.75% of the national population or less – which, in 2012 for example, would have been the thirty least populous states. In other words, *none of the variables included in the regression model predict a state's vote trend deviation when the state's population represents more than 1.75% of the national population.* The effects of political experience on vice presidential HSA therefore are not unqualified and direct, nor are the effects of home state population. Rather, these findings suggest that population and political experience matter when explaining a candidate's HSA – but only when a candidate hails from a relatively less-populous state.

An illustration may help to make the results of our analysis more intuitive. Based upon the evidence from our models, if we assume that a vice presidential candidate hails from a state that accounts for 1.5% of the nation's population, the marginal effect of political experience is 0.13. The marginal effect increases to 0.15 if the state comprises 1% of the nation's population, and increases again to 0.17 if the state comprises 0.5% of the nation's population. Thus, as state population decreases, the effect of political experience on the size of a vice presidential HSA increases. To illustrate this point further, consider the following hypothetical example: Model 4 predicts that a vice presidential candidate who lives in a state comprising 0.5% of the US population and has twenty years of elected political experience serving constituents in that state would receive a total marginal effect of 3.4 (0.17 x 20 years = 3.4 marginal effect). In other words, in the vice presidential candidate's home state his party's presidential ticket would perform 3.4% better than otherwise expected, controlling for other variables.

Having clarified the relationship between state population and the vice presidential HSA, our next objective is to evaluate the merits of the competing explanatory models – specifically, to determine whether a four- or five-election lag is preferable when measuring the vice presidential HSA, and to determine whether the interactive effect described above improves model fit in comparison to the Dudley and Rapoport models. We make these determinations based upon the adjusted R^2 value that each model generates.[17]

First, with respect to measuring the dependent variable, the five-election lag HSA models clearly are preferable because they explain more variance than the four-election lag models. In the Dudley and Rapoport models, the four-election lag produces an adjusted R^2 value of 0.063, while the five-election lag produces an adjusted R^2 value of 0.072. In the Devine and Kopko models, the four-election lag produces an adjusted R^2 value of 0.093, and the five-election lag produces an adjusted R^2 value of 0.12. Perhaps it is not surprising that models using a five-election lag to measure HSA explain more variance than models using four-election lags, since outlier elections have more statistical leverage in the latter and therefore are more likely to bias HSA estimates. The evidence presented here suggests that the five-election lag of the Lewis-Beck and Rice HSA scores is preferable to the four-election lag.

In terms of overall model fit, the Devine and Kopko models clearly perform best. In both cases, these models – which differ from the Dudley and Rapoport models by adding a measure of state political experience and its interaction with state population – have higher adjusted R^2 values. Model 4, which uses a five-election lag to measure the vice presidential HSA, explains the most variance of any model. To be specific, the joint relationship between state population and political experience explains approximately five percentage points more of the variance in the dependent variable than the Dudley and Rapoport model, which excludes these measures.

Discussion

Despite the superior performance of the Devine and Kopko models, due caution is in order. After all, the model with the highest adjusted R^2 value explains only 12% of the variance in the dependent variable. Substantively, this means that 88% of the variance can be attributed to factors not accounted for in our models. At first, then, one might believe that our models do a rather poor job of predicting the dependent variable. But we suspect that this performance says more about the weakness of the vice presidential HSA than the weakness of our models. Recall our earlier description of the Lewis-Beck and Rice equation, as essentially accounting for deviations in a state's presidential voting trends relative to national voting trends. The methodology *assumes* that such deviations in a (vice) presidential candidate's home state are attributable to the unique appeal of the home state candidacy, and therefore – in the case of systematic and positive deviation – it is capable of revealing a general (vice) presidential HSA. However, if there is no systematic HSA then non-zero values generated by the Lewis-Beck and Rice method are likely to reflect the influence of other factors related to presidential voting – for instance, economic conditions (at the individual or aggregate level), voter characteristics (e.g., party identification, ideology, gender, race, age, etc.), and evaluations of the presidential candidates – that may become more or less relevant in a given electoral or geographic context.

Since we find evidence of only a conditional vice presidential HSA – limited to relatively less-populous states and candidates with extensive political experience in the state – perhaps it should come as no surprise that our models predicting HSA scores based on running mate characteristics explain only 12% of the variance. In essence, the problem may not be our models or the Lewis-Beck and Rice equation, but the fact that vote choice generally is not a function of running mate characteristics, even in the vice presidential candidate's home state.

For illustrative purposes, consider Lyndon Johnson's vice presidential candidacy in 1960. The Lewis-Beck and Rice score for Johnson is –14.71, using the five-election lag. This is quite shocking, on its face. Did Lyndon Johnson's candidacy really *cause* the Democratic Party to do nearly fifteen points worse in Texas in 1960 than it would have without Johnson on the ticket? Would Kennedy have won Texas in a landslide, rather than a squeaker, had he not selected Johnson as his running mate? It is hard to imagine this being the case. Perhaps a more plausible explanation for this score, and other negative estimates for that matter, is that Johnson's candidacy had no discernible effect on home state vote share because voters in a state as large as Texas – the sixth most-populous in 1960 – are not influenced by home state vice presidential candidacies.

Then what might account for Texas's –14.71 score in 1960? Perhaps the most likely and obvious answer is the 1960 Democratic Party presidential candidate, John F. Kennedy. Kennedy was widely known to Texans, and southerners generally, as a northeastern, Catholic, liberal – not the traditional nominee of the party they had long supported, and perhaps divergent enough to inspire a deviation from past voting patterns within that state and region, particularly. We discuss this possibility, and other reasons why Johnson may have been ill-equipped to deliver a HSA, in Chapter 6. For the time being, though, the evidence presented in this chapter speaks clearly to such an example: vice presidential candidates who come from very large states, or who lack extensive experience in elected office within that state, should not expect to earn a HSA.

Of course, our main empirical conclusion about the vice presidential HSA – that it occurs not generally but under narrow conditions – is based upon one method of operationalization and therefore could be no more than a methodological artifact. Indeed, as noted earlier in this chapter, there are many ways to measure the HSA. To provide appropriate scrutiny for our conclusions, in the next section we measure the vice presidential HSA using an entirely different methodology: fixed effects regression models. In addition to serving as an opportunity to correct or confirm our initial conclusions, this analysis also represents an unprecedented opportunity to directly compare distinct methods of measuring the vice presidential HSA, for purposes of better informing future research on the subject.

An alternative approach: Fixed effects regression

Most studies of presidential or vice presidential HSA that do not use the Lewis-Beck and Rice equation instead use regression models (e.g., Campbell 1992; Campbell, Ali, and Jalalzai 2006; Garand 1988; Holbrook 1991; Kahane 2009; Mixon and Tyrone 2004; Powell 2004; Rosenstone 1983). Typically, these are pooled, state-level models that use a variety of independent variables – including home state variables – to predict vote choice in a given set of elections. The regression coefficient and p-value associated with the home state variables provide direct measures of the statistical significance, magnitude, and direction of the HSA. For example, if the vice presidential home state variable has a p-value of 0.03 and a regression coefficient of 1.5, we would conclude that, on average, a presidential ticket performs 1.5% better in the running mate's home state, controlling for other factors associated with vote choice – and this effect is statistically significant. If, on the other hand, this variable has a p-value of 0.05 (or worse), for the purposes of conventional significance – or 0.1 (or worse), for the purposes of marginal significance – and a regression coefficient of 1.5, we would conclude that, on average, a presidential ticket does not perform better in the running mate's home state; effectively, the change in performance amounts to zero since the p-value indicates a null finding.

A fixed effects regression approach to operationalizing the HSA has considerable value. First, a regression model allows researchers to directly evaluate the strength of a home state variable[18] relative to that of other variables potentially influencing vote choice, by referencing the regression coefficients. Second, regression models produce a goodness-of-fit statistic – such as adjusted R^2 – that allows researchers to measure and compare the overall predictive power of various models to determine which ones are most effective at explaining vote choice. Third, unlike the Lewis-Beck and Rice equation, fixed effects regression models do not require excluding observations from analysis when multiple candidates – presidential or vice presidential – share the same home state. A regression model, therefore, maximizes the number of candidacies that can be included in an analysis of the HSA.

Nonetheless, regression models do have significant limitations, most notably in terms of data availability and time frame restrictions. Most pooled, state-level analyses of the HSA in presidential elections begin with 1960 (e.g., Holbrook 1991) or 1972 (e.g., Kahane 2009; Mixon and Tyrone 2004), in order to incorporate economic indicators not available – at least in reliable form – prior to those years.[19] As a result, these regression models only permit an examination of presidential elections over the course of a few decades, and no farther back in time than the mid- to late-twentieth century.

Fixed effects regression analyses generally find evidence of a statistically significant presidential HSA. The average vice presidential HSA – although not statistically significant – is estimated by Garand (1988) to be 3%, while Holbrook (1991) and Rosenstone (1983) estimate it to be 1% and 2.5% respectively, and not statistically significant in either case. Powell (2004), however, estimates a model of state-level, two-party vote deviations and finds evidence of a statistically significant vice presidential HSA.[20] In addition, Campbell (1992) and Campbell, Ali, and Jalalzai's (2006) models of presidential vote choice yield evidence of a statistically significant vice presidential HSA, resulting in a marginal effect of 2.57% and 2.07%, respectively. Notably, Campbell (1992) and Campbell, Ali, and Jalalzai (2006), operationalize their dependent variables so as to incorporate state population, rather than using it as an independent predictor. Thus, increasing values in the dependent variable denote HSAs in less populous states. Their results, then, are consistent with studies of vice presidential HSA that make use of the Lewis-Beck and Rice equation and find significant differences based on population, rather than contradicting them. It is also important to note that none of these studies used observations from before 1932 or after 2004.

Data and methodology

To maximize the comprehensiveness of our analysis, we test three different fixed effects regression models predicting state-level, Democratic Party vote share (percentage of the two-party vote): one model that includes all elections from 1884 through 2012, a second model that includes observations from 1960 through 2012, and a third model that includes observations from 1972 through 2012. In several respects – including the number and recency of observations, as well as the range and sophistication of control variables – these models represent the most comprehensive regression-based analysis of the HSA to date.

Unfortunately, due to data limitations, it is impossible to estimate a regression model that includes reliable economic indicators for observations dating to 1884. For this reason, our first model accounts for the following independent variables, where i refers to an individual state in t election year:

- β_1 Democratic vice presidential home state $_{it}$ (0=No; 1=Yes)
- β_2 Republican vice presidential home state$_{it}$ (0=No; 1=Yes)
- β_3 Democratic presidential home state$_{it}$ (0=No; 1=Yes)
- β_4 Republican presidential home state$_{it}$ (0=No; 1=Yes)
- β_5 Incumbent president's party$_{it}$ (0=Democrat; 1=Republican)
- β_6 Average Congressional delegation DW-NOMINATE scores, previous midterm election$_{it}$ (-1=most liberal; 1=most conservative)[21]
- β_7 Democratic Party vote share in previous presidential election$_{it}$

For Models 2 and 3, we include several economic indicators[22] in addition to the independent variables used in Model 1. These indicators include:

- β_8 National unemployment rate in year$_t$
- β_9 State unemployment rate in year$_{it}$
- β_{10} Percentage change in national personal disposable income since previous year$_t$
- β_{11} Percentage change in state personal disposable income since previous year$_{it}$
- Interaction variables: (β_5 x β_8); (β_5 x β_9); (β_5 x β_{10}); (β_5 x β_{11})

The inclusion of the lagged vote variable (β_7) and economic indicators (β_8 through β_{11}) is consistent with state-level forecasts of presidential election returns (see Bartels and Zaller 2001; Berry and Bickers 2012; Jerôme and Jerôme-Speziari 2012, 2013; Klarner 2012, 2013). It is also important to note that since the Democratic Party's share of the two-party vote is the dependent variable in all three models, we include home state variables for both Democratic and Republican presidential and vice presidential candidates, in order to identify average HSAs for each type of candidacy. While the Lewis-Beck and Rice equation allows for an individualized measure of each candidate, a regression model of this nature must distinguish between either Democratic and Republican candidates, or incumbent and non-incumbent candidates; this has been the standard practice in previous studies that implement the regression method.[23]

Empirical results

Table 4.3 presents the results of our fixed effects regression models.[24] Depending on the year of analysis, Democratic vice presidential candidates earned, on average, a HSA of 1.2%–1.8%, while Republican vice presidential candidates earned an average HSA of 0.95%–1.44%. The regression coefficients associated with the home state variables are positively signed and greater in magnitude than the average HSA score as calculated by the Lewis-Beck and Rice measure. However, none of the vice presidential home state variables achieve conventional levels of statistical significance. As such, we do not have confidence that these averages are statistically distinguishable from zero.[25] These results confirm

Table 4.3: Fixed effects models of Democratic two-party vote share

Variables	(Model 1) Observations 1884–2012	(Model 2) Observations 1960–2012	(Model 3) Observations 1972–2012
Dem. VP home state	1.244 (1.671)	1.763 (1.855)	1.497 (1.816)
Rep. VP home state	−0.95 (1.713)	−1.278 (1.857)	−0.911 (1.824)
Dem. presidential home state	3.855* (1.723)	6.581*** (1.866)	7.357*** (1.828)
Rep. presidential home state	−1.992 (1.745)	−4.524* (1.99)	−3.673+ (1.938)
Incumbent president's party	−0.383 (0.543)	−14.578*** (2.698)	−13.492*** (2.608)
Congressional midterm ideology	−15.395*** (1.26)	−15.327*** (1.861)	−12.931*** (2.015)
Dem. two-party vote share, previous election	0.469*** (0.026)	−0.105** (0.04)	−0.01 (0.048)
National unemployment rate	–	−1.433*** (0.379)	−0.91* (0.391)
State unemployment rate	–	0.818* (0.351)	0.571+ (0.348)
% change in national PDI	–	−1.062*** (0.234)	−0.882*** (0.249)
% change in state PDI	–	0.097 (0.177)	−0.146 (0.202)
Incumbent party x national unemployment	–	2.1*** (0.516)	2.097*** (0.51)
Incumbent party x state unemployment	–	−0.452 (0.361)	−0.351 (0.352)
Incumbent party x % change in national PDI	–	−0.383 (0.281)	−0.5+ (0.283)
Incumbent party x % change in state PDI	–	0.077 (0.217)	0.338 (0.235)
Constant	26.963*** (1.487)	58.2*** (3.271)	61.897*** (3.978)
N	1,565	696	550
Adj. R^2	0.5582	0.5619	0.6482

Note: Model accounts for fixed effects of states (estimates omitted).
"*** denotes p < .001; ** denotes p < .01; * denotes p < .05; + denotes p < .10.

the null finding of the t-test presented earlier in this chapter when using the Lewis-Beck and Rice method. Thus, regardless of the time period under analysis, or the method of analysis, our conclusion is the same: we find no evidence of a statistically significant vice presidential HSA.

The results presented in Table 4.3 can also be used to evaluate the presidential HSA – which, although it is not the focus of our analysis, certainly is relevant and worthy of mention. The evidence concerning presidential HSA largely confirms findings from previous research. In the observation period 1884–2012, we find evidence of a statistically significant presidential HSA, but only for Democratic candidates. However, when examining elections in recent history (1960–2012 or 1972–2012), both Democratic and Republican presidential candidates earn a statistically significant HSA, in general. Based on the model coefficients for the modern era, Democratic presidential candidates typically enjoy a 6.6%–7.4% advantage in their home state, while Republican presidential candidates typically enjoy a 3.7%–4.5% advantage in their home state.[26]

The evidence presented thus far directly challenges the belief held by many political observers, commentators, and strategists – as documented in previous chapters – that vice presidential candidates can be expected to deliver an electoral advantage in their home state. Across multiple time frames and methods of analysis, our consistent finding is that the average vice presidential HSA is statistically indistinguishable from zero. Still, our previous analysis, using the Lewis-Beck and Rice equation, suggests that vice presidential HSAs occur only under identifiable conditions – namely, when running mates come from relatively less populous states and have extensive experience in elected office within that state. To confirm this finding, one might ask whether we find similar evidence of a conditional effect when analyzing results from the fixed effects regression models.

To properly test the effects of state population and political experience on vote share, it is necessary that we interact these variables with both the Democratic and Republican vice presidential home state variables. In Appendix B, we reestimate Model 1 from Table 4.3 to include interactions for state population and candidate political experience.[27] This additional analysis requires two three-way interaction terms, six two-way interaction terms, and five lower-order interaction variables. Unfortunately, because we are comparing a relatively small number of home state observations to non-home state observations throughout a 128-year period (which includes sixty-six vice presidential candidacies), and this analysis requires numerous two- and three-way interaction terms (thus further dividing the small number of home state observations with which we begin), deriving precise estimates for candidates who hail from less populous states simply is not possible. In more concrete terms, the home state variables and interaction terms in this analysis have enormous confidence intervals – far too large to permit meaningful interpretation. All of this is in stark contrast to the models presented in Table 4.2, which only relied on observations from vice presidential home states and included a single interaction term.

To illustrate the limitations of the model in Appendix B, we use its estimates to predict the Democratic Party's two-party vote share in both of the 2012 running mates' home states: Delaware, for Vice President Joe Biden (Democrat); and Wisconsin, for vice presidential candidate Representative Paul Ryan (Republican). The fixed effects model predicts a Democratic two-party vote share of 63.81% for the Obama/Biden ticket in Delaware, with a 95% confidence interval of 54.19%–73.43% (a nineteen-point spread). The actual Democratic two-party vote share in Delaware was 59.45%, which is clearly within the model's margin of error, but not particularly impressive given how large the confidence interval is. In Paul Ryan's case, the model predicts a Democratic two-party vote share of 53.17%, with a 95% confidence interval of 46.07%–60.26% (a fourteen-point spread). The actual Democratic two-party vote share in Wisconsin in 2012 was 53.52% – very close to our model's estimate, but again this is difficult to take seriously given the size of the confidence interval.

The size of these confidence intervals is almost certainly attributable to having a small number of home state observations and a large number of interaction terms in the model, as required in order to test the conditional effect of state population and political experience on vote share. While it is unfortunate, then, that we cannot directly compare our finding of a conditional, rather than general, vice presidential HSA between the Lewis-Beck and Rice model and the fixed effects regression model, to focus on this discrepancy would be to miss the larger point. Despite major differences between these two sets of analyses – from independent and dependent variables, to the number of observations, to the use of pooled versus exclusively home state datasets – both lead us to the same fundamental conclusion: vice presidential candidates, in general, do not provide a statistically significant HSA. Based upon either method of analysis, and using various time frames, we cannot reject the null hypothesis that running mates have no effect on home state voting.

Conclusion

This chapter provides an unprecedented, multi-method analysis of the vice presidential HSA. The results of our analysis yield no evidence that presidential tickets perform better than expected in the vice presidential candidate's home state, although we do find evidence of improved performance in the presidential candidate's home state. When using the Lewis-Beck and Rice equation, however, we find evidence of a *conditional* vice presidential HSA; specifically, a presidential ticket performs significantly better than expected in a vice presidential candidate's home state when that state is relatively less populous and the candidate has extensive experience in elected office within it. This empirical finding is entirely consistent with the friends and neighbors hypothesis advanced by V. O. Key.

While we use multiple methods in this chapter to test whether vice presidential candidates influence home state voting, our analysis is still limited in two important respects. First, to this point we have relied exclusively upon aggregate, specifically state-level, data, to test the vice presidential HSA. While state-level data provide useful indications of electoral behavior and are more readily accessible than individual-level data, the fact remains that vote choice is an *individual*-level behavior. If we draw conclusions about the effect of vice presidential candidates on the behavior of home state voters based upon aggregate data alone, we risk an error in deduction known as the "ecological fallacy." Our conclusions about the vice presidential HSA, therefore, should draw upon analysis of individual- as well as state-level data.

Second, we are mindful that an exclusive focus on vote choice in presidential elections may overlook more varied and subtle ways in which vice presidential candidates could provide a "home state advantage" to their presidential ticket. In the next chapter, then, we introduce the first large-scale individual-level analysis of the vice presidential HSA – based upon data from the American National Election Studies – that incorporates alternative indicators beyond vote choice: such as voter turnout, political participation, and candidate evaluations. Such an analysis extends the multi-method approach introduced in this chapter. Also, it provides an additional opportunity to reject or once more confirm our fundamental conclusion – that vice presidential candidates, in general, do not enjoy an electoral advantage in their home state.

Notes

1 For further information on the distribution of pork barrel projects (i.e., distributive policy) to an elected official's state or geographic region, see Evans (2004); Ferejohn (1974); Lee (2003); Shapiro, Swenson, and Donno (2008); Shepsle and Weingast (1981); Weingast, Shepsle, and Johnsen (1981).

2 See Devine and Kopko (2013); Disarro, Barber, and Rice 2007); Kahane (2009); Mixon and Tyrone (2004). Garand (1988) confirms this finding for Democratic presidential candidates only.

3 For an extensive treatment of descriptive measures of HSA, see Tubbesing (1973).

4 Reliable state vote percentages are unavailable for eight candidacies occurring prior to 1832. Also, we exclude the 1856 Republican vote in New Jersey because the Republican Party did not exist in the previous presidential election; the 1860 Democratic vote in Georgia, because the Republican Party did not appear on the state ballot in that election; and the 1864 Republican vote in Tennessee, because the state had seceded and did not vote in that year's election.

5 Lewis-Beck and Rice used raw vote share to calculate HSA scores. However, subsequent studies have used two-party votes share in recognition of the fact that third-party candidacies sometimes substantially reduce the vote percentage earned by a presidential ticket, thereby distorting direct comparisons of past and present party performance (Devine and Kopko 2011, 2013; Dudley and Rapoport 1989). For our analysis, we use two-party vote share.

6 We discuss the validity of this assumption later in the chapter.

7 Due to complications arising from the Reconstruction period, however, Lewis-Beck and Rice, Dudley and Rapoport, and other scholars researching presidential and/or vice presidential HSA use three-election and four-election trends for the 1884 and 1888 presidential elections, respectively.

8 Indeed, Dudley and Rapoport found that parties favored geography over all other types of ticket-balancing (i.e., ideology, religion, state versus federal experience) in vice presidential selections since 1884.

9 In fact, Heersink and Peterson (2014) introduce their own method of measuring the HSA, through synthetic controls (Abadie, Diamond, and Hainmueller 2010). This method yields an estimated average vice presidential HSA of 2.78%, which is distinguishable from zero. While the authors employ an innovative statistical technique to estimate these scores, and the distribution of their estimates generally match those derived by the Lewis-Beck and Rice equation – the scores are correlated at $r = 0.502$ ($p < 0.001$) – in our view their estimates may be skewed upward as a result of variables used to weight the synthetic control units. The authors concede that they extrapolated measures of partisanship for control units using gubernatorial election returns, and gubernatorial elections typically occur in non-presidential election years (Abadie, Diamond, and Hainmueller 2010, 14). This measure of state partisanship introduces time-variant bias into the weighting process because states vary in the years in which they hold gubernatorial elections. Furthermore, there is not a theoretically obvious relationship between numerous weight variables used to construct synthetic controls and a state's two-party vote share – e.g., "percentage of females and African-Americans between the ages of 5 and 18 that were enrolled in school … size of farms in acres, the total number of acres employed in agriculture, and the number of manufacturing establishments in each state" (Abadie, Diamond, and Hainmueller 2010, 17). These variables result in pairings between home states and synthetic controls that lack face validity. To name a few examples: Wisconsin in 2012 is said to most resemble Iowa, Mississippi, and Hawaii; Delaware in 2008 and 2012 is said to most resemble Florida; and Texas in 1980 is said to most resemble Arkansas, Utah, and Massachusetts.

10 This results in the exclusion of Levi Morton (1888), Whitelaw Reid (1892), Thomas Marshall (1916), Charles Fairbanks (1916), Henry Cabot Lodge, Jr. (1960), Sargent Shriver (1972), Spiro Agnew (1972), and Lloyd Bentsen (1988). We also exclude James Sherman (1912) because the Progressive Party ticket headed by Theodore Roosevelt – a fellow New Yorker – earned more electoral votes than the Republican Party in that state, thus warranting its treatment as a major party.

11 There are some minor discrepancies in the scores derived for each candidate when comparing the four-election versus five-election lags. However, it is important to note that the scores are highly correlated at 0.98 ($p < .001$) and, generally speaking, quite similar.

12 The scores range from –12.11% to +12.53% using the four-election lag equation, and –14.71% to +13.32% using the five-election lag equation. Based upon the scores reported using the four-election lag equation, 54.4% of the candidates (N=31) received a positive HSA, while 57.9% of candidates (N=33) received a positive HSA using the five-election lag equation.

13 It has been the accepted practice in the HSA literature to measure state population as a percentage of the national population. Operationalizing population in this

manner helps to account for temporal changes in population throughout our period of analysis. One could argue, however, that the raw population count of a given state may be a better indicator of friends and neighbors voting, especially given that the US population has steadily increased over time and it should be easier to make personal connections within a state when the population is small. We are not convinced that this approach is a better measurement. But given the temporal span of our analysis, advancements in travel, and the ability to personally meet voters over the course of a public official's career, a raw population count could result in biased estimates. For example, a raw population count would treat a relatively populous state in 1884 like a relatively less populous state in the twenty-first century, given the natural population growth of the US in that time period. In light of these problems, we believe it is more appropriate to measure state population as a percentage of national population, consistent with Lewis-Beck and Rice (1983) and Dudley and Rapoport (1989).

14 We calculated the number of years in elected office by subtracting the first year the candidate served in an elected office from the last year he or she served in that office. For example, we coded John Edwards, whose only experience in elected office was serving as North Carolina's senator from 1999–2005, as having five years of state political experience when he was selected as John Kerry's running mate in 2004 (2004–1999=5). To determine which years, and in which offices, the vice presidential candidates served, we relied principally on two sources: the *Biographical Directory of the United States Congress* (http://bioguide.congress.gov) and the National Governors Association website (www.nga.org). Accessed February 23, 2015.

15 For further discussion as to why it is necessary to correct for observations that are not independent and identically distributed, see Huber (1967), Moulton (1990), and Rogers (1993).

16 A one-tailed significance test, using a 90% confidence interval, is appropriate because we posit a directional hypothesis regarding the effect of state population and political experience.

17 We report both the R^2 and adjusted R^2 in Table 4.2. The inclusion of the R^2 statistic is useful when comparing our findings here to previous studies in the HSA literature. For example, Lewis-Beck and Rice (1983) and Dudley and Rapoport (1989) only report an R^2 statistic for their analyses. However, we believe the adjusted R^2 is a better indication of a model's ability to explain variance in the dependent variable. R^2 statistics increase with the addition of new variables into a model. This is true even if a new variable is not statistically significant (the only time it will not increase the R^2 statistic is when a coefficient is equal to zero). The adjusted R^2 statistic, however, corrects for the addition of new variables relative to the number of observations. See, for example, Kohler and Kreuter (2005, 195–196) and Remler and Van Ryzin (2015, 316–317).

18 These variables are usually binary variables where a Democratic candidate's home state is coded as 1, and otherwise 0; and a Republican candidate's home state is coded as 1, and otherwise 0. Alternatively, Holbrook (1991) employed a trichotomous measure where –1 represents a non-incumbent party candidate, 0 for non-home states, and 1 for the incumbent party candidate's home state.

19 Unfortunately, many states did not systematically collect state-level economic indicators before 1960. Even the Bureau of Labor Statistics (BLS) did not systematically

calculate state-level unemployment statistics until 1976. Before 1976, and again in many cases not until 1960, each state calculated its own state-level unemployment rate, and according to the BLS, "Those estimates are not comparable to the official BLS series and may not be comparable across states or over time for a given state" (personal correspondence with the authors, 2013).

20 According to Powell's (2004) regression-based estimates, vice presidential candidates earned an average HSA of 3.01% between 1932–2000, increasing to 3.35% for elections held between 1972 and 2000. However, Powell's operationalization of the dependent variable, which differs considerably from other HSA studies, may be problematic. As Powell notes, "the dependent variable … measures the difference between a candidate's percentage of the two party vote in a particular state and the percentage of the national two-party vote for the same candidate" in a single election year (p. 122). As we noted earlier in this chapter when discussing the vice presidential candidacy of John Nance Garner, using a single election to estimate state versus national vote trend deviations may lead to biased estimates. In addition, based upon the sample sizes reported in his article, Powell appears to double-count many states as the unit of analysis in his pooled models (i.e., counting two-party vote shares for Democrats and Republicans separately, as unique observations for each state). Powell states that "The unit of analysis in this study is each state in the 18 presidential elections from 1932 to 2000" (p. 122). In his model of vote deviation between 1932 and 2000, he reports a sample size of 1,735. Given that Powell accounts for the average state presidential vote share in the past two elections as an independent variable, this practice results in the censoring of observations from Alaska and Hawaii for the 1960 and 1964 elections, respectively. If each state is counted only once, this should result in 882 observations between 1932 and 2000. The reported sample size suggests that many states are included more than once as observations from the same election year, which, among other things, violates the OLS assumptions of independent and identically distributed observations (see endnote 15).

21 DW-NOMINATE scores were obtained from www.voteview.com. Accessed February 23, 2015.

22 Personal disposable income and unemployment statistics were obtained directly from the US Bureau of Economic Analysis and US Bureau of Labor Statistics, respectively.

23 As previously noted, an alternative approach is to operationalize the dependent variable as the incumbent party's two-party vote share, in which case the home state variables would represent the home state of an incumbent party versus non-incumbent party candidate. There is no substantive difference between operationalizing these variables in terms of a specific party versus the incumbent party in any given set of elections. We opt for the former measure because we believe it allows for a more intuitive interpretation of model results. One could, on the other hand, employ a trichotomous home state variable, following Holbrook (1991). However, the results we present here are not substantively different when employing two dichotomous home state variables versus one trichotomous variable. In that case, using two separate measures is preferable because it allows us to identify partisan differences without distorting our substantive conclusions.

24 A Hausman test confirmed that a fixed effects model was appropriate as compared with a random effects model ($p < 0.001$). As such, we account for the fixed effects of states in these models (estimates of state effects omitted).

25 In an unreported analysis, we estimate the models in Table 4.3 using a trichotomous home state variable similar to Holbrook (1991), where –1 represents a Democratic candidate home state candidate, 0 for non-home state, and 1 for Republican candidate home state. Using those models, the average HSA scores for all vice presidential candidates are 0.79% (observations 1884–2012), 1.11% (observations 1960–2012), and 0.64% (observations 1972–2012). In each of these three model estimates, the home state variable fails to attain statistical significance.

26 When presidential HSA is operationalized as a trichotomous variable, the average HSA is 2.46% (observations 1884–2012), 5.75% (observations 1960–2012), and 6.1% (observations 1972–2012). All presidential HSA variables across the three models were statistically significant at $p \leq 0.05$.

27 We report the reestimation of Model 1 (of Table 4.3) in Appendix B because that model yields the highest number of vice presidential candidate observations. We also estimated Models 2 and 3 from Table 4.3 to account for an interactive effect, and found that the results were not substantively different from those reported for Model 1. As a further precaution, we also estimated the interactive effect using the trichotomous home state variable for Models 1 through 3, and again there were no substantive differences in comparison to what we find when reestimating Model 1 using two dichotomous home state variables.

5

An empirical analysis of the vice presidential home state advantage (individual-level data)

In 2008 Mississippi was the poorest state in the nation, with a median income of $36,446 – $1,500 lower than the next poorest state (West Virginia), and nearly half that of the wealthiest state (New Hampshire).[1] Mississippi was also a strongly Republican state, voting in that year's presidential election for John McCain by a margin of 13.2% at the same time that his Democratic opponent, Barack Obama, won the national popular vote by 7.2%. In fact, the six states with the lowest median income levels in 2008 – Mississippi, West Virginia, Louisiana, Arkansas, Tennessee, and Kentucky – each voted for McCain, and each by lopsided margins ranging from 13.1% to 19.8%.[2] Based upon these data, it would be tempting to draw the conclusion that – contrary to conventional wisdom about the relationship between income and party preference – poorer people tend to vote *Republican*.[3] In fact, one decade ago a popular book titled *What's the Matter with Kansas?* suggested just such a conclusion, arguing that the Republican Party had come to dominate lower-income, rural states such as Kansas by convincing working-class whites to vote based on social issues such as abortion and gun control rather than on economic issues (see Frank 2004).

Such conclusions, however, are products of what scholars call an "ecological fallacy," or an error in causal attribution whereby group characteristics are inaccurately ascribed to individual group members. In this case, despite what seems to be overwhelming evidence of a relationship between low income levels and Republican voting – based on state population characteristics and election outcomes – the truth is that low-income voters *are* – as conventional wisdom would suggest – more likely to vote for the Democratic Party. How could this be? Aggregate, in this case state-level, data cannot capture the individual-level relationship between variables such as income and vote choice, and may lead to inaccurate conclusions. Suppose, for instance, that low-income residents of a relatively poor state such as Mississippi strongly prefer the Democratic candidate but represent a smaller proportion of presidential voters than middle- and upper-income voters, who overwhelmingly prefer the Republican candidate. In this example, the Republican candidate might very well win the state, perhaps even by a large margin, and in doing so give the false impression of having attracted strong support from low-income voters. This is essentially what happened in Mississippi in 2008.

According to exit polls conducted on Election Day 2008,[4] Barack Obama won 76% of Mississippi voters making under $15,000 in annual income and 59% making between $15,000–$30,000. McCain, however, won a slight majority (53%) of Mississippi voters making $30,000–$50,000 and an overwhelming majority of voters making $50,000–$75,000 (71%), $75,000–$100,000 (77%), and $100,000 or more (75%). While Obama won approximately two-thirds of the vote among Mississippians making less than $30,000, those voters made up only 32% of the state electorate. Voters making more than $50,000, on the other hand, made up 46% of the state electorate and approximately three-quarters of them voted for McCain. The remaining voters were essentially split between the two candidates. Thus, even though the Republican candidate lost badly among low-income voters in Mississippi, he was able to win handily in the nation's poorest state due to a combination of differences in turnout and victory margins among low- versus high-income group members.

More comprehensive individual-level analyses confirm the relationship between low income levels and Democratic voting that is obscured by reliance upon state-level data. Most notably, Larry Bartels (2006), in an article brilliantly titled "What's the Matter with *What's the Matter with Kansas?*," refutes Thomas Frank's characterization of low-income white voters by demonstrating – through American National Election Studies (ANES) data – that their preference for the Democratic Party has remained relatively constant in recent years while economic issues have continued to exert much greater influence on their vote choice than social issues. In fact, social issues most influence voting among high-income earners.[5]

What does all of this have to do with the vice presidential home state advantage (HSA)? Since the analyses presented in Chapter 4 use aggregate-level data – specifically, state and national two-party vote shares – to estimate and explain the effects of a home state candidacy on vote choice – which is, in fact, an *individual-level decision* – it is possible that our conclusions about the vice presidential HSA to this point are in fact based upon no more than an ecological fallacy. For instance, whereas the evidence that we have presented suggests that voters are generally unaffected in their vote choice by the candidacy of a home state running mate, perhaps these voters are in fact quite polarized about that candidate and motivated to vote on the basis of their feelings toward him or her. If so, and the percentage of voters motivated by favorable versus unfavorable evaluations of the running mate are roughly equal, then the home state candidate's effect on aggregate vote share would essentially cancel out and give the false impression of being irrelevant to individual vote choice within that state.

Is this a likely explanation for our findings? We think not. However, the possibility of committing an ecological fallacy should always be taken seriously when using aggregate-level data and without taking steps to address this issue accepting our conclusions about the vice presidential HSA will necessarily involve a somewhat uncomfortable leap of faith. Moreover, if an analysis of the vice presidential HSA based upon individual-level data confirms the fundamental conclusions presented so far in this book, the case for accepting those conclusions will be much stronger. In this chapter we present such an analysis – indeed, the first of its kind in the HSA literature – that also capitalizes on individual-level behavioral and attitudinal measures to test alternative indicators of the vice presidential HSA.

Data and methodology

To conduct an individual-level analysis of the vice presidential HSA, we make use of an extraordinary dataset called the American National Election Studies (ANES) Cumulative Data File. The cumulative file comprises responses from ANES surveys conducted among large, nationally representative respondent samples during each presidential election campaign and most midterm Congressional election campaigns held between 1948 and 2008.[6] The items included in ANES surveys intentionally have been kept similar across the time series, so as to facilitate longitudinal comparisons. Because of this, the cumulative file is able to be presented as an integrated dataset in which nearly all variables report data from multiple if not each of the 1948–2008 surveys. For example, the respondent's state of residence is reported in variable VCF0901 for each of the 1952–2008 presidential elections,[7] and vote choice in each presidential election is reported in variable VC0704 – coded 1 for a Democratic vote, 2 for a Republican vote, 3 for a third party vote, and 0 for non-voting, regardless of the election year.

Using these two variables we can estimate the direct relationship between living in a vice presidential candidate's home state and individual vote choice in a presidential election. To be more precise, we begin by generating a new variable in the dataset coded 1 for living in the home state of a vice presidential candidate in a given election year, 0 for not living in that state, and missing for invalid home state data. If, for instance, a respondent to the 1968 ANES were from Maine, the home state of Democratic running mate Edmund Muskie, or Maryland, the home state of Republican running mate Spiro Agnew, the respondent would be coded as 1 on this variable. All other respondents would be coded as 0, or missing if no state data are reported. The same coding scheme can be used to generate a separate *presidential* home state variable that allows us to estimate the presidential HSA and draw comparisons to the vice presidential HSA. If, in the case of this additional variable, a 1968 respondent reported living in California or Minnesota – the home states of Republican presidential candidate Richard Nixon and Democratic presidential candidate Hubert Humphrey, respectively – he or she is coded as 1. Residents of any other state, including vice presidential home states, are coded as 0 on this variable. Moreover, we can

Table 5.1: Number of respondents from a vice presidential or presidential candidate's home state, 1952–2008 ANES

	Vice president – Rep.		Vice president – Dem.		President – Rep.		President – Dem.	
Election year	Home state	N	Home state	N	Home state	N	Home state	N
1952	California	143	Alabama	58	Kansas	23	Illinois	77
1956	California	144	Tennessee	13	Kansas	29	Illinois	55
1960	Massachusetts	31	Texas	42	California	84	Massachusetts	31
1964	New York	120	Minnesota	35	Arizona	12	Texas	72
1968	Maryland	28	Maine	22	California	151	Minnesota	27
1972	Maryland	56	Maryland	56	California	225	South Dakota	38
1976	Kansas	0	Minnesota	50	Michigan	90	Georgia	54
1980	Texas	127	Minnesota	32	California	144	Georgia	40
1984	Texas	153	New York	189	California	262	Minnesota	54
1988	Indiana	41	Texas	143	Texas	143	Massachusetts	37
1992	Indiana	88	Tennessee	88	Texas	186	Arkansas	33
1996	New York	87	Tennessee	49	Kansas	11	Arkansas	24
2000	Wyoming	5	Connecticut	17	Texas	137	Tennessee	42
2004	Wyoming	0	N. Carolina	0	Texas	84	Massachusetts	57
2008	Alaska	0	Delaware	20	Arizona	42	Illinois	29

Data come from the ANES Cumulative Data File. Available for download at: www.electionstudies.org.

disaggregate these two variables into four party- and candidate-specific variables distinguishing between residents of a Democratic versus Republican vice presidential or presidential home state.

After generating the new home state variables we can test for statistically significant vice presidential and presidential HSAs by comparing vote choice between residents and non-residents of vice presidential or presidential home states, respectively. If, for example, individuals are more likely to support a presidential ticket when it includes a running mate from their home state – in other words, if the vice presidential HSA is generally applicable – we would expect to find that the proportion of respondents voting for the Democratic (Republican) presidential ticket is greater among residents of the Democratic (Republican) running mate's home state than among residents of other states, in general, and that the difference is statistically significant.

Respondent sample

To draw general conclusions about the vice presidential, as well as presidential, HSA, however, our data must include a large number of respondents from the candidates' home states (for purposes of statistical power), and a wide range of individual candidacies (since, as indicated by the evidence in Chapter 4, the occurrence and size of a vice presidential HSA may vary by state and candidate characteristics).[8] To determine whether these conditions have been satisfied, Table 5.1 presents the number of respondents included in the ANES cumulative data file who reported living in the same state as a vice presidential or presidential candidate in the 1952–2008 presidential elections.

In terms of vice presidential candidates, twenty-six of thirty cases (86.7%) are represented in the data by home state respondents – the exceptions being Kansas in 1976 (Bob Dole), Wyoming in 2004 (Dick Cheney), North Carolina in 2004 (John Edwards), and Alaska in 2008 (Sarah Palin). While the missing states tend to be less populous, not surprisingly, less populous states are represented at other points in the data – for instance, Wyoming in 2000 (Dick Cheney) and Delaware in 2008 (Joe Biden). Presidential candidates, on the other hand, are represented by home state respondents in all thirty cases (100%) – including less populous states such as Arizona in 1964 (Barry Goldwater) and Kansas in 1996 (Bob Dole). In terms of total cumulative file respondents, 1,837 come from vice presidential home states (1,023 for Republican candidates versus 814 for Democratic candidates) and 2,293 come from presidential home states (1,623 for Republican candidates versus 670 for Democratic candidates). As a percentage of the 28,730 respondents in the cumulative file for whom a home state is recorded, vice presidential home state respondents constitute 6.39% and presidential home state respondents constitute 7.98%. In many election years, despite their overall disadvantage, vice presidential home state respondents actually outnumber presidential home state respondents; this is true in six of the fifteen individual elections and in terms of total home state respondents for Democratic candidates. Vice presidential home states are, in short, well-represented in our data.

Survey measures

In addition to testing for the possibility of an ecological fallacy, the ANES cumulative file offers another major benefit: an extensive battery of variables measuring individual demographics, political attitudes, and political behaviors other than vote choice. The availability of such variables is significant for two reasons. First, rather than simply testing for differences in the proportion of Democratic (Republican) vice presidential home state respondents voting for the Democratic (Republican) ticket, in comparison to residents of other states, we can construct models of vote choice that statistically control for relevant individual characteristics such as party identification and standard demographics. In other words, we can test the relationship between home state residence and vote choice, independent of other factors influencing the individual's outcome on the dependent variable, to determine with greater precision whether a HSA actually exists.

Second, the availability of attitudinal and behavioral measures in the ANES cumulative file allows us to address a second concern about our prior analyses. To this point in the research, we have conceptualized the vice presidential HSA strictly in terms of vote choice – specifically, as an increase in two-party vote share won by the running mate's ticket in his or her home state, relative to state and national voting trends. This approach is quite natural; vote choice is the most important outcome in any political campaign, and it is almost exclusively the outcome of interest in HSA research.[9] However, a comprehensive analysis of the HSA should go beyond vote choice to examine whether – and, if so, how – *patterns* of electoral behavior and attitudes change in response to the selection of a home state candidate. Even if individuals are no more likely to vote for a presidential ticket that includes a home state candidate, one might reasonably expect them to differ on other important election-related outcomes – such as voter turnout, political participation, campaign interest, and candidate evaluations – due to greater familiarity with the candidate, attended by stronger opinions about his or her candidacy, and an increased focus on the campaign within the individual's immediate information environment. Alternative indicators of HSA, such as those just listed, may also be more susceptible to variation than vote choice – a discrete and deep-seated preference for most voters – and thus more sensitive to the subtle effects of a home state candidacy. Another major objective of this chapter, therefore, is to systematically compare residents versus non-residents of a vice presidential or presidential candidate's home state on a wide range of electoral behaviors and attitudes, in order to comprehensively characterize the HSA.

Independent variables

The ANES cumulative data file contains nearly 1,000 variables, including literally dozens of variables that could qualify as statistical controls in vote choice models or alternative indicators of HSA. Our process for selecting and employing an appropriate range of control variables and dependent variables is governed by a few guiding principles. First, to maximize statistical power and make possible the inclusion of all available candidacies, we have limited the control variables to those for which data are available in each of the 1952–2008 presidential election surveys. Second, to maintain a reasonable level of consistency across models, we have selected a limited range of control variables with a plausibly direct and substantial relation to each of the dependent variables – including vote choice and alternative indicators of HSA such as voter turnout and candidate evaluations – to serve as a common "base model" rather than varying the controls to fit each dependent variable intricately. Third, we permit minor variations in the base model to account for qualitative differences in the dependent variable – specifically, for differences between dependent variables that are partisan versus non-partisan in nature.[10]

In addition to the vice presidential and presidential home state variables already described, we include the following control variables in our base model: Party Identification, coded from 1, Strong Democrat, to 7, Strong

Republican (M = 3.60; SE = 0.01); Age, coded continuously from 17 to 99 (M = 45.8, SE = 0.1); Gender, coded 0 for female and 1 for male (M = 0.44, SE = 0); Non-White, coded 0 for white and 1 for any other race or ethnicity (M = 0.2, SE = 0); Education, coded from 1 for eight grades or less, to 7 for an advanced degree (M = 3.61, SE = 0.01); Household Income, coded from 1 for the 0–16th percentile to 5 for the 96–100th percentile (M = 2.86, SE = 0.01); South, coded 0 for living outside the southern census region and 1 for living within the southern census region (M = 0.34, SE = 0). For each variable, invalid responses – including "Don't Know" or "Refused" – are coded as missing observations.

To this base model we add several variables not included in the ANES cumulative file, to control for state and national conditions likely to influence political behavior and attitudes. First is the "Battleground" measure introduced in Chapter 3, which ranks each state from most competitive (1) to least competitive (48 or 50, depending on the election year) based upon the average difference between two-party vote shares in that state over the three preceding presidential elections. For each election year, the state with the smallest average difference in two-party vote share is rated as the most competitive, and the state with the largest average difference is rated as least competitive. This variable should have no direct bearing on partisan outcomes such as vote choice, and so it is omitted from those models; however, it is likely to have a significant effect on non-partisan outcomes such as voter turnout and campaign interest – with greater competitiveness leading to greater engagement in the election – and so it is included in those models.[11]

Second is a pair of variables measuring economic conditions at the state and national level, in terms of change in personal disposable income (PDI). Economic conditions have been shown to exert a substantial impact on many political attitudes and behaviors, particularly vote choice, and even more so at the aggregate than the individual level (see Lewis-Beck *et al.* 2008, Chapter 13). While a more standard measure of economic conditions would be unemployment, state and national unemployment statistics are not available prior to 1960 and were not reliably reported in many states until 1972.[12] Statistics on state and national changes in PDI, on the other hand, are available from the Bureau of Economic Analysis for the years 1948 onward. To test their effects on participatory attitudes and behaviors, the "State PDI" and "National PDI" variables are included as direct predictors in each model with a non-partisan outcome. The effect of economic conditions on partisan outcomes, however, should be conditioned by which party holds power at the time that the economy improves or worsens, as a matter of retrospective evaluation (see Fiorina 1981). Therefore, when including the PDI variables in partisan outcome models we interact each with an "Incumbent Party" variable coded 1 when a Democrat is president, and 2 when a Republican is president. The Incumbent Party variable also is included as a direct predictor in partisan outcome models, to capture more general effects of party incumbency on vote choice. Values for the National

PDI and Incumbent Party variables are uniform across all respondents within a given election year. The State PDI and Battleground variables, on the other hand, are coded to match specific conditions in a respondent's home state in a given election year.

Dependent variables

The dependent variables that we analyze in this chapter include several for which data are available across each of the 1952–2008 presidential elections. In addition to "Presidential Vote" – coded 0 for a Republican vote, 1 for a Democratic vote, and missing otherwise – these dependent variables include a range of behavioral and attitudinal measures that serve as alternative indicators of the HSA. First is "Voter Turnout," coded 0 for not voting in that year's presidential election, 1 for voting, and missing otherwise. Second is a battery of political participation variables, including dichotomous measures of whether a respondent reported: trying to influence the votes of others during a campaign ("Influence"); attending campaign rallies or political meetings ("Rallies"); working for a party or candidate during a campaign ("Volunteer"); donating money to a party or a candidate's campaign ("Donate").[13] Each of these variables is coded 0 for not participating in the specified activity, 1 for participating, and missing otherwise. The third dependent variable, "Interested in Campaign," is coded 0 for reporting being "Not much interested" or "Somewhat interested" in a political campaign in a given presidential election year, 1 for being "Very much interested," and missing otherwise. Another attitudinal variable, "Care Who Wins," asks respondents whether they care who wins that year's presidential election. Responses are coded 0 for "Don't care very much" or "Don't Know," 1 for "Care a good deal," and missing otherwise.

To enlist a broader range of HSA indicators, we also test several candidate evaluation variables included in many but not all of the presidential election years covered by the ANES cumulative file. We do so with some caution, however, since, as noted above, any tests based on such data will be characterized by decreased statistical power and a more limited range of candidacies. To highlight this fact, we present the results of these analyses separately from those of the dependent variables described above.

The first set of additional dependent variables – "Thermometer: Democratic Presidential," "Thermometer: Republican Presidential," "Thermometer: Democratic Vice Presidential," "Thermometer: Republican Vice Presidential" – comprises feeling thermometer ratings of each party's presidential and vice presidential candidates in a given election year, included in each of the 1968–2008 ANES. Feeling thermometers require respondents to rate their attitudes toward a given target – in this case a candidate – on a scale ranging from 0 (coldest, or most negative, feelings) to 100 (warmest, or most positive, feelings), with a score of 50 indicating neutral feelings. Our coding preserves the scores reported for each respondent in the cumulative file except to recode values listed by ANES as "97–100 degrees" to 100; "Don't know" and "Don't recognize" responses to a neutral score of 50; invalid responses as missing.[14]

A second set of candidate evaluations, included in the 1952–2004 ANES, calculates the relative number of likes and dislikes reported by a respondent about that year's Democratic presidential candidate ("Affect: Democratic Presidential") and Republican presidential candidate ("Affect: Republican Presidential"). Respondents were given the open-ended opportunity to list up to five things that they liked and five things that they disliked about each candidate. The ANES "affect" variable subtracts the number of dislikes reported by each respondent from the number of likes, to create a general affect scale ranging from –5 (maximum negative, or five dislikes and no likes) to +5 (maximum positive, or five likes and no dislikes) for a given target. We recode invalid affect scores as missing, and otherwise retain the ANES coding.

Finally, the 1980–2008 ANES include a battery of questions asking respondents whether they have felt various forms of specific affect toward each presidential candidate. For our third set of dependent variables we isolate the item asking whether a Democratic or Republican presidential candidate has made the respondent feel "proud." Pride is particularly relevant to our analysis of the vice presidential HSA – much more so than other affect measures such as anger, fear, and hope – since it taps the assumption that individuals see a home state vice presidential candidate as "one of our own" and are motivated by this sense of shared identity. Unfortunately, we cannot test this assumption directly because the ANES do not measure affect toward vice presidential candidates. However, if feelings of pride in a home state running mate are extended to the presidential candidate who selected him or her, our analysis should show that vice presidential home state respondents score significantly higher on this measure. To test this relationship we use two new dependent variables – "Proud: Democratic Presidential" and "Proud: Republican Presidential" – coded 0 for reporting "No, haven't felt proud," 1 for reporting "Yes, have felt proud," and missing otherwise.

If vice presidential candidates enjoy a competitive advantage in their home state, we should find evidence that ANES respondents are more likely to support a presidential ticket on which a native son or daughter serves as running mate. However, if our aggregate-level evidence from previous chapters is accurate, this chapter's individual-level analysis should show that there is no statistically significant difference in vote choice between residents and non-residents of the running mate's home state. Moreover, our evaluation of alternative indicators of the vice presidential HSA affords an unprecedented opportunity to detect whether the effects of a home state candidacy extend to more subtle shifts in election-related attitudes and behaviors such as voter turnout, political participation, campaign interest, and candidate evaluations. Even if running mates do not earn greater support for their ticket in the home state, it might be the case that their candidacies inspire greater civic engagement and thus a different type of "home state advantage."

Empirical analysis

Table 5.2 presents descriptive statistics, as well as preliminary statistical tests, comparing respondents who did or did not live in the home state of a vice presidential candidate or a presidential candidate in a given presidential election year, for each dependent variable included in the 1952–2008 ANES. Columns 1 and 6 list the average percentage of home state respondents – vice presidential and presidential, respectively – scoring 1 on the dependent variable; Columns 2 and 7 do the same for non-home state respondents; Columns 3 and 8 report the difference between each set of percentages; Columns 4 and 9 report statistically significant differences between home state and non-home state respondents derived from difference of proportions tests (two-tailed).[15] The purpose of this table, however, is not to provide definitive evidence of the HSA but to begin our analysis with initial evidence that is more intuitive than the multivariate regression models to follow.

The preliminary evidence presented in Table 5.2 shows no indication of a vice presidential HSA; the only statistically significant difference between vice presidential home state and non-home state respondents is a *lower* level of turnout among the former which might be attributable to intervening variables not accounted for in a difference of proportions test. There is, however, evidence of a *presidential* HSA; presidential home state respondents are 5.5%–5.9% more likely to vote for a native son, and the differences are statistically significant. Also, presidential home state respondents are significantly more likely to try to influence another person's vote, according to difference of proportions tests. We must bear in mind, though, that these results are not conclusive since they estimate the direct effects of home state candidacies without accounting for relevant control variables such as party identification and standard demographics. A more definitive evaluation of the home state advantage is made possible by multivariate regression analysis, the results of which we present next.

Table 5.3 presents results from multivariate logistic regression models predicting election-related behaviors and attitudes measured in each of the 1952–2008 presidential election year surveys. The independent variables in each model comprise the "base model" described earlier in this chapter, with appropriate variations to account for partisan versus non-partisan dependent variables.[16] The statistics reported in Table 5.3 include the coefficient and standard error associated with each variable. Because these are logistic regression models, however, the coefficients represent log odds ratios and cannot be interpreted directly and intuitively as with linear regression coefficients. Statistical significance

Table 5.2: Descriptive comparison and difference of proportions tests for vice presidential and presidential home state versus non-home state respondents, 1952–2008 ANES

	Vice presidential home state?				
Dependent variable	(1) Home state	(2) Non-Home state	(3) Difference	(4) Significance	(5) N
Presidential vote – Dem.	50.87%	49.92%	0.95%	–	17,639
Presidential vote – GOP	48.29%	50.12%	–1.83%	–	17,639
Voter turnout	71.88%	74.83%	–2.95%	**	25,297
Participation: Influence	35.66%	33.98%	1.68%	–	25,093
Participation: Rallies	7.23%	7.69%	–0.46%	–	25,084
Participation: Volunteer	4.13%	4.01%	0.12%	–	25,068
Participation: Donate	8.72%	9.77%	–1.05%	–	25,051
Interested in campaign	69.07%	67.81%	1.26%	–	26,966
Care who wins election	33.59%	33.98%	–0.39%	–	27,937
	Presidential home state?				
Dependent variable	(6) Home state	(7) Non-Home state	(8) Difference	(9) Significance	(10) N
Presidential vote – Dem.	55.7%	49.80%	5.9%	*	17,639
Presidential vote – GOP	55.28%	49.75%	5.53%	***	17,639
Voter turnout	74.68%	74.64%	0.04%	–	25,297
Participation: Influence	36.49%	33.88%	2.61%	*	25,093
Participation: Rallies	7.54%	7.67%	–0.13%	–	25,084
Participation: Volunteer	4.13%	4.01%	0.12%	–	25,068
Participation: Donate	10.07%	9.68%	0.39%	–	25,051
Interested in campaign	70%	67.71%	2.29%	–	26,966
Care who wins election	36.19%	33.75%	2.44%	–	27,937

Descriptive statistics report the percentage of respondents (converted from proportions for ease of interpretation) who score 1 on the dependent variable. The "Significance" column reports results from difference of proportions tests.

***Denotes significant at p<0.001; ** denotes significant at p<0.01; * denotes significant at p<0.05; + denotes significant at p<0.1; - denotes not significant.

Dependent variable coding: Presidential vote – Dem (Republican = 0, Democrat = 1, missing otherwise); Presidential vote GOP (Democrat = 0, Republican = 1, missing otherwise); Voter turnout (Did not vote = 0, Voted = 1, missing otherwise); Participation (No = 0, Yes = 1, missing otherwise); Interested in campaign ("not much" or "somewhat interested" = 0, "very much interested" = 1, missing otherwise); Care who wins ("don't care very much" or "don't know"= 0, Care a good deal = 1, missing otherwise).

Table 5.3: Predictors of election-related behavior and attitudes, 1952–2008 ANES

Parameter	(Model 1) Presidential Vote choice	(Model 2) Voter Turnout	(Model 3) Participation: Influence	(Model 4) Participation: Rallies	(Model 5) Participation: Volunteer	(Model 6) Participation: Donate	(Model 7) Interested In campaign	(Model 8) Care Who wins
VP home state: General	–	−0.011	0.049	−0.074	0.005	−0.099	0.007	0.151*
	–	(0.11)	(0.068)	(0.135)	(0.155)	(0.082)	(0.088)	(0.074)
Pr. home state: General	–	−0.077	0.047	−0.129	0.068	−0.104	0.126*	0.16*
	–	(0.108)	(0.058)	(0.149)	(0.136)	(0.084)	(0.077)	(0.069)
VP home	0.108	–	–	–	–	–	–	–
state: Republican	(0.301)	–	–	–	–	–	–	–
VP home state:	−0.015	–	–	–	–	–	–	–
Democrat	(0.170)	–	–	–	–	–	–	–
Pr. home	−0.405**	–	–	–	–	–	–	–
state: Republican	(0.134)	–	–	–	–	–	–	–
Pr. home state:	0.179	–	–	–	–	–	–	–
Democrat	(0.192)	–	–	–	–	–	–	–
Party identification	−0.876***	−0.034**	0.014	−0.011	0.011	0.032	−0.01	−0.003
	(0.039)	(0.011)	(0.011)	(0.029)	(0.034)	(0.027)	(0.013)	(0.021)
Age	−0.003	0.033***	−0.001	0.004*	0.009***	0.024***	0.025***	0.016***
	(0.002)	(0.001)	(0.002)	(0.002)	(0.002)	(0.004)	(0.002)	(0.001)
Gender	−0.064	0.079	0.344***	0.132*	−0.034	0.118*	0.271***	0.001
	(0.052)	(0.075)	(0.044)	(0.052)	(0.103)	(0.053)	(0.025)	(0.022)
Non-White	1.422***	−0.168*	−0.039	0.203⁺	0.044	−0.142⁺	0.098	0.366***
	(0.172)	(0.069)	(0.073)	(0.112)	(0.127)	(0.083)	(0.063)	(0.078)
Education	0.083⁺	0.349***	0.202***	0.264***	0.222***	0.29***	0.218***	0.194***
	(0.044)	(0.02)	(0.02)	(0.026)	(0.036)	(0.038)	(0.017)	(0.021)
Household Income	−0.14***	0.362***	0.122***	0.157***	0.233***	0.501***	0.143***	0.11***
	(0.037)	(0.016)	(0.016)	(0.042)	(0.042)	(0.045)	(0.015)	(0.014)

Table 5.3: (*cont.*)

Parameter	(Model 1) Presidential Vote choice	(Model 2) Voter Turnout	(Model 3) Participation: Influence	(Model 4) Participation: Rallies	(Model 5) Participation: Volunteer	(Model 6) Participation: Donate	(Model 7) Interested In campaign	(Model 8) Care Who wins
South	–0.646***	–0.453***	0.062	–0.251**	–0.111	–0.235**	0.145***	0.118**
	(0.095)	(0.07)	(0.039)	(0.087)	(0.078)	(0.079)	(0.037)	(0.043)
Change in PDI: State	0.017	–0.017	0.006	0.015	–0.006	–0.017	–0.006	–0.008
	(0.027)	(0.013)	(0.007)	(0.016)	(0.023)	(0.016)	(0.007)	(0.01)
Change in PDI: National	0.027	–0.054*	–0.023	–0.034	–0.001	0.029	–0.041	–0.103***
	(0.244)	(0.025)	(0.021)	(0.03)	(0.034)	(0.059)	(0.029)	(0.03)
Incumbent party	0.168	–	–	–	–	–	–	–
	(0.891)	–	–	–	–	–	–	–
Incumbent*state PDI	–0.025	–	–	–	–	–	–	–
	(0.023)	–	–	–	–	–	–	–
Incumbent*national PDI	–0.035	–	–	–	–	–	–	–
	(0.125)	–	–	–	–	–	–	–
Battleground	–	–0.006*	0	–0.001	0.001	0.001	–0.001	–0.001
	–	(0.003)	(0.002)	(0.003)	(0.004)	(0.002)	(0.001)	(0.002)
Constant	3.47*	–1.616***	–1.841***	–4.024***	–5.172***	–6.274***	–2.835***	–0.284
	(1.771)	(0.266)	(0.197)	(0.262)	(0.42)	(0.399)	(0.199)	(0.23)
Log-pseudolikelihood	–6,821.963	–11,706.761	–14,738.316	–6,235.778	–3,957.052	–6,851.499	–15,544.883	–15,853.925
N	16,197	22,817	22,641	22,635	22,617	22,607	24,255	25,115

Entries are logistic regression coefficients, robust standard errors clustered by year are included in parentheses.

*** Denotes significant at $p<0.001$; ** denotes significant at $p<0.01$; * denotes significant at $p<0.05$; + denotes significant at $p<0.1$.

Dependent variable coding: Vote choice (Republican = 0, Democrat = 1, missing otherwise); Voter turnout (Did not vote = 0, Voted = 1, missing otherwise); Participation (No = 0, Yes = 1, missing otherwise); Interested in campaign ("not much" or "somewhat interested" = 0, "very much interested" = 1, missing otherwise); Care who wins ("don't care very much" = 0, "care a good deal" = 1, missing otherwise).

is the primary focus of this analysis, specifically for the vice presidential and presidential variables.[17]

Vote choice models

The results presented in Column 1 of Table 5.3 confirm our previous findings: there is no statistically significant relationship, in general, between living in a vice presidential candidate's home state and voting for his or her presidential ticket. If there were such a relationship, we would expect – given that the dependent variable in this model is coded 0 for Republican presidential vote choice and 1 for Democratic presidential vote choice – that the Democratic vice presidential home state variable would be statistically significant and positively signed, and that the Republican vice presidential home state variable would be statistically significant and negatively signed. Instead, neither variable is significant.

This is not to say that home states are irrelevant to presidential voting, though. The Republican presidential home state variable is statistically significant and correctly signed in the vote choice model. This finding is consistent with previous aggregate-level analyses of the presidential HSA, however it is inconsistent with the Democratic presidential home state variable which fails to reach conventional levels of statistical significance. Why the discrepancy? The answer is unclear, but it could be an issue of statistical power: Democratic presidential candidates are the least represented by home state respondents in our data, including vice presidential candidates, at 670 – nearly 1,000 less than Republican presidential candidates, at 1,623. It is also possible that Republicans have happened to nominate presidential candidates with stronger appeal to home state voters, but it is hard to believe that such a difference would be systematic between parties.

Of greater importance than resolving this discrepancy, for the purposes of our analysis, is the fact that we find evidence of a statistically significant presidential HSA, contrasted with no evidence of a significant vice presidential HSA. This is the storyline that emerges from decades of research in the HSA literature, including research presented in Chapter 4 of this book, and here it is corroborated by our individual-level analysis.

Alternative HSA models

The results from the alternative indicator models in Columns 2–8 further challenge any notion of a vice presidential HSA. Vice presidential home state respondents are no more likely than respondents from other states to vote in the presidential election, engage in acts of political participation, or express interest in a political campaign. However, the same respondents *are* significantly more likely to care who wins the presidential election. We do, then, find some indication that vice presidential candidates influence electoral attitudes in their home

Table 5.4: Descriptive comparison and difference of means or proportions tests for vice presidential and presidential home state versus non-home state respondents, 1952–2008 ANES (partial)

	Vice presidential home state?				
Dependent variable	(1) Home state	(2) Non-Home state	(3) Difference	(4) Significance	(5) N
Therm: Dem. vice presidential	61.15	54.54	6.61	***	21,492
Therm: Rep. vice presidential	57.88	50.96	6.92	***	21,508
Therm: Dem. presidential	58.25	57.4	0.85	–	21,561
Therm: Rep. presidential	59.21	57.6	1.61	–	21,555
Affect: Dem. presidential	0.14	0.26	–0.12	–	24,558
Affect: Rep. presidential	0.21	0.10	0.11	–	24,588
Proud: Dem. presidential	34.02%	37.95%	–3.93%	+	15,190
Proud: Rep. presidential	43.75%	44.17%	–0.42%	–	15,260
	Presidential home state?				
Dependent variable	(6) Home state	(7) Non-Home state	(8) Difference	(9) Significance	(10) N
Therm: Dem. vice presidential	58.49	54.66	3.83	***	21,492
Therm: Rep. vice presidential	51.22	51.14	0.08	–	21,508
Therm: Dem. presidential	63.28	57.31	5.97	***	21,561
Therm: Rep. presidential	59.99	57.48	2.51	***	21,555
Affect: Dem. presidential	0.52	0.14	0.38	***	24,558
Affect: Rep. presidential	0.09	0.11	–0.02	–	24,588
Proud: Dem. presidential	49.84%	37.56%	12.28%	***	15,190
Proud: Rep. presidential	48.84%	43.83%	5.01%	**	15,260

Descriptive statistics report the mean feeling thermometer rating (1968–2008), mean affect score (1952–2004), or percentage of proud responses (1980–2008) for respondents in the relevant ANES surveys.

The "Significance" column reports results from difference of means or difference of proportions tests. ***Denotes significant at $p<0.001$; ** denotes significant at $p<0.01$; * denotes significant at $p<0.05$; + denotes significant at $p<0.1$; - denotes not significant.

Dependent variable coding: Feeling Thermometers (0 for most negative feelings through 100 for most positive feelings, "Don't know" and "Don't recognize" recoded to 50, missing otherwise); Affect (–5 for five candidate dislikes and 0 candidate likes, through +5 for 0 candidate dislikes and five candidate likes, missing otherwise); Proud ("No, haven't felt proud" = 0, "Yes, have felt proud" = 1; missing otherwise).

state. That evidence is quite limited, though, and it does not translate into actual changes in electoral behavior.

Presidential home state respondents also are significantly more likely to care who wins the presidential election, and to express interest in a political campaign. Aside from its significant effect on vote choice for Republican candidates, though, the presidential HSA does not extend to other election-related behaviors tested in these models; respondents from a presidential candidate's home state are no more likely to vote in the presidential election or to engage in acts of political participation.[18]

Candidate evaluation models

The evidence of a vice presidential HSA is so underwhelming that it is reasonable to wonder whether running mates *are* more popular in their home state, after all – and, if so, whether that popularity extends to the presidential candidate who selects him or her for the ticket. In order to measure home state effects on candidate evaluations, in Table 5.4 we begin our analysis of the second group of dependent variables – included in some but not all of the 1952–2008 ANES surveys – by presenting preliminary evidence including descriptive statistics and difference of proportions tests. The order and formatting of this table are the same as in Table 5.2. Also, as with Table 5.2, the purpose of presenting this evidence is to make our analysis of the dependent variables more intuitive. Definitive evaluations of the HSA are reserved for the multivariate regression analyses that follow.

The evidence presented in Table 5.4 indicates that vice presidential candidates are significantly more popular among home state respondents. However, the running mate's popularity does not extend to the presidential candidate heading the same ticket; vice presidential home state respondents show no statistically significant differences in terms of presidential candidate thermometer ratings, general affect toward the presidential candidate, or pride in the presidential candidate. Presidential candidates also are significantly more popular among their home state respondents; in addition to giving the candidate higher feeling thermometer ratings, on average, presidential home state respondents are more likely to report feeling proud of that candidate and, in the case of Democratic candidates but not Republicans, exhibit more positive general affect toward him. Of course this evidence is not conclusive since it does not control for factors that tend to influence candidate evaluations and might be associated with living in a given state, such as party identification and standard demographics. To provide a more rigorous test of the relationship between home state candidacies and candidate evaluation, next we consider results from the multivariate regression models.

Table 5.5 presents a series of linear and logistic regression models – for continuously-coded and dichotomous dependent variables, respectively – predicting presidential or vice presidential candidate evaluations. Because each

Table 5.5: Predictors of vice presidential and presidential candidate evaluations, 1952–2008 ANES (partial)

Parameter	(1) Therm: GOP VP	(2) Therm: Dem VP	(3) Therm: GOP Pres.	(4) Therm: Dem Pres.	(5) Affect: GOP Pres.	(6) Affect: Dem Pres.	(7) Proud: GOP Pres.	(8) Proud: Dem Pres.
VP home state: Republican	5.614**	–0.062	0.465	0.619	0.153	0.187	0.04*	0.01
	(1.708)	(1.85)	(1.206)	(2.006)	(0.172)	(0.136)	(0.014)	(0.043)
VP home state: Democrat	–1.294	7.874+	–0.113	0.697	0.068	0.073	–0.025	0.001
	(1.133)	(3.588)	(1.396)	(1.622)	(0.123)	(0.112)	(0.045)	(0.02)
Pr. home state: Republican	0.127	0.293	1.695+	–1.917	0.093	–0.143	0.037	–0.029
	(0.426)	(1.238)	(0.801)	(1.357)	(0.096)	(0.096)	(0.033)	(0.026)
Pr. home state: Democrat	–2.243	3.480*	–3.726*	5.17*	–0.083	0.341*	–0.016	0.106
	(1.26)	(1.382)	(1.56)	(2.124)	(0.144)	(0.149)	(0.016)	(0.056)
Party identification	4.611***	-4.09***	6.725***	-6.699***	0.552***	-0.519***	0.085***	-0.08***
	(0.491)	(0.366)	(0.418)	(0.307)	(0.03)	(0.03)	(0.004)	(0.006)
Age	0.09**	0.057**	0.073***	0.021	0.001	0.002	0.002	0.001**
	(0.024)	(0.018)	(0.01)	(0.023)	(0.002)	(0.001)	(0.001)	(0)
Gender	–0.738+	–1.383*	–0.835*	–2.002***	–0.041	–0.146***	0.023	–0.041*
	(0.374)	(0.451)	(0.359)	(0.416)	(0.043)	(0.027)	(0.012)	(0.012)
Non-White	–0.845	1.935	–4.069*	8.505**	–0.466***	0.524***	–0.075*	0.103*
	(1.283)	(1.322)	(1.714)	(2.224)	(0.109)	(0.103)	(0.023)	(0.038)
Education	–0.702+	1.143***	–1.428**	0.268	–0.126**	0.021	0.018+	0.019**
	(0.379)	(0.159)	(0.35)	(0.375)	(0.034)	(0.021)	(0.008)	(0.005)
Household income	0.739+	–0.294	1.518***	–1.494***	0.106***	–0.088**	0.031***	–0.016***
	(0.38)	(0.342)	(0.226)	(0.322)	(0.021)	(0.023)	(0.006)	(0.003)
South	3.607***	–1.781*	5.229***	–2.809*	0.415***	–0.368***	0.044**	0.017
	(0.658)	(0.75)	(0.484)	(1.061)	(0.049)	(0.079)	(0.009)	(0.014)
Change in PDI: State	–0.163	–0.401	–1.239*	–0.662	–0.008	–0.089***	–0.027	0.002
	(0.418)	(0.433)	(0.409)	(0.777)	(0.026)	(0.02)	(0.015)	(0.018)

Change in PDI: National	−1.361	−0.549	1.184	−0.726	−0.119	−0.071	0.02	0.018
	(0.821)	(0.883)	(1.529)	(1.004)	(0.174)	(0.094)	(0.031)	(0.045)
Incumbent party	−13.814+	−6.296	−5.96	−8.42+	−0.134	−0.365	0.162	0.005
	(6.489)	(4.198)	(6.758)	(4.457)	(0.785)	(0.301)	(0.107)	(0.188)
Incumbent* state PDI	0.21	0.138	0.798*	0.167	0.009	0.047*	0.017+	−0.002
	(0.263)	(0.229)	(0.3)	(0.44)	(0.018)	(0.016)	(0.008)	(0.009)
Incumbent* national PDI	1.149	0.379	0.144	0.835	0.02	0.005	−0.016	−0.013
	(0.729)	(0.634)	(0.924)	(0.693)	(0.1)	(0.054)	(0.02)	(0.025)
Constant	47.983***	75.212***	29.861*	96.448***	−1.069	3.333***	−0.344*	0.596+
	(7.913)	(6.171)	(12.285)	(5.6)	(1.335)	(0.522)	(0.128)	(0.296)
R^2/Log-pseudolikelihood	0.193	0.168	0.306	0.315	0.273	0.273	0.193	0.165
N	19,262	19,246	19,307	19,316	22,040	22,040	13,408	13,347

Entries are linear regression coefficients (Models 1–6) or logistic regression coefficients (Models 7–8). Robust standard errors clustered by year are included in parentheses. Models 1–4 include observations from 1968–2008, Model 5 includes observations from 1952–2004, and Model 6 includes observations from 1980–2008. ***Denotes significant at $p<0.001$; ** denotes significant at $p<0.01$; * denotes significant at $p<0.05$; + denotes significant at $p<0.1$.Dependent variable coding: Feeling Thermometers (0 for most negative feelings through 100 for most positive feelings, "Don't know" and "Don't recognize" recoded to 50, missing otherwise); Affect (−5 for five candidate dislikes and 0 candidate likes through +5 for 0 candidate dislikes and five candidate likes, missing otherwise); Proud ("No, haven't felt proud" = 0, "Yes, have felt proud" = 1, missing otherwise).

dependent variable is partisan in nature, the independent variables are uniform across each model – including the four partisan-specific home state variables and the two economic interaction variables, while excluding the Battleground variable. The statistics reported in this table once more include coefficients and robust standard errors. The feeling thermometer and affect models yield linear regression coefficients amenable to direct interpretation, whereas the pride models yield log odds ratios not amenable to direct interpretation.

Vice presidential candidates are, in fact, more popular among residents of their home state, according to this analysis. The Republican vice presidential home state variable is a statistically significant predictor of the Republican vice presidential feeling thermometer ($p < 0.05$), while the Democratic vice presidential home state variable is a marginally significant predictor of the Democratic vice presidential feeling thermometer ($p = 0.053$). The linear regression coefficient for each variable permits us to quantify its effect; Republican running mates score 5.61 points higher on a 0–100 feeling thermometer in their home state, and Democratic running mates score 7.87 points higher. The effect of a home state candidacy, however, is almost totally isolated. Vice presidential home state respondents rate the presidential candidates no differently on the feeling thermometer than respondents from other states, and the same is true for the opposing vice presidential candidates. These findings are significant for two reasons: first, they provide actual evidence that running mates are generally more popular in their home state, whereas that fact is usually assumed; second, they indicate that the vice presidential candidate's popularity in his or her home state has no effect on feelings toward other members of the presidential tickets.

The remaining models provide further evidence for the latter conclusion. In all but one instance, there is no statistically significant relationship between residence in a vice presidential candidate's home state and affect – in general or specifically in terms of pride – toward the presidential candidate on either ticket. The only exception is found in the model predicting pride in a Republican presidential candidate; there, the Republican vice presidential home state variable is statistically significant and positively signed. Perhaps, then, pride in a "native son" running mate is transferred to the presidential candidate who selected him. However, this is the only finding to indicate such an effect; every other model of affect toward the presidential candidates yields a null result.

Living in a presidential candidate's home state has somewhat similar effects. The Democratic presidential home state variable is a statistically significant predictor of the Democratic presidential candidate's feeling thermometer ($p < 0.05$), and the Republican presidential home state variable is a marginally significant predictor of the Republican presidential candidate's feeling thermometer ($p = 0.06$). Based upon the regression coefficients, the associated increase in feeling thermometer ratings is 5.17 for a Democratic presidential candidate and 1.7 for a Republican presidential candidate. In other models, the Republican presidential home state variable fails to attain statistical significance. The Democratic presidential home state variable, on the other hand, reaches conventional significance levels in three other models; it is associated with more positive ratings on the Democratic vice presidential candidate's feeling thermometer (+3.48), more negative ratings of the Republican presidential candidate (–3.73), and more positive general affect toward the Democratic presidential candidate (+0.34). To some extent, then, we see evidence that living in a presidential candidate's home state has more far-reaching effects than living in a vice presidential candidate's home state; whereas the latter influences only evaluations of the home state candidate, the former – at least in Democratic cases – influences evaluations of other presidential and vice presidential candidates as well.

Discussion

From these results we observe a general pattern that is consistent with our prior analyses of the vice presidential, as well as presidential, HSA. Vice presidential candidates tend to be more popular within their home state, but their candidacy has no bearing on residents' evaluations of other participants in the race. Presidential candidates are also more popular in their home state. The difference is that – in Democratic, but not Republican, cases – we find evidence of their candidacies influencing home state residents' attitudes toward the presidential tickets as a whole. Compared to those who live in other states, respondents from a Democratic presidential candidate's home state evaluate his running mate more positively, evaluate his opponent more negatively, and express more positive general affect toward their "native son." Put simply, a presidential home state candidacy has the demonstrated potential to influence electoral evaluations *in general*, whereas a vice presidential home state candidacy seems relevant to evaluating only the native candidate. The reason, we suspect, is an obvious one indicated by our discussion in Chapter 1: presidents are far more powerful and consequential political actors than vice presidents, and so voters generally base their votes on characteristics of the presidential candidates. Running mates *can* influence home state electoral behavior, but as the evidence from Chapter 4 indicates, these effects are conditional rather than general.

Conclusion

This chapter's analysis of the vice presidential HSA is unique in two important respects. First, to address the possibility that previous conclusions about the vice presidential HSA – in this book and within the associated literature, generally – are based upon an ecological fallacy, we test the effects of a home state candidacy using individual- rather than aggregate-level data. Second, to identify broader and perhaps more subtle effects of a home state candidacy on political attitudes and behaviors, we test alternative indicators of the vice presidential HSA – including voter turnout, political participation, election attitudes, and candidate evaluations.

The evidence from this analysis confirms and expands upon our previous characterizations of the vice presidential HSA. Individuals who live in a vice presidential candidate's home state are not more likely to vote for that candidate's presidential ticket, nor are they more likely to vote in the presidential election, engage in acts of political participation, or express interest in a political campaign. We do find evidence that these individuals are more likely to care who wins the presidential election, but there is no indication that this translates into actual behavioral changes. Vice presidential candidates *are* significantly more popular among home state residents, according to our analysis of feeling thermometer ratings, but the presidential candidates who selected them are rated no differently by the same respondents, nor are the opposing presidential and vice presidential candidates. Furthermore, we find only limited evidence of a change in general affect toward the presidential candidate and no difference in expressed pride.

Presidential candidates, on the other hand, seem to enjoy a HSA. Republican and Democratic presidential candidates earn a significantly higher percentage of the vote among home state residents, although only the former retains this advantage after accounting for intervening variables. Presidential home state respondents also express more interest in a political campaign and care more about who wins the presidential election, but they are not more likely to vote in the election or to engage in acts of political participation. In terms of candidate evaluations, presidential candidates are more popular among home state residents (at conventional significance levels for Democratic candidates and marginal levels for Republican candidates). The effect of a home state candidacy is limited to the "native son" for Republican presidential home state respondents, but for Democratic presidential home state respondents we find evidence of a wider effect. In a Democratic presidential candidate's home state, respondents express more positive general affect toward that candidate while rating the Democratic running mate more favorably and the Republican presidential candidate more negatively on feeling thermometers. In short, there is substantial but inconsistent evidence that living in a presidential candidate's home state influences attitudes toward the election in general, and vote choice in particular, while the evidence is almost entirely consistent in showing that vice presidential candidates do not influence election-related attitudes or behaviors, including vote choice.

The widespread perception of a vice presidential HSA – among historians, journalists, campaign advisers, and presidential candidates – documented in the first three chapters of this book does not withstand empirical scrutiny. Neither the aggregate-level analysis presented in Chapter 4 nor the individual-level analysis presented in this chapter show any evidence that vice presidential candidates, in general, enhance the performance of their presidential ticket in the home state. However, this does not exclude the possibility of a HSA in presidential elections. Our aggregate-level analysis of 1884–2012 election returns in Chapter 4 indicates that presidential candidates earn a statistically significant advantage in their home state, and our individual-level analysis of 1952–2008 ANES survey data in this chapter indicates that Republican presidential candidates, at least, earn a statistically significant HSA. Vice presidential candidates may also earn a statistically significant HSA – according to our analysis from Chapter 4 – but the effect is conditional: the home state must be relatively less populous and the candidate must have substantial experience in elected office within the state.

This pattern of results seems to reflect a fundamental reality of presidential elections too often ignored, or temporarily suppressed, in the fevered strategizing of "veepstakes" speculation and campaign decision-making: voters generally vote for presidential candidates and not their running mates. Rarely will a home state vice presidential candidacy alter this reality.

Notes

1 See: www.census.gov/hhes/www/income/data/statemedian/. Data file: "Median Household Income by State – Single-Year Estimates." Accessed June 3, 2014.
2 See: www.presidency.ucsb.edu/showelection.php?year=2008. Accessed February 23, 2015.
3 For that matter, the same data could be used to argue that wealth is positively associated with voting for Democrats; indeed, twelve of the fourteen states with the highest median income levels in 2008 voted for Barack Obama.
4 See: www.cnn.com/ELECTION/2008/results/polls/#val=MSP00p1. Accessed February 23, 2015.
5 Also see Gelman *et al.* (2007) for an individual-level analysis of the relationship between income and vote choice in relatively rich versus poor states, which yields similar findings.
6 The ANES Cumulative Data file is publicly available for download on the ANES website, www.electionstudies.org. Accessed February 23, 2015. Since our interest is in presidential elections, the subsequent analysis excludes data from midterm election years.
7 Since home state residence is not reported in the 1948 data, we exclude that year from analysis.
8 This, by the way, is almost certainly why studies of the presidential or vice presidential HSA typically rely upon aggregate-level data despite the well-known dangers of committing an ecological fallacy. National election surveys often do not include respondents from each state, and when candidates' home states are represented in the data the number of home state respondents still may be too small to detect statistically significant differences. Moreover, the states most likely to be included, and represented by many respondents, are large states – which, according to our analysis, are least likely to yield a vice presidential HSA. Time series data help to mitigate this problem by allowing researchers to pool together home state respondents from across election years. However, collecting longitudinal data is costly and logistically complex, and this limits the availability of individual-level datasets capable of appropriately testing the HSA. The ANES cumulative file is a rare example of such a dataset, and exceptional in that it includes applicable data for presidential elections dating back to 1952.

9 A qualified exception is found in Devine and Kopko (2013), where we analyze differences in voter turnout between vice presidential or presidential home states and non-home states. However, our measurement of the "turnout advantage" in that article is not an end in itself; instead, we use it as an independent variable in models predicting the HSA, to determine whether such advantages are driven by processes of voter mobilization versus voter conversion. An exclusive focus on vote choice is also the norm within the friends-and-neighbors literature, more broadly, but there are some exceptions. Aspin and Hall's (1987) analysis of voting for trial court judges, although primarily focused on vote choice, also shows that voter turnout for a judicial retention election is higher in a judge's home county. A subsequent research note finds the same for judicial elections at the appellate court level (Aspin and Hall 1989). In Thielemann's (1993) analysis of the friends and neighbors effect in Texas Supreme Court elections, campaign financing rather than vote choice is the dependent variable.

10 For example, when predicting partisan outcomes such as presidential vote choice, we disaggregate the home state variables by party – e.g., Republican Vice Presidential Home State versus Democratic Vice Presidential Home State – since living in a vice presidential home state, *per se*, should not predict voting for a Democratic candidate over a Republican candidate. Conversely, when predicting non-partisan outcomes such as voter turnout or campaign interest, we use unified home state variables – "Vice Presidential Home State" and "Presidential Home State" – since living in a Democratic versus Republican running mate's home state should not condition the outcome, and disaggregating in this case would needlessly mitigate statistical power. Other variables exclusive to models with a non-partisan dependent variable include measures of home state competitiveness and interactions of the incumbent party with economic conditions – both of which we describe in this section.

11 Note that the Battleground variable is coded to indicate decreasing competitiveness as it increases in value. Therefore, we expect a negative relationship between it and measures of electoral engagement, since the consequences of engagement are more significant in close races.

12 See Chapter 4 for more on our economic variables.

13 The variable measures used by ANES do not specify whether these acts of political participation occurred within the context of the presidential campaign or a different state or local campaign. However, the opportunity to participate in state and local campaigns is available within each state and so a statistically significant increase among residents of a vice presidential candidate's home state should be a valid indicator of HSA. The same logic applies to our treatment of the campaign interest variable.

14 Separate tests of the feeling thermometers in which "Don't know" and "Don't recognize" responses are coded "missing" rather than "neutral" reveal no substantive differences from the results reported in this chapter. We prefer to recode these responses in order to preserve the cases and maximize statistical power in subsequent analyses.

15 We convert the proportions used in our statistical analysis to percentages in this table (multiplying each proportion by 100) in order to make the presentation of results more intuitive.

16 We use a general weight variable (VCF0011) from the ANES cumulative file when testing each model. Also, since observations within a given year are not independent

of one another, we cluster by year when testing each model. As a result, our estimates of statistical significance for each independent variable are calculated using robust standard errors.

17 To maintain this focus, we do not discuss the performance of other predictors which are intended to serve as statistical controls. It is worth noting, though, that each control is marginally significant in at least one model presented in this chapter, except for the interaction of incumbent party and national PDI.

18 With regard to voter turnout, this evidence seems to challenge Devine and Kopko's (2013) finding of a statistically significant "turnout advantage" for presidential candidates. Since that positive finding derives from aggregate-level data, and turnout is an individual-level decision, it may be more appropriate to accept the null finding from this individual-level analysis. However, this analysis uses a much shorter time frame (1952–2008 as opposed to 1884–2012), and survey respondents are notorious for reporting much higher turnout rates than election data – such as those used in our 2013 study – show to be true. Resolving the discrepancy between these results is a worthy goal for future research, but not an immediate concern for this analysis since our primary focus is upon the vice presidential HSA.

6

Did LBJ really "deliver" Texas ... and the South?

John F. Kennedy, then a forty-two-year-old senator from Massachusetts, announced his candidacy for the Democratic Party's presidential nomination on January 2, 1960. The next morning he appeared on NBC's *Meet the Press*. What he met there may be better described as great skepticism. *New York Times* columnist James Reston, for one, seemed incredulous at the thought of this young man's audacious quest against party stalwarts many years his senior (in age and political experience) to assume leadership of the free world. Forgoing a serious discussion of Kennedy's candidacy, Reston used his first question to ask whether the senator would instead accept his party's *vice* presidential nomination if it were offered. (Kennedy had, after all, waged a vigorous but unsuccessful campaign for that nomination at the 1956 Democratic National Convention.) It was only the third question of the interview, and the first of four consecutive questions on this matter.

"I'm not going to accept the vice presidential nomination," Kennedy said, flatly. He explained:

> Looking at the history of the last 60 years, I don't recall a single case where a vice presidential candidate contributed an electoral vote. I think [Republican presidential candidate Thomas] Dewey lost California in 1948 with [Governor Earl] Warren at the height of his popularity as vice president[ial candidate]. I know [Republican presidential candidate] Wendell Willkie lost Oregon in 1940 with [Senator] Charles McNary, the most popular figure in the history of Oregon. *A vice presidential candidate does not contribute. People vote for the presidential candidate on both sides. That's what's going to happen in 1960. They presume that the presidential candidate is going to have a normal life expectancy. They don't say, "We don't like the presidential candidate, but we'll vote for the vice presidential candidate."* [emphasis added][1]

John F. Kennedy's public assessment of the vice presidential home state advantage (HSA) was, if anything, even more emphatic than the one we have presented in this book (and quite at odds with his later actions and private comments concerning the selection of Lyndon Johnson, as detailed in this chapter). On the fundamental point, of course, we agree: vice presidential candidates generally do not provide an electoral advantage in their home state. Based upon the evidence presented in Chapter 4 and the logic of the friends and neighbors hypothesis, however, we do not deny the vice presidential HSA altogether but rather treat it as conditional; a significant advantage *is* likely if the running mate: (1) comes from a relatively less populous state; and, (2) has extensive experience in elected office within that state. It is because most running mates do not meet these criteria that we observe a general null effect. Thus, while expectations of a vice presidential HSA are usually unwarranted and irrelevant to the outcome of the presidential election, a real and decisive advantage *is possible* under extraordinary conditions – namely, in addition to the two criteria just cited, the election in the home state must be relatively competitive and the Electoral College vote must be close enough to hinge upon the outcome of not just one state, but a small state with relatively few electoral votes.

To make more concrete these two critical points about the vice presidential HSA – its conditional nature and its potential significance – in this chapter and the next we analyze specific elections in which that advantage might have had a consequential effect. First, in this chapter we use survey data to evaluate the most famous alleged vice presidential home state, or for that matter home region, advantage in presidential history: that of Texas's Lyndon Johnson in 1960. As noted in previous chapters, the notion that Johnson "delivered" Texas and the South that year is widely accepted even among individuals who dismiss the vice presidential HSA in general – so much so that the matter is not subjected to empirical scrutiny but rather accepted as obvious fact. If true, Johnson's HSA is problematic for our analysis because his candidacy fails one of the two conditions we have identified as determinative of that advantage: Texas in 1960 was not a relatively less-populous state, but the sixth most-populous in the nation. However, our analysis of 1960 survey data indicates that Johnson was not very popular among Texans and southerners, and in all likelihood did not deliver the presidential vote in their states. The potentially decisive impact of a vice presidential HSA is more clearly demonstrated in Chapter 7, where we analyze how Al Gore might have won the 2000 presidential election by selecting a different running mate with extensive elected experience in a less-populous state.

"We couldn't have won the South without Johnson"

John Kennedy's comments on *Meet the Press*, excerpted above, are supremely ironic for two reasons. First, and tragically so, he did not reach normal life expectancy but in fact was assassinated in November 1963 and succeeded by Vice President Lyndon Johnson. Second, based on the historical record there is no doubt that Kennedy selected Johnson primarily to secure electoral votes in

Texas and throughout the South. In other words, as with so many other presidential candidates, campaign strategists, and journalists, there seems to have been a profound disconnect between Kennedy's conclusions about the vice presidential HSA *in general* (at least as professed in public) and its applicability to *specific* cases.

Vice presidential selection

Kennedy defeated Johnson on the first ballot at the 1960 Democratic National Convention, with a bare majority of 806 votes (53%). Despite his stature as the US Senate's majority leader, and an exceptionally powerful one at that, in the race for his party's nomination Texas's Lyndon Johnson was, in effect, a sectional candidate – he had strong support from the southern states but little support from outside the region. In a Gallup poll conducted in late 1959, Johnson placed third among Democrats nationally, but first among southerners – with 31% (his nearest competitor, former Illinois Governor Adlai Stevenson, had 20% support). In the East, Midwest, and West, however, he placed no higher than fifth, with no more than 7% support.[2] Also in late 1959, Gallup polled Democratic Party county chairmen throughout the US and found that Johnson placed third overall but first among southern chairmen with 40% support, compared to 21% for his nearest competitor, Missouri Senator Stuart Symington. Among county chairmen in "Dixiecrat" states – the four that had voted for the splinter Democratic segregationist ticket in 1948 – Johnson's support was even higher, at 47%.[3] Johnson's southern support held strong at the 1960 Democratic National Convention as well; of the southern delegations' 352 votes, Johnson won 281.5, or 79.97%. But outside the South he picked up only 127.5 votes – 31.17% of a delegate total that fell far short of securing Johnson the presidential nomination.

John Kennedy, after winning that nomination, immediately turned his attention to choosing a running mate. His decision to select Johnson clearly was made with expectations of a vice presidential home state, and region, advantage in mind. As Kennedy would later explain to House Speaker Sam Rayburn, also from Texas, "it would be easier for the Democrats to carry Texas and the South if Johnson were on his ticket" (Potter 1964, 18). Doing so, every Democrat knew, was essential given the growing sectional rift within the party that was primarily – but not exclusively – centered upon civil rights for African-Americans. The once-solid Democratic South had fractured in recent years, at least at the presidential level, with the Dixiecrat revolt of 1948 and Republican Dwight Eisenhower's victory in four southern states in 1952 and five in 1956, both times including Texas. To win what was expected to be a very close race in 1960 against Republican nominee and incumbent Vice President Richard Nixon required holding together, to the maximum extent possible, the party's awkward North-South coalition solidified in the New Deal era.

Kennedy's seizure upon sectional considerations seems to have been immediate and overriding. On the morning that he decided upon Johnson, the nominee instructed his brother and campaign manager Robert F. Kennedy "to get a reading on the number of electoral votes that could be won in the Northern industrial states 'plus Texas'" (Potter 1964, 17). Robert – whose spiteful relationship with LBJ was later the subject of a book aptly titled *Mutual Contempt* (Shesol 1997) – clearly got the message. Returning to his hotel room, he called upon top campaign advisers Ken O'Donnell and Pierre Salinger. "How many electoral votes are we going to get if we capture the East, Northeast, and the solid South?" RFK shouted when the two men entered. Salinger, understanding the implication, responded with horror: "Are you talking about nominating Lyndon Johnson? You're not going to do that!" Pressed to explain the elevation of a southerner anathema to northern liberal delegates, particularly integrationists and labor leaders, "Bobby's response was to point out that Johnson had great strength in the South" (Caro 2012, 124).

Later, John Kennedy called the campaign's leadership to his hotel room to announce the decision and draw up plans for preventing a liberal revolt on the Convention floor. Johnson's biographer Robert Caro (2012, 126) explains Kennedy's thinking and the impression made upon his staff in this meeting:

> As soon as the nomination was won, Kennedy had begun counting the Electoral College votes necessary to win the real prize, the presidency – and even a quick, preliminary look at those votes showed that without Texas' twenty-four votes, and at least a few of the other southern votes, in his column, Jack Kennedy stood almost no chance at all of defeating Richard Nixon or any other Republican candidate. Extended analysis was not required, [campaign adviser Lawrence] O'Brien was to explain [to delegates and party leaders who questioned the decision].

Southern skeptics of Kennedy and northern skeptics of Johnson could not help but find the logic of this pairing persuasive. John Connally, an LBJ confidante and later governor of Texas, told Johnson: "He'll never beat Nixon in Texas unless you're on the ticket" (Caro 2012, 118). House Majority Whip Hale Boggs assured an LBJ aide about his state that, in Caro's (2012, 128) paraphrase, "Johnson's presence on the ticket would guarantee that Louisiana wouldn't vote Republican again." Liberals at the Convention who, upon hearing of Kennedy's decision, planned to nominate alternative vice presidential candidates and force a floor fight, also resigned themselves to what seemed a necessary strategic compromise. In Caro's (2012, 141) words, "the liberal bravado faded in the face of reality. The reality was the numbers: the figures in the Electoral College were all that mattered now." One defiant insurgent, Michigan Governor Soapy Williams, challenged Connecticut Senator Abe Ribicoff on the Convention floor: "Why retreat … from principle?" To which Ribicoff responded simply, "We want to win" (Caro 2012, 142). Democrats nominated Johnson for vice president, and the campaign was on.

Vice presidential advantage

Johnson spent most of the campaign barnstorming through southern states. In October he set off on a 3,500-mile whistlestop tour of the South, on a train called the "LBJ Special." At each stop, once "The Yellow Rose of Texas" finished playing over the train's loudspeakers, Johnson would emerge proudly sporting a ten-gallon hat. Following "introductions that emphasized that he was from the South and the significance of that fact," Johnson would deliver speeches that were characteristically energetic, and "very southern in their message" (Caro 2012, 145). "Why, oh why, should the great state of Virginia ever vote Republican?" Johnson said in that state, and likewise in others. The Republican Party "has no interest in Virginia or any other southern state. What excuse have you got for not voting with the party of your fathers" (Caro 2012, 145–146)? Afterward, LBJ and his wife Lady Bird would typically invite local officials to their parlor car for photos, as well as to "charm them, and warn them what would happen to the South if Nixon won – or if Kennedy won without its support" (Caro 2012, 148).

On Election Day, Kennedy's shrewd electoral calculation seemed to pay off. The Democratic ticket won with 303 electoral votes to the Republicans' 219, including all but four southern states – Florida, Tennessee, and Virginia, all voting Republican, and Mississippi, which voted for an independent slate of electors that ultimately cast its votes for segregationist Virginia Senator Harry F. Byrd. Most notably, Texas returned to the Democratic column for the first time since 1948 – and that by the slim margin of 46,000 votes, or 2%. Texas did not, however, make the difference in the election; without its twenty-four electoral votes, Kennedy still would have won nine votes more than the 270 required for election. Yet if Johnson could be credited with holding just one of the three southern states contributing at least ten electoral votes to Kennedy's total – Georgia, Louisiana, and North Carolina – or any combination of two or more southern states, then it was he who delivered the election in 1960.

It would be the unmistakable judgment of history, and of contemporaries, that Lyndon Johnson had done his job – that, as Kennedy's running mate, he had delivered Texas and most of the South, and in turn the election itself. Johnson "had been put on the Kennedy ticket to hold [the South] for the Democrats," noted the *US News & World Report*. "Mr. Johnson did the job" (Caro 2012, 155). Political columnists Robert Novak and Roland Evans agreed: "John F. Kennedy could not have been elected President without the South. Could he have carried enough southern states to win" without Johnson as his running mate? "Probably not" (Caro 2012, 155). Philip Potter (1964, 20), writing in the *Reporter*, offered a similar assessment: "Probably no other combination could have won for the Democrats in 1960."

No judgment of Johnson's impact is more noteworthy, however, than that of the presidential candidate who selected him. "You've got to admit that I was right," President John F. Kennedy told White House aide Ken O'Donnell in 1962. "We couldn't have carried the South without Johnson" (Potter 1964, 20).

"Lyndon Benedict Johnson"

The preceding narrative suggests that Johnson was exceptionally popular among southerners, and Texans in particular – enough so to convince thousands of voters in multiple states to cast their votes for a presidential nominee they would have otherwise rejected in order to elevate to the vice presidency a running mate who was "one of us."[4] Yet there is good reason to question whether LBJ was in fact popular enough to have such an effect. This is not to say that he was *unpopular*; Johnson was, after all, also reelected to a third term in the US Senate with 58% of Texas's vote in 1960,[5] and we have shown that he received strong support from southern party elites in the 1960 nomination race as well as from rank-and-file southern Democrats. In keeping with the scientific method, however, we do not assume – based on conventional wisdom and circumstantial evidence – that Johnson's candidacy provided the Democratic ticket with an electoral advantage in his home state and region; rather, we test whether there is sufficient evidence to reject the null hypothesis that Johnson had no such effect. Our analysis focuses particularly on the *degree* to which Johnson was popular in his home state and region, since voters are unlikely to cast a presidential vote on the basis of vice presidential preference except under extraordinary conditions. Was Johnson, then, exceptionally popular among Texans and southerners – to the point where his presence on the ticket might reasonably be expected to alter presidential voting in large numbers? Or was Johnson's popularity limited to the point where, like most vice presidential candidates, he could win elections in his home state but not redirect thousands of presidential votes?

Ambition

Lyndon Johnson was, without question, popular enough to win elections in Texas. First elected to the US House of Representatives in a 1937 special election, Johnson went on to win reelection five times before being elected to the US Senate in 1948. It was not the first time Johnson had attempted to win a Senate seat; in 1941 he lost a special election to a fellow Democrat by 1,300 votes. His victory in the 1948 Democratic Party primary for Senate was so narrow, at eighty-seven votes, and so tainted by charges of election fraud, that it earned him the derisive nickname "Landslide Lyndon." Nonetheless, he was reelected to the Senate in 1954 with 85% of the vote.

By 1957, however, Johnson had turned his sights toward the presidency. Keenly aware of the challenges faced by a southern aspirant to the highest office in the nation – even after winning the 1964 presidential election with 61.1% of the vote, he still believed that another southerner would not be elected president in his lifetime (see Caro 2012, 115) – Johnson began shifting his position on civil rights. After voting against civil rights legislation for twenty years, Johnson as Senate majority leader played a key role in passing the first such legislation since Reconstruction: the Civil Rights Act of 1957. Hoping to please both sides of the sectional divide on civil rights, Johnson used his institutional authority to dilute the bill's provisions but also was one of only five southern senators – out of twenty-two – to vote for its passage. In 1960 Johnson used his parliamentary expertise to bypass southern obstructionists and bring a new civil rights bill to the Senate floor, leading Georgia's Richard Russell – a longtime ally – to angrily accuse him in session of "lynching the orderly procedure in the Senate of the United States" (Unger and Unger 1999, 233). Speaking to the Texas delegation at that year's National Convention, in a debate with Kennedy, Johnson went so far as to boast about his efforts to pass civil rights legislation. The delegates from Florida and Mississippi were so repelled by this appeal that they switched their Convention votes from LBJ to their respective state governors (Caro 2012, 108).

The calculation behind Johnson's shift toward a more moderate stance on civil rights was obvious. Supporters and opponents alike knew he was a man of boundless ambition, determined to win the nomination and the presidency in 1960, and that, as the *New York Times* said at the time, he could not succeed in doing so with a "Dixiecrat record on civil rights" (Unger and Unger 1999, 207). Noting that Johnson "not only voted with the South on civil rights, but he was a southern strategist" until 1957, biographer Robert Caro said: "He always had this true, deep compassion to help poor people and particularly poor people of color, but even stronger than the compassion was his ambition."[6] The influence of ambition was also apparent to Johnson's contemporaries. Senate aide Howard Schumann confessed: "Well, one doesn't know whether he was a liberal or a reactionary. Probably he was neither. He probably was just an extraordinary parliamentarian who was an opportunist and who sensed the wind and then went in that direction."[7] Labor leader Joseph L. Rauh, Jr., concurred: "It wasn't that he was a conservative or a radical or anything else; it was simply that he was trying to be all things to all people" (Caro 2012, 77). Johnson himself explicitly denied the "conservative" label cherished by his southern colleagues in Congress, instead describing himself as a "man in the middle, progressive and prudent without being radical" (Unger and Unger 1999, 240).

"Betrayal"

To many southerners, LBJ's shift on civil rights was a betrayal – not just an unwelcome change of heart but a calculated attempt to sell them out in pursuit of his presidential ambitions. In the lead-up to the passage of the Civil Rights Act of 1957, Johnson's office received a telegram from the segregationist Texas Citizens Council in Houston, reading: "We are told you are ready to sell out the South. Is this true?" (Unger and Unger 1999, 212). In response to the civil rights legislation that Johnson helped to bring before the Senate in 1960, the *Florida Times-Union* labeled him "the southern Benedict Arnold." A headline in the *Augusta Herald* read: "South is betrayed by Johnson for the sake of his own ambition." (Unger and Unger 1999, 235).

These feelings of betrayal were only exacerbated by Johnson's agreement to run on the Democratic ticket alongside John F. Kennedy – a northeastern Catholic who favored civil rights – and perhaps more so by his unapologetic defiance of those in the South who might have expected him to use his leverage to rein in Kennedy's liberalism and dilute the Democratic platform. In an August 1 article titled "Johnson takes his stand: Vice-Presidential nominee seeks unity within party but not on South's terms," the *New York Times* reported on a major campaign rally in Tennessee – attended by only four of the ten southern governors that Tennessee Governor Buford Ellington had invited – that

> Senator Lyndon B. Johnson has put the South on notice that he will not bargain away the Democratic platform's liberal principles to win the region's support .... In a news conference yesterday, in the speech last night and in conversations with political leaders, the Texan displayed no tendency to avoid or to compromise the two issues that most trouble Southerners [civil rights and Kennedy's Catholicism].

"I'm not here tonight as a Texan speaking to Tennesseans," Johnson told the crowd, invoking their shared southern identity in order to declare its irrelevance.

> I come as an American – to speak to my fellow Americans ... Wherever I go, I will never speak as a Southerner to Southerners or as a Protestant to Protestants or as a white to whites. I will speak only as an American to Americans – whatever their region or their religion or their race.[8]

It was a courageous approach, born perhaps of decency or perhaps of ambition to win, and probably both. However, for southerners alienated by the Kennedy candidacy or the Democratic platform, and for those who suspected Lyndon Johnson of betraying the South, his defiance likely provided confirmation rather than comfort.

Antipathy toward Johnson, often explicitly focused on the theme of betrayal, was particularly intense in his home state of Texas. Indeed, "signs with the word 'Judas' on them had been waved at his every appearance in Texas" during the campaign (Caro 2012, 149). At a meeting of the Dallas County Democratic Executive Committee, attended by Kennedy and Johnson, a speaker called LBJ "Lyndon Benedict Johnson." Worst of all was a November 4 incident at Dallas's Adolphus Hotel, where Lyndon and Lady Bird Johnson had come to address a Democratic rally. Upon entering the hotel lobby, the Johnsons were mobbed by a gathering of pro-Nixon demonstrators – many of them self-professed Democrats – holding signs that read, among other things, "Let's Beat Judas," and "LBJ – Counterfeit Confederate." The mob spat upon and shouted at the couple, and one woman even seized Lady Bird's gloves and tossed them in a gutter. Sensing a political opportunity as television cameras rolled, LBJ refused police assistance and calmly endured this abuse for the half-hour it took him and his wife to advance through the crowd, a mere twenty-five yards to the hotel elevator. The media coverage elicited sympathy from northerners who saw LBJ "spat on by the very people he was supposed to be one of" (Unger and Unger 1999, 252), and, more importantly, from Texans who were mortified to be publicly associated with such gross incivility. According to Ted Sorenson, adviser to a Kennedy campaign that feared it was losing in Texas, this "undoubtedly helped switch more than the 23,000" votes that provided the Democratic margin of victory in Texas (Caro 2012, 150). In Caro's judgment, "The incident turned the tide in Texas" (Caro 2012, 150).

The preceding evidence – while primarily anecdotal and circumstantial, like much of the evidence of Johnson's popularity in the previous section – suggests that he may not have been as popular in Texas, and in the South at large, as typically assumed. Johnson's moderate stance on civil rights legislation and his unqualified support for Kennedy provided bases for disaffection among the conservative southern Democrats he was put on the ticket to win over. Perhaps more importantly, they fed into a plausible and unattractive narrative about Johnson – that in order to achieve his political ambitions he had betrayed the principles and the people of the South. For that matter, even southern moderates and liberals who supported civil rights or did not fear Kennedy's Catholicism might have found Johnson's opportunism distasteful. How widespread were these concerns, though? Were they outweighed by positive evaluations of Johnson in other areas? More to the point, was Johnson extremely popular among Texans and southerners – as most historical accounts assume and as we would expect if he were to have delivered his home state and region for Democrats in 1960 – or were their opinions of him more muted or even polarized?

These questions cannot be resolved by the subjective perceptions of campaign observers and participants, or by anecdotal evidence that fails to measure the balance and intensity of opinion toward LBJ in Texas and the South in 1960. To do so requires systematic analysis of data measuring the attitudes and behaviors of actual voters in that state and region during that year's presidential campaign, and of a sufficient quantity and quality to permit appropriate statistical analysis. Unfortunately, data collection efforts such as these were far rarer in 1960 than they are today. To our knowledge there is only one publicly available data source competent to the task: the American National Election Studies.

Empirical analysis: ANES, 1960

As noted in the previous chapter, the American National Election Studies (ANES) has conducted large, nationally representative surveys of Americans in each presidential election campaign since 1948. These quadrennial surveys are commonly known as the "ANES Time Series." In addition to the time series, the ANES has periodically conducted panel studies over four-year periods spanning two presidential elections and one Congressional midterm election. Respondents in these panel studies are surveyed at least once during each election campaign, thereby enabling researchers to analyze longitudinal changes and their causes at the individual level. The first such panel study was, fortuitously, conducted between 1956–1960. Therefore, in addition to the 1960 ANES Time Series, we also have the option of studying the 1960 presidential election using the 1956–60 ANES Panel Study.[9]

Data and methodology

Our analysis uses responses to the 1960 wave of the 1956–1960 ANES Panel Study, because it contains a greater number of respondents in total than the 1960 ANES Time Series (1,514 versus 1,181), as well as a greater number of respondents from Texas (fifty-nine versus forty) and the South (377 versus 295).[10] This, in turn, maximizes generalizability and statistical power when analyzing causal relationships, particularly within geographic subsets.

To measure attitudes toward Lyndon Johnson, we make use of a survey item asking respondents to list, in open-ended fashion, up to two opinions about the vice presidential candidates. Specifically, after listing up to five open-ended likes and dislikes about the two major parties and their presidential nominees, respondents were asked: "How about the candidates for Vice-President? Aside from their parties, do you have any strong opinions about either of them? (How is that?)" ANES researchers coded responses to this question, for Johnson and for Republican running mate Henry Cabot Lodge, Jr., using an extensive series of master codes detailed in the dataset's codebook and appendix,[11] then tallied responses into a single variable for each candidate. In the case of Lyndon Johnson, respondents were coded as "Pro-Johnson" for two positive responses; "Anti-Johnson" for two negative responses; or "Pro-Con Johnson" for one positive and one negative response. Many respondents (683) indicated that they did not have strong opinions about Johnson, and so they were coded as "No opinion about Johnson," while 267 initially said they had a strong opinion but provided no substantive responses and were coded as "DK [Don't Know] about Johnson."

Using this measure, we can gauge the valence of opinion toward Johnson – overall and within geographic subsets – and referring to the master codes for each of the two component measures we can assess the substantive content of respondents' opinions. Unfortunately, the 1960 panel study – and for that matter, the 1960 time series, which includes identical variables – includes no other measures of attitudes toward the vice presidential candidates, such as the feeling thermometers added to the ANES in 1968.[12] While more such measures would be preferable, certainly what is available provides a reasonable quantitative and substantive indicator of attitudes toward the 1960 vice presidential candidates.

Moreover, the 1960 panel study includes items that can shed light on the electoral significance of the vice presidential candidates despite not asking about them directly. First, included in the master codes for the party and presidential candidate likes and dislikes are several capturing responses that mention the vice presidential candidates. Second, the data include measures asking respondents who reported ever "chang[ing] their mind" about Kennedy or Nixon, and why they had done so – with one option coded as "Selection of Vice-Presidential Candidate."

To evaluate the electoral significance of Johnson's selection, we also make use of several election-related behavioral and attitudinal measures, including: vote choice (Nixon = 0, Kennedy = 1); turnout (did not vote = 0, voted = 1); voting for a candidate versus voting against an opponent ("Against other party" = 1, through "For own candidate" = 5); political participation (no activities = 0, through participation in all five listed activities = 5);[13] caring who wins the election ("Don't care at all" = 1, through "Care very much" = 5); expecting a close presidential race (expecting one candidate to "Win by a lot" = 1, through "Very close race" = 5). First, we evaluate these dependent variables using comparisons of means or proportions by region and state. Then, using regression analysis, we estimate the region- and state-specific effect of Johnson evaluations for each outcome by interacting those evaluations with a dummy variable reporting whether the respondent lived in a southern state (non-Southern = 0, Southern = 1),[14] in the full sample; or whether the respondent lived in Texas (non-Texan = 0, Texan = 1), among southern respondents only.

To isolate independent effects in regression analyses, we add statistical controls for relevant intervening variables including party identification ("Strong Democrat" = 1, through "Strong Republican = 7); attitudes toward federal intervention to integrate public schools ("Disagree strongly" = 1, through "Agree strongly" = 5); age (coded continuously); sex (male = 0, female = 1); education (none = 0, through college degree = 7).

Our expectations for this analysis are straightforward. If Lyndon Johnson delivered Texas and much of the South in the 1960 presidential election, we would expect to find that contemporary opinions of him were significantly more positive among southerners versus non-southerners, and especially positive among Texans. Also, we would expect to find that the effect of Johnson evaluations on key political attitudes and behaviors would be significantly stronger, and positively so, among southerners as compared to non-southerners and among Texans as compared to non-Texans in the South. Finally, we would expect to find that when given the opportunity to explain their opinions about the Democratic Party and presidential candidate John Kennedy, in open-ended fashion, or to explain changes in their opinion about Kennedy over the course of the campaign, many southerners and Texans would cite the selection of Lyndon Johnson as Kennedy's running mate. Evidence consistent with those expectations would provide an empirical basis for rejecting the null hypothesis that Johnson did not provide the Democratic ticket with an electoral advantage in his home state and region. Evidence inconsistent with those expectations would fail to provide an empirical basis for rejecting that null hypothesis.

Empirical results

Only 35.2% of ANES respondents reported having strong opinions about Lyndon Johnson in 1960. This percentage was much higher among Texans (63.6%), but actually lower among southerners (33.1%) than non-southerners (35.9%). Surprisingly, more respondents reported strong feelings about Republican vice presidential candidate Henry Cabot Lodge in the overall sample (46.6%) and among southerners (34.9%), although not among Texans (45.5%).

The nature of those opinions runs counter to what one would expect if Lyndon Johnson had delivered Texas and the South in 1960. First, and to provide a summary measure of Johnson evaluations, we analyze mean ratings on the ANES trichotomous variable, coded 1 for "Anti-Johnson;" 2 for "Pro-Con Johnson;" and, 3 for "Pro-Johnson." Southerners' mean rating (2.09) is actually *lower*, or more negative, than that of non-southerners (2.29), while Texans (1.8) are the most negative of all. In each case the differences are statistically significant at $p < 0.05$, based on difference of means testing. This pattern of results does not change when adding "Don't know" and "No opinion" responses to the neutral category, "Pro-Con Johnson," to include more respondents – what we refer to as the "expanded" Johnson opinion variable.

Next, we separately compare "Anti-Johnson" and "Pro-Johnson" opinions across geographic subsets. The pattern of results is essentially the same. The percentage of respondents expressing strong *negative* opinions of Lyndon Johnson is highest among Texans (60%), and higher among southerners (42.9%) than among non-southerners (31.8%). Each of these differences is statistically significant at the conventional $p < 0.05$ level. Conversely, the percentage of respondents expressing strong *positive* opinions of Johnson is lowest among Texans (40%), and lower among southerners (52.1%) than among non-southerners (60.6%). In this case, the differences reach only marginal levels of statistical significance, $p < 0.10$.

To determine whether this pattern of results is attributable to intervening variables, we estimate a series of logistic regression models separately predicting classification as "Anti-Johnson" or "Pro-Johnson." The dependent variable in each model is coded 1 for classification as "Anti-Johnson" or "Pro-Johnson," depending on the model being tested, and 0 otherwise (including "Pro-Con Johnson," "Don't Know," and "No opinion"). A dichotomous variable is included in each model to indicate whether a respondent lived in the South (coded 1 for South, 0 otherwise), or whether a respondent lived in Texas (coded 1 for Texas, 0 otherwise). The South variable is included in tests of the full respondent sample only, and the Texas variable is included in tests of southern respondents only. Covariates in each model include: party identification;

Table 6.1: Predictors of opinions of Lyndon Johnson, 1960 ANES Panel Study data

Parameter	(1) US.: Pro-Johnson	(2) South: Pro-Johnson	(3) US.: Anti-Johnson	(4) South: Anti-Johnson
Party identification	−0.138***	−0.226*	0.095*	0.232**
	(0.032)	(0.092)	(0.038)	(0.087)
Integration opinion	0.063	0.134	−0.067	0.09
	(0.045)	(0.12)	(0.055)	(0.13)
Sex	−0.553***	−0.783*	−0.188	−0.430
	(0.145)	(0.329)	(0.176)	(0.381)
Age	0.022***	0.032**	0.004	0.012
	(0.005)	(0.011)	(0.007)	(0.013)
Education	0.349***	0.342***	0.277***	0.413***
	(0.053)	(0.103)	(0.062)	(0.126)
South	−0.374*	–	0.431*	–
	(0.188)	–	(0.217)	–
Texas	–	0.347	–	1.705***
	–	(0.391)	–	(0.408)
Constant	−3.091***	−3.961***	−3.437***	−5.402***
	(0.437)	(0.949)	(0.525)	(1.19)
Log-pseudolikelihood	−584.827	−121.864	−435.353	−92.264
N	1,090	263	1,090	263

Entries are logistic regression coefficients, standard errors are in parentheses.
***Denotes significant at $p<0.001$; ** denotes significant at $p<0.01$; * denotes significant at $p<0.05$; + denotes significant at $p<0.1$.
Dependent variable coding: Pro-Johnson (1 for only positive opinions about Johnson, 0 for any other valid response); Anti-Johnson (1 for only negative opinions about Johnson, 0 for any other valid response).

opinions on school integration; sex; age; education. Table 6.1 presents the results from each model.

In short, these models' results depart minimally from our previous findings. Southerners are significantly more likely than non-southerners to express strong negative opinions about Lyndon Johnson (Column 3), while Texans are significantly more likely than southerners not from Texas to do so (Column 4). Southerners are also significantly less likely to express strong positive opinions about Lyndon Johnson (Column 2) than non-southerners, but Texans do not differ significantly from other southerners in this respect (Column 1).

This pattern of results is counterintuitive, to say the least, given traditional accounts of LBJ's role in the 1960 election. Rather than proving exceptionally popular in his home state and region, by any method of measurement and analysis Johnson's popularity actually *decreases* with increasing proximity to his home state. Nor is this pattern attributable to general negativity toward the election, and its candidates, within southern states. Using the original or expanded measure of vice presidential opinion, Henry Cabot Lodge's mean rating is higher than Lyndon Johnson's in the full sample (2.88 original versus 2.48 expanded), among southerners (2.83/2.35), and among Texans (2.48/2.27). In each case, the difference between candidate means favors Lodge and is statistically significant at $p < 0.05$. While we do not claim that Johnson was actually *unpopular* in Texas and in the South, particularly given his reelection to the Senate in 1960, these results certainly provide no evidence to warrant rejecting the null hypothesis that Johnson provided no electoral advantage in his home state and region. In the previous section, we offered some thematic explanation for why southerners might have lacked enthusiasm about Johnson. Next we consider the substance of opinions expressed about Johnson to evaluate that explanation.

Table 6.2 summarizes all substantive opinions expressed about Lyndon Johnson by Texas respondents to the 1960 ANES Panel Study. Its purpose is to provide a sampling of pro- and anti-Johnson themes from those respondents most familiar with him, rather than an exhaustive analysis of all substantive opinions. Texans provided nearly twice as many negative opinions about Johnson as positive opinions: twenty-nine to fifteen, respectively.[15] In terms of positive responses, we observe no dominant theme; a small plurality of respondents (three) commends Johnson as a "Good man" with strong qualifications. In terms of negative responses, a theme clearly emerges and it echoes the Johnson counter-narrative from the preceding section: nine of twenty-eight negative opinions, nearly one third, describe Johnson as "Lack[ing] integrity. Unprincipled, opportunistic. Dishonest. Too ambitious." No other substantive opinion, positive or negative, is cited even half as frequently among Texans. Perhaps even more remarkable is the fact that no Texan referenced – positively or negatively – the themes supposed to make Johnson more popular in the South: civil rights policy or sectional interests/identity.

To enhance generalizability, we also analyze substantive responses among all southern respondents and report the results here in the text. Johnson opinions are much more favorable among southerners generally than among Texans – eighty-five positive to sixty-nine negative. The dominant positive response among southerners, referenced in twenty-four cases, is "Good man. Well-qualified for the job." Only two southerners made any positive reference to Johnson's civil rights stance – one because Johnson "Is in favor of desegregation" and one because Johnson "Is against desegregation," indicating how muddled his position on the issue had become. In terms of regional identity, three southerners referenced Johnson's willingness to help groups including "middle class or white collar workers, or … sectional interests, veterans, etc." but it is impossible to know which of these groups were specified; meanwhile, one southerner described him as a "Well-known figure, popular hero." Only one southern respondent described Johnson as a "Man of integrity, principle" or "Ambitious" in a positive sense. Conversely, fourteen of sixty-eight negative responses – 20.3% – referenced Johnson's ambition negatively, qualifying for the "Lacks integrity" code previously cited. The next most frequent reference

Table 6.2: Open-ended statements of opinion about Lyndon Johnson, by Texas respondents to the 1960 ANES Panel Study (ANES master codes)

Frequency	Pro-Johnson opinion
3	Good man. Well-qualified for the job. R has heard good things (unspecified). Experienced (NA what kind).
1	Successful record. Was a good senator, representative.
2	Other experience and ability.
1	Educated. Scholarly. Intelligent, smart.
1	Like him as a person. Like his face. Nice personality. Pleasant. Good sense of humor.
1	Familiar with world situation, military situation. Knows how to handle other countries (unspecified which).
	Experience abroad, travel. Foreign counties respect him.
2	He's a Democrat, the Democratic nominee, a good Democrat.
1	I just like him (no specified content).
3	Other miscellaneous (positive).
Frequency	**Anti-Johnson opinion**
2	Not a good man. Not qualified for the job. R has heard bad things about him. Mediocre, inexperienced (NA what kind of experience lacking).
1	Weak, weak-looking. Indecisive, no self-confidence, vacillating. People don't have confidence in him.
4	A politician. Too much in politics.
9	Lacks integrity. Unprincipled, opportunistic. Dishonest. Too ambitious.
1	Doesn't understand the problems facing us. Poorly informed.
1	Don't like him as a person. Doesn't have a nice personality.
1	Insincere.
1	Other negative domestic policy reference.
3	Bad speaker. Don't like his speeches, campaign tactics.
4	I just don't like him. Don't like him at all (no specific content).
1	Other miscellaneous (negative).

(eight) expressed general dislike. No southerners characterized Johnson as too conservative on policies including civil rights, but three criticized him as "Too liberal, too radical. For New (Fair) Deal. Would listen to radical (Northern) wing of party" and one said "Don't like his stand on civil rights – not firm enough on segregation." Another southerner described Johnson as "Evasive, don't know where he stands on issues."

If Lyndon Johnson was exceptionally popular among Texans and southerners in 1960, enough so to deliver the presidential vote across these states and for the reasons typically cited, certainly we would expect the balance and substance of opinion expressed about him to differ dramatically from the evidence just presented. The divergence of that evidence from traditional narratives is not necessarily indicative of Johnson's unpopularity or detrimental effect on Kennedy's performance in southern states; rather, we believe it is indicative of the *absence* of a significant, positive effect on presidential voting, much like we claim for vice presidential candidates generally and particularly for those who, like Johnson, come from highly-populated states.

As further evidence of this conclusion, consider two additional measures found in the 1960 ANES Panel Study. First, respondents were given the opportunity to report up to five likes and five dislikes about each of the major parties and their presidential candidates. The ANES master codes for each set of party and candidate (dis)likes include multiple that are specific to the vice presidential candidates, including: "Johnson"; "Kennedy's relationship to vice-presidential candidate"; "Would listen to Southern Democrats (Johnson)"; "Don't like the men around him, his associates, Johnson." If Johnson significantly influenced voting decisions in the 1960 election, particularly among southerners, certainly one would expect his name to come up frequently when respondents were given the open-ended opportunity to explain their feelings about the Democratic Party and John Kennedy. Instead, the ANES data reveal only thirty-four references to Lyndon Johnson – including six from southerners and three from Texans, of which four and two, respectively, were negative.[16] Again, the implication of this evidence is that Johnson was not a significant influence on presidential evaluations and voting in 1960. A second indicator is found in a series of questions asking respondents "Have you ever felt differently about Kennedy than you do now?" – and, if so, "Why?" Only 118 of 972 respondents with a valid response (12.1%), including thirty-nine of 277 southerners (14.1%), reported ever feeling differently about Kennedy. Of those respondents, only two cited "Selection of Vice-Presidential Candidate" as the reason for this change – including one southerner – and both reported voting for Nixon.

Our analysis would be incomplete without a more direct test of Lyndon Johnson's impact on election-related outcomes in the 1960 presidential election. In Table 6.3 we present a comparison of vote choice and other dependent variables indicative of a home state or region advantage, among respondents from the South versus non-South, and from Texas versus other southern states. First, in terms of vote choice, the percentage of Democratic voters does not differ significantly across voters in the South (49.55%) versus non-South (49.41%), or in Texas (52.38%) versus the rest of the South (48.9%), according to difference of proportions tests. These results are reassuring of the data's generalizability, since they closely mirror actual election results; if anything, the Texas sample is slightly more pro-Kennedy than the actual Texas electorate in 1960 (50.5% Kennedy – 48.5% Nixon). On other election-related outcomes, however, we find substantial differences between geographic subsets. Southern respondents were significantly *less* likely than non-southern respondents to vote in the presidential election, participate in political activities, report voting for rather than against a candidate, care who won the election, and expect a close election. However, in comparison to respondents from other southern states, Texans were significantly *more* likely to vote and to vote for rather than against a candidate, but only marginally more likely to participate in political activities, care who won, and expect a close election. In short, these initial results suggest a striking lack of

Table 6.3: Descriptive comparison and difference of means/proportions tests for election-related outcomes in the South and Texas, 1960 ANES Panel Study data

	All respondents				
Dependent variable	South	Non-South	Difference	Significance	N
Presidential vote – Democratic	49.55%	49.41%	0.14%	–	1,149
Voter turnout	61.8%	82.11%	−20.31%	***	1,512
Positive vote	51.08%	72.61%	−21.53%	***	1,480
Political participation	0.61	0.92	−0.31	***	1,411
Care who wins election	3.33	3.59	−0.26	**	1,417
Expect close election	3.67	3.92	−0.25	***	1,076
	Southern respondents only				
Dependent variable	Texas	Non–TX South	Difference	Significance	N
Presidential vote – Democratic	52.38%	48.9%	3.48%	–	224
Voter turnout	74.58%	59.43%	15.15%	*	377
Positive vote	63.79%	48.72%	15.07%	*	370
Political participation	0.8	0.57	0.23	+	352
Care who wins election	3.67	3.27	0.4	+	347
Expect close election	3.91	3.62	0.29	+	246

Descriptive statistics report the respondent mean, or percentage of respondents (converted from proportions for ease of interpretation) who score 1, on the dependent variable. The "Significance" column reports results from difference of means or proportions tests.

***Denotes significant at $p<0.001$; ** denotes significant at $p<0.01$; * denotes significant at $p<0.05$; + denotes significant at $p<0.1$; - denotes not significant.

Dependent variable coding: Presidential vote – Democratic (Republican = 0, Democrat = 1); Voter turnout (Did not vote = 0, Voted = 1); Positive vote (Voted against other party = 1, through Voted for own candidate = 5); Political participation (0–5 election-related activities); Care Who Wins Election (Don't care at all = 1, through Care very much = 5); Expect Close Election (Win by a lot = 1, through Very close race = 5).

enthusiasm about the 1960 election among southerners generally (undercutting the notion of a home region advantage) but a great deal of relative enthusiasm among Texans (supporting the notion of a HSA).

However, it would be an unwarranted inferential leap to attribute Texas's distinctiveness on these measures to Lyndon Johnson's vice presidential candidacy *prima facie*, since other state-level factors – including differences in mass party identification, strength of party organizations, distribution of campaign resources, and so on – could be responsible. To evaluate whether Johnson's candidacy caused geographic differences in vote choice and other election-related outcomes, in Table 6.4 we present results from a series of logistic and linear regression models. The key independent variable in each model is the interaction of Johnson opinions with a dummy variable representing residency in

Table 6.4: Predictors of election-related behavior and attitudes, 1960 ANES Panel Study data

Parameter	(1) Presidential vote choice	(2) Voter turnout	(3) Positive vote	(4) Political participation	(5) Care who wins	(6) Expect close race
All respondents						
Party identification	–1.003***	0.122**	0.089**	0.059***	0.061***	0.046***
	(0.06)	(0.04)	(0.031)	(0.015)	(0.018)	(0.014)
South	–1.823*	–0.649	–1.007+	–0.084	–0.183	–0.135
	(0.772)	(0.598)	(0.515)	(0.279)	(0.33)	(0.257)
LBJ opinion	0.334+	0.188	–0.015	0.028	0.113	0.032
	(0.182)	(0.175)	(0.136)	(0.064)	(0.076)	(0.06)
South * LBJ opinion	0.167	–0.183	0.082	–0.103	0.012	–0.033
	(0.354)	(0.277)	(0.239)	(0.13)	(0.153)	(0.119)
Constant	3.018***	1.264**	1.0**	0.709***	3.183***	3.668***
	(0.446)	(0.414)	(0.33)	(0.158)	(0.188)	(0.148)
Log-pseudolikelihood	–326.957	–452.975	–611.627	–	–	–
Adjusted R^2	–	–	–	0.028	0.014	0.02
N	939	1,125	1,100	1,115	1,081	851
Southern respondents						
Party identification	–0.838***	0.022	0.069	0.026	0.087*	0.088*
	(0.148)	(0.064)	(0.06)	(0.027)	(0.041)	(0.035)
Texas	–0.77	1.252	0.704	0.437	–0.128	0.688
	(1.367)	(1.122)	0.923	(0.414)	(0.601)	(0.492)
LBJ opinion	0.425	0.027	0.106	–0.051	0.09	0.118
	(0.349)	(0.259)	(0.242)	(0.111)	(0.168)	(0.136)
Texas * LBJ opinion	0.585	–0.244	–0.027	–0.138	0.288	–0.154
	(0.697)	(0.523)	(0.446)	(0.198)	(0.29)	(0.234)
Constant	1.005	0.717	–0.143	0.637*	2.926***	3.101***
	(0.859)	(0.613)	(0.572)	(0.264)	(0.398)	(0.332)
Log-pseudolikelihood	–86.165	–163.123	–182.93	–	–	–
Adjusted R^2	–	–	–	0.002	0.018	0.034
N	192	279	274	275	266	193

Entries are logistic or linear regression coefficients, standard errors are in parentheses.
***Denotes significant at p<0.001; ** denotes significant at p<0.01; * denotes significant at p<0.05; + denotes significant at p<0.1.
Dependent variable coding: Presidential vote choice (Republican = 0, Democrat = 1); Voter turnout (Did not vote = 0, Voted 1); Positive vote (Voted against other party = 1, through Voted for own candidate = 5); Political participation (0–5 election-related activities); Care who wins election (Don't care at all = 1, through Care very much = 5); Expect close race (Win by a lot = 1, through Very close race = 5).

the South, for tests including all respondents; or Texas, for tests including only southern respondents. Each model also controls for party identification.[17] If Johnson's candidacy had a geographically specific causal effect on Democratic voting, voter turnout, and so forth, in the 1960 presidential election, the interaction should be statistically significant and positive. If Johnson's candidacy is not responsible for any observed geographic differences, the interaction should not be statistically significant.

The interactive effect is not statistically significant in any model from Table 6.4, suggesting that Johnson evaluations did not cause geographic discrepancies in election outcomes. Party identification, on the other hand, is statistically significant in each of the full-sample models and three of the six southern models; Democratic identification is associated with voting for Kennedy, and in each other significant case it is associated with higher levels of electoral enthusiasm or engagement, independent of attitudes toward Johnson. To summarize this analysis and all that precedes it, there is simply no direct evidence in the available data to support the claim that LBJ provided an electoral advantage in Texas and the South in 1960, and in turn "delivered" the presidential election.

Empirical analysis: Kennedy-Johnson campaign polling

Our findings are so at odds with conventional accounts of Lyndon Johnson's role in the 1960 presidential election that we are hesitant to rest our claims exclusively on data from one source – even if that source is the most reputable survey in American politics research, the ANES. To gain additional empirical leverage – recognizing that no other public data sources exist capable of facilitating individual-level analysis of Johnson evaluations and their causal effects – we turn to internal polls conducted within key southern states on behalf of the Kennedy-Johnson campaign in 1960, each made available through the candidates' respective presidential libraries.

Texas

The first such poll, titled "A Survey of the Presidential Election in Texas in 1960," was conducted by Louis Harris & Associates in late August and early September among a representative sample of 985 Texans. Included in this survey were two questions directly measuring attitudes toward Lyndon Johnson. The first asked Texans which candidate they would prefer for vice president: Johnson or Henry Cabot Lodge. A minority of respondents, 48%, selected Johnson – hardly what one would expect from a favorite son so beloved that he would swing thousands of votes in that state to the Democratic ticket. Johnson, did, however, win a plurality on this question as 37% of respondents chose Lodge and 15% were undecided. Excluding undecided Texans increased Johnson's advantage over Lodge to 56%–44% – better, but still underwhelming for a Democratic US senator from Texas running against a Republican United Nations ambassador from Massachusetts, and hardly indicative of an intense demand that would spill over to presidential voting. Indeed, Johnson preferences seem to have had a relatively weak effect on presidential preference; 23% of respondents who preferred Johnson for vice president intended to vote for Nixon, while only 14% who preferred Lodge intended to vote for Kennedy.

The second relevant measure from the Texas survey asked respondents to rate the jobs done by Johnson, Kennedy, and Nixon, in their respective public offices. Johnson performed well on this measure: 28% Excellent, 41% Pretty Good, 17% Only Fair, 8% Poor, 6% Unsure. However, Johnson's ratings are nearly identical to Texans' ratings of Vice President Nixon: 27% Excellent, 36% Pretty Good, 20% Only Fair, 10% Poor, 7% Unsure. Comparing either candidate to Kennedy is difficult since his "Not sure" percentage is 34%. Excluding those "Not sure" of Kennedy's performance, however, again yields ratings nearly identical to, or actually slightly better than, Johnson's: 27% Excellent, 47% Pretty Good, 20% Only Fair, 6% Poor. Once more, Johnson proves not to be exceptionally popular among Texans. For that matter, the perception that Texans were deeply skeptical of Kennedy is not evident in these data; respondents were, at worst, undecided on him.

Louisiana

A second poll, titled "Louisiana Opinion in Presidential Race as of Late September,"[18] was conducted by Dallas's Southland Center between September 21 and September 28, 1960, among a representative sample of 1,000 Louisianans. Included in this survey was a "sensitive attitude scale" designed to measure the direction and strength of attitudes toward both major party presidential and vice presidential candidates, as well as various national and state political leaders. Specifically, respondents were first asked whether they had heard or read about a given political figure; if so, respondents were asked to rate how much they liked or disliked that figure, on a scale ranging from +3, the highest or best rating, to –3, the lowest or worst rating.

Since Louisiana is a southern state and a neighbor to Texas, one would expect Lyndon Johnson to have proven exceptionally popular in comparison to his three counterparts in the presidential race, each from Massachusetts or California. In fact, Johnson is not the most popular candidate and by some measures he performs the worst. He earns the lowest percentage of favorable ratings (+1, +2, or +3) statewide: 74%, compared to Kennedy's 80%, Lodge's 77%, and Nixon's 76% – and ties with Nixon for the lowest percentage of +3 ratings: 29%, compared to Kennedy's 40% and Lodge's 36%. Johnson also earns the second-highest percentage of unfavorable ratings (–1, –2, or –3) statewide – 15%, compared to Nixon's 19%, Kennedy's 14%, and Lodge's 9% – and the worst rating from 6% of respondents, just ahead of Kennedy and Nixon at 7% each but behind Lodge at 2%.[19] A regional breakdown shows similar patterns. Johnson is last, or tied for last, in terms of total favorable ratings and +3 ratings in Orleans Parish, the north, and the southeast. Johnson also has the most total unfavorable ratings and second-most –3 ratings in the north (to Lodge); the second-most total unfavorable and –3 ratings in the southwest; but the second-fewest total unfavorable and –3 ratings in Orleans and the southeast (to Lodge).

Johnson does not rate as the most popular candidate in the race by any measure, statewide or within any region of Louisiana. Moreover, Johnson is not propping up Kennedy in this southern state but lagging behind him on nearly every rating. Kennedy earns a higher percentage of total favorable responses and +3 ratings statewide and in every region of Louisiana, as well as a lower percentage of total unfavorable responses and –3 ratings in the Southwest region closest to Johnson's Austin home base, and in the north. Johnson's total unfavorable and –3 ratings are slightly lower in Orleans and the southeast, but in either region Kennedy's +3 ratings nearly double Johnson's (54%–29% and 42%–25%, respectively).

Internal polling data from the Kennedy-Johnson campaign provides no evidence that Lyndon Johnson was exceptionally popular among Texans or southerners in 1960, and therefore likely to have delivered those states' votes in the presidential election. In fact, across nearly all measures available in the ANES or internal polling data, Johnson's performance is virtually the same as – if not worse than – his counterparts in that election. It is hard to imagine a pattern of results less amenable to the hypothesis that Johnson's vice presidential candidacy delivered Texas and the South to the Democratic ticket in 1960.[20]

Conclusion

In Chapter 4, we presented estimates of the vice presidential HSA in the 1884–2012 presidential elections. Lyndon Johnson's HSA is estimated at –14.71, which, at first glance, suggests that his vice presidential candidacy *decreased* Democratic voting in Texas substantially in 1960. However, as we explain later in that chapter, the Lewis-Beck and Rice equation is designed to capture deviations in state voting patterns, which may be attributable to a vice presidential candidacy or other factors when observed in a given state; the assumption, which we find credible, is that any *systematic* vice presidential HSA would be evident if, *on average*, the home state deviated from normal voting patterns in a way that significantly and positively affected the running mate's presidential ticket. Yet we do not observe such a systematic advantage when using any of three different research methodologies – including ones based upon state- and individual-level data – in Chapter 4 and Chapter 5. In fact, the only time we observe a statistically significant relationship between vice presidential candidate characteristics (political experience) and the vice presidential HSA is when the running mate hails from a relatively less-populous state. For running mates from relatively populous states, candidate characteristics – e.g., service as a senator or governor, political experience, incumbency – exhibit no statistically significant effect on the HSA. Individual HSA estimates for a candidate such as Lyndon Johnson, whose home state was among the most populous in the nation, therefore seem to reflect other factors – e.g., the presidential candidates, state demographic changes, state parties and interest groups, regional economic conditions, etc. – particular to that election year and geographic context, rather than the intrinsic allure of a home state vice presidential candidacy.

Thus, our view of the Johnson candidacy is not that he hurt the Democratic ticket in Texas, but – given our finding that vice presidential HSAs generally do not occur in relatively populous states – it is that he *did not* provide a significant home state, or region, advantage in that election. In all likelihood, Texans and southerners were effectively voting for a presidential candidate, not for a vice presidential candidate – an outcome ironically consistent with John Kennedy's January 1960 comments on *Meet the Press* and inconsistent with his reasons for actually selecting Johnson.[21]

The evidence presented in this chapter – to our knowledge, the first individual-level empirical analysis of LBJ's home state/region effect in 1960 to use data from public surveys and internal campaign polling – strongly supports that conclusion. Despite winning strong support from southerners at the National Convention, as well as in pre-Convention polling of Democrats, and despite winning reelection to the Senate in Texas in 1960, we find no empirical basis for rejecting the null hypothesis that Lyndon Johnson provided no electoral advantage in his home state and region. Indeed, there is no evidence in the three available data sources to indicate that Lyndon Johnson was very popular among Texans and southerners, in general, at the time of the 1960 presidential election. Johnson's popularity actually *decreases* with increasing proximity to his home state in the 1960 ANES Panel Study data, while he performs the same as or worse than other participants in the presidential race according to most measures available from internal Kennedy-Johnson campaign polls. Perhaps most importantly, there is no evidence in the ANES data of a causal relationship whereby attitudes toward Johnson were associated with geographically specific differences in vote choice or other election-related attitudes and behaviors. Johnson's perceived impact on this historic election is legendary, the classic example of a decisive vice presidential HSA. But, scientifically speaking, there is no direct evidence that LBJ "delivered" the votes of Texans and southerners in 1960.

Notes

1 See: www.nbcnews.com/video/meet-the-press/53389282#53389282. Accessed July 30, 2014.

2 See: www.jfklibrary.org/Asset-Viewer/Archives/JFKCAMP1960-1047-017.aspx. Accessed February 23, 2015.

3 See: www.jfklibrary.org/Asset-Viewer/Archives/JFKCAMP1960-1047-017.aspx. Accessed February 23, 2015..

4 Indeed, the typical assessment of Johnson's impact – illustrated in multiple of the preceding quotes – suggests that not just any southerner could have had such an effect but, in Kennedy's words, "We couldn't have carried the South without *Johnson*" (emphasis added). Democrats had, after all, lost Texas and three other southern states in 1952 with Alabama Senator John Sparkman on the ticket; then in 1956 lost Texas and four other southern states with Tennessee Senator Estes Kefauver on the ticket. If Kennedy wanted to improve upon those performances, and particularly to pick up Texas, he could have chosen among many credible alternatives to Johnson in that state, let alone elsewhere in the South. In 1960, Democrats held nearly every major office in Texas – including the governorship, both US Senate seats, and all but one of its twenty-two seats in the US House of Representatives. But it was Johnson who Kennedy believed, along with most political elites and observers at and since that time, had the unique ability to appeal to voters from Texas and throughout the South.

5 It is important to note, however, that Johnson faced a relatively weak Republican opponent in this race: John Tower, then an obscure professor at Midwestern University in Wichita Falls who had lost his only other bid for political office when running for the Texas House of Representatives in 1954. Tower would go on to defeat Johnson's appointed replacement in the US Senate, William A. Blakley, in a May 1961 special election. Tower initially won a 31% plurality in the first round of voting against a fragmented field of seventy-seven candidates, including five Democrats that won at least 9% of the vote. In the subsequent run-off election, he narrowly defeated Blakley with 50.6% of the vote, aided by the abstention of many liberal Democrats who considered Blakley too conservative (see, for instance, Richards 2012, 223). Tower would go on to be reelected three times to the US Senate, but is best known for being appointed and then rejected for confirmation as US secretary of defense in 1989, largely on account of his alleged philandering and alcoholism.

6 See: http://blogs.loc.gov/loc/2013/02/last-word-author-robert-caro-on-lbj/. Accessed February 23, 2015.

7 See: www.pbs.org/wgbh/americanexperience/features/transcript/lbj-transcript/. Accessed February 23, 2015.

8 See: www.jfklibrary.org/Asset-Viewer/Archives/JFKCAMP1960-1047-017.aspx. Accessed February 23, 2015.

9 Both datasets are available for download from the Data Center of the ANES website, www.electionstudies.org. Accessed February 23, 2015.

10 A creative alternative would be to combine data from the two surveys into a new, common dataset. However, our analysis of the individual responses and interview information (e.g. date and interviewer) indicate that many, if not most, respondent interviews used in the 1960 panel study wave were also used in the time series survey. For instance, all but four of the Texans included in the time series survey also appear in the panel study wave – whereas twenty-three Texans in the panel study are unique to that dataset. Since the number of respondents, particularly in Texas and the South, to be gained from combining datasets is so minimal, and since the panel study sample is larger overall and within key states, we opt to use the panel data only.

11 See: www.electionstudies.org/studypages/anes_panel_1956to1960/anes_panel_1956to1960.htm. Accessed February 23, 2015.

12 Feeling thermometers were introduced to the ANES in 1964, but were not applied to measuring attitudes toward the vice presidential candidates until 1968.

13 The five possible reported activities include each of those discussed in our analysis of ANES data in the previous chapter: attempting to influence another person's vote; donating money to a campaign or party; attending a political meeting or rally; volunteering on behalf of a party or candidate; wearing campaign paraphernalia.

14 States coded as "southern" include each of the eleven former members of the Confederate States of America: Alabama, Arkansas, Florida, Georgia, Louisiana, Mississippi, North Carolina, South Carolina, Tennessee, Texas, and Virginia.

15 This, of course, would not necessarily mean that opinions in Texas ran 2:1 against Johnson. Of the many respondents who offered no strong opinion of Johnson, quite possibly a majority would express mild support if pressed to register an opinion or vote for him if forced to choose in an election.

16 In the 1956 wave of the panel study, the Democratic Party and nominee (dis)likes included forty-two references to Tennessee Senator Estes Kefauver, seven of which came from southerners.

17 To maximize degrees of freedom in this analysis, we use only one essential control variable. However, adding other controls – age, sex, education, and integration attitudes – does not change any substantive results.

18 See: www.jfklibrary.org/Asset-Viewer/Archives/JFKCAMP1960-0980-006.aspx. Accessed February 23, 2015.

19 These percentages are not significantly distorted by unfamiliarity with the candidates. At least 94% of respondents report having heard or read about each candidate, and only 5%–8% fail to rate a given candidate.

20 Further confirmation of these results comes from an August 1960 Gallup poll, in which a national sample of respondents was asked to rate their attitudes toward each of the four presidential and vice presidential candidates on a ten-point scale, ranging from least favorable (1) to most favorable (10). The poll's director, George Gallup, used this measure to create an "Enthusiasm Quotient" by calculating the percentage of respondents who rated each candidate at the two highest points on the scale: 9 or 10. Remarkably, Henry Cabot Lodge performed best on the "EQ" measure nationally, with 45% to Nixon's 43%, Kennedy's 42%, and Johnson's 30%. Even more remarkable is the fact that Lodge (35%) scored slightly higher than Johnson (34%) among *southern* respondents. Kennedy also fared slightly better than Johnson among southern respondents, with an EQ rating of 37%. Nixon was the only candidate to rate lower among southerners, with 17%. Nationally, Johnson scored higher than Lodge only among Democrats (42% to 33%, respectively); among every other group (Easterners, Midwesterners, Westerners, Republicans, Independents, Protestants, Catholics), Lodge was rated sixteen to forty-one percentage points higher than Johnson (see Gallup 1960).

21 One could argue that Johnson did not provide a home state or region advantage, *per se*, but was popular enough among American voters in general to have provided the margin of victory in Texas as well as other southern and non-southern states. Again, the available survey evidence provides no basis for accepting such a claim. First, difference of means testing indicates that Johnson scored significantly lower on the ANES vice presidential evaluation measure than his Republican opponent, Henry Cabot Lodge, among all respondents to the 1960 panel wave – 2.24 to 2.88, respectively, when excluding "No opinion" responses ($p < 0.001$) and 2.1–2.46

when coding "No opinion" responses as neutral ($p < 0.001$). As discussed in the previous endnote, Gallup polls from the 1960 election also report that Lodge was more popular than Johnson; the former scored fifteen percentage points higher than the latter on the polling firm's "enthusiasm quotient" (45% to 30%), and Lodge even scored slightly higher than Kennedy and Nixon (Gallup 1960). Furthermore, Johnson performs slightly worse on the ANES vice presidential evaluation measure than his predecessor, Estes Kefauver, whose mean scores among respondents to the 1956 panel wave were 2.33 (excluding "No opinion") and 2.15 (including "No opinion"). In short, Lyndon Johnson was an average to below average vice presidential candidate in terms of national popularity, relative to his contemporaries.

7

Has the vice presidential home state advantage ever decided an election?

On November 3, 2004 – in the afternoon following Election Day – President George W. Bush, Vice President Dick Cheney, and their families, walked onto the stage of the Ronald Reagan Building and International Trade Center in Washington, DC, to thunderous applause and chants of "Four more years!" from their supporters. This was the final Bush-Cheney campaign rally – it was their victory rally. Just ninety minutes earlier, Democratic Party nominee Senator John F. Kerry had conceded defeat in a speech delivered at Boston's historic Faneuil Hall, ending his quest for the White House and confirming Bush's reelection. President Bush, basking in his success after a hard-fought campaign, looked on as Vice President Cheney took the podium to offer introductory remarks. As the crowd's cheers subsided, Cheney began: "Thank you all. It's an honor for me to be here along with Lynne and our whole family on this very special afternoon. This was an historic election, and" – he added, in full deadpan – "once again I have delivered the state of Wyoming for the Bush-Cheney ticket."[1] The crowd erupted in laughter, along with members of the Bush and Cheney families, at this rare yet unmistakable flash of humor from the vice president.

Cheney's tongue-in-cheek remarks were notable for two reasons. First, prior to the election there had been speculation that President Bush would replace Cheney on the 2004 ticket with a more electorally advantageous running mate; in fact, on at least three occasions Cheney had offered to leave the ticket if it would help the reelection effort, and Bush had given serious thought to the possibility (Baker 2013, 282–284; Bush 2010, 86–87). Second, Cheney's overt reference to the vice presidential home state advantage (HSA) is striking. Indeed, the fact that he was *not* selected for the purpose of delivering an electoral, and particularly a home state, advantage is so obvious and so contrary to conventional wisdom as to make his remark plainly a joke. Cheney's home state of Wyoming overwhelmingly voted in favor of the Republican presidential ticket in 2004, and – having done so in every presidential election since 1968 – there was no reason to believe that it would have voted differently without Cheney on the ticket.

Cheney did, of course, meet the two requirements of friends and neighbors voting discussed in Chapter 4. First, he hailed from a small state (the least populous in the nation, in fact) and served for ten years as Wyoming's at-large member of the US House of Representatives. But even if Wyoming's three electoral votes were cast for John Kerry in the 2004 election, the Bush-Cheney ticket still would have secured a majority of votes in the Electoral College. Wyoming's electoral votes were simply inconsequential in the 2004 election. This fact, and Cheney's facetious introduction, illustrates an important point: a vice presidential HSA, even when it occurs, is irrelevant to the outcome of a presidential election *unless* the state is competitive enough to have voted for a different party in the event that a native son or daughter had not been chosen for the ticket. For that matter, the election itself must be close enough for one state to make the difference in the Electoral College.

Given the narrowness of these conditions – and, according to the empirical evidence presented in this book, the highly conditional nature of vice presidential HSAs in general – it is only reasonable to ask: do vice presidential HSAs ever actually *matter*? Has there ever been a plausible instance in which they *could have* or actually *did* decide the outcome of a presidential election? Or is the possibility of such an occurrence so remote, and so lacking in precedent, as to render the subject unworthy of serious historical and prospective attention?

We endeavor to answer those questions in this chapter – to determine, based upon analysis of electoral data and characteristics associated with actual vice presidential finalists, whether a presidential candidate has ever had a genuine opportunity to change the outcome of an election by way of the vice presidential HSA. Specifically, we estimate whether, and if so, when: (1) a running mate has ever delivered a home state that was decisive in securing a majority of Electoral College votes for his or her party's presidential ticket; and, (2) a presidential candidate has ever *failed to capitalize* on a potentially decisive HSA by not selecting a different vice presidential finalist as his running mate.

Answering the first research question is relatively straightforward. To do so we need to systematically examine historical election results and determine if, and when, a vice presidential home state provided the decisive margin in the Electoral College. Additionally, though, we must consider whether these cases were qualified by factors that might inhibit friends and neighbors voting and thus render them inappropriate as examples of a decisive vice presidential HSA.

The second research question is more complicated because it requires us to employ statistical forecasting models and engage in an analysis of counterfactual, or "what if," history. To answer this question, we must identify instances in which: (1) a change in the electoral votes of one state would have delivered the presidential election to the opposing major political party; and, (2) a finalist in the vice presidential selection process came from a potentially decisive state. Then, in order to plausibly claim the potential for a decisive vice presidential HSA, given our prior analyses, also we must determine: (3) whether the state in question was relatively less-populous; and, (4) whether the candidate in question had sufficient experience in elected office within that state to bring about friends and neighbors voting. After identifying the cases that meet these conditions, we employ a variation of the Lewis-Beck and Rice model presented in Chapter 4 to impute counterfactual HSA estimates for vice presidential finalists who were *not* selected for their party's presidential ticket. These estimates then enable us to project whether a counterfactual vice presidential candidacy would have changed the outcome in the Electoral College.

Our immediate objective in this analysis is to determine, on a credible empirical basis, whether a vice presidential HSA *could have made the difference* in a presidential election. More broadly, our objective is to shed light on the electoral importance of the vice presidential HSA and the conditions under which presidential candidates can maximize its strategic significance. The analysis shows that under the most extraordinary of conditions and with just the right type of candidate, a decisive vice presidential HSA *is* possible – not just in a theoretical sense but, according to our analysis, as a matter of historical precedent.

A historical analysis of potentially decisive vice presidential HSAs

It is quite unlikely that one state – let alone a vice presidential candidate's home state – will determine the outcome of any given presidential election. In 2012, for instance, Mitt Romney would have fallen nine electoral votes short of victory even if he had scored a major upset in the nation's largest state, California. Instead, Romney lost the state by 23.1% – a margin far too great for any vice presidential nominee to overcome. The 2012 election is emblematic of most presidential elections in American history; usually, they are not decided by one state's electoral votes. Indeed, Adkison (1982) found that only 30% of presidential elections held between 1900 and 1980 were decided by the outcome in a single state – and of those elections, only 29% could have changed hands if the losing candidate had won the vote of a larger vice presidential home state. Of course, Adkison's limited time frame does not account for many close elections in American history, both prior to 1900 (e.g., 1800, 1876) and since 1980 (e.g., 2000, 2004). To provide a more comprehensive record of presidential elections decided by a single state, and to better understand the role of vice presidential home states in presidential elections, we extend Adkison's analysis to include all presidential elections from 1789 through 2012.

Historical introduction

Between 1789 and 2012, the United States held fifty-seven presidential elections. However, given that George Washington won the first two presidential elections without opposition, and the same was largely true of James Monroe in 1820, this leaves us with fifty-four competitive presidential elections to examine. Of these elections, 24.1% (N=13) would have been won by a different candidate if a single state – usually the largest state in the union – completely changed the allocation of its electoral votes from the candidate that received a majority of all Electoral College votes to the runner-up.[2] And of those thirteen elections, seven were so close that a major party vice presidential candidate's home state *could have* influenced the election's outcome.[3] By this we mean that: (a) the winning ticket would have failed to secure a majority in the Electoral College had it not won the vice presidential candidate's home state; or, (b) the losing ticket would have secured a majority in the Electoral College had it won the vice presidential candidate's home state. Essentially, the vice presidential candidate's home state could have altered the Electoral College outcome in 13% of competitive presidential elections, or 12.3% of all presidential elections.

At first, this may seem highly consequential; approximately one of every eight presidential elections has been effectively decided by a vice presidential candidate's home state. Upon closer examination of these seven elections, however, it is clear that we cannot reasonably attribute the Electoral College outcome to a decisive vice presidential HSA. Take, for example, the presidential elections of 1796 and 1800. In both cases it is difficult to evaluate the influence of vice presidential home states due to three historical idiosyncrasies that differentiate early presidential elections from modern ones. First, there were far fewer states in the union at the time of the 1796 and 1800 presidential elections – sixteen, to be exact – and this, in itself, increased the statistical probability of a vice presidential home state deciding the Electoral College outcome, in comparison to modern elections. Second, these elections were conducted before the ratification of the Twelfth Amendment, and thus represent a fundamentally different presidential election system than what most modern Americans would recognize. Under this system, each elector cast two votes on behalf of his state. The candidate receiving the most votes was elected president, and the runner-up was elected vice president. Because of the way the Electoral College operated at this time, technically every candidate – even a running mate – was a presidential candidate. Third, many states during this time selected electors based upon the vote of the state legislature. This was true of New York and South Carolina in 1796 and 1800, home to Thomas Jefferson's and John Adams's running mates, respectively. The average voter in these states had little say in the selection of his state's electors, and therefore had no direct way of voting for a candidate who was "one of us." In short, there was no opportunity for friends and neighbors voting to occur in these vice presidential home states, and we cannot draw meaningful inferences about the electoral influence of running mates from these two cases.[4]

Historical examples

After the ratification of the Twelfth Amendment, the first election in which a vice presidential home state could have made a difference in the Electoral College was the election of 1812. In this election, James Madison and his running mate – Elbridge Gerry – received 128 electoral votes, while DeWitt Clinton of New York and his running mate, Jared Ingersoll, received eighty-nine votes. Madison carried Gerry's home state of Massachusetts and Ingersoll's home state of Pennsylvania. But if Clinton had carried either Massachusetts or Pennsylvania he would have received a majority in the Electoral College. At the time, however, Pennsylvania was the second-largest state in the union, and Massachusetts was the third largest state. Neither state met the first condition necessary for friends and neighbors voting and, as such, it is unlikely that a vice presidential candidate had any meaningful effect on the outcome.

The vice presidential candidate most likely did not "deliver" a decisive home state in 1848, either. This three-way presidential race between Zachary Taylor, Lewis Cass, and Martin Van Buren resulted in Taylor winning 163 electoral votes to Cass's 127; Van Buren failed to carry any states as the Free Soil candidate. The one state that could have changed the outcome of this election was New York – also the most populous state in the union. New York cast its thirty-six electoral votes for the Whig ticket comprised of Zachary Taylor, from Louisiana, and Millard Fillmore, a former US representative and then the comptroller of New York. Not only does New York fail to meet the first requirement of friends and neighbors voting due to its population, but New York was also Van Buren's home state. As our previous research demonstrates (Devine and Kopko 2013), presidential candidates, on average, receive a statistically significant HSA. In fact, Van Buren received the second-highest vote total in New York – about 6,000 more than Cass.[5] If there was a HSA in the 1848 election, it was probably due to Van Buren receiving a presidential HSA to secure a second-place finish. Simply put, it is hard to imagine that Millard Fillmore's candidacy resulted in Taylor winning New York's electoral votes, given that another presidential candidate hailed from that state and New York was too populous to accommodate friends and neighbors voting.

New York played a similar role in the election of 1880. That year, the winning ticket consisted of Republicans James A. Garfield of Ohio and Chester A. Arthur, another vice presidential candidate from New York. If Garfield's opponent, Pennsylvania's Winfield Hancock, had carried New York, then the Democratic ticket would have won the presidential election. However, New York was far too populous to facilitate friends and neighbors voting – again, it was the most populous state in the union. The same is true of the 1888 presidential election. New York was the only state that could have altered the outcome of that election, and it, too, was the home state of Republican vice presidential candidate Levi P. Morton. Benjamin Harrison, the Republican presidential nominee, could not have won the election without New York's electoral votes. However, New York remained the nation's most populous state, and it was also the home state of incumbent Democratic President Grover Cleveland. Therefore, it seems implausible to claim that the Republican victory was attributable to a vice presidential HSA in New York; friends and neighbors voting was unlikely given the state's population, and any inclination to vote for a home state vice presidential candidate surely would have been overwhelmed by the inclination to vote for a home state presidential one.

In the twentieth century, not a single presidential election was decided by the electoral votes of a vice presidential candidate's home state. In fact, following the election of 1888, it would be 112 years until the next example occurred. In 2000, the bitter, contested election between George W. Bush and Al Gore was ultimately decided by the outcome of Florida's electoral votes. The Bush-Cheney ticket won the election with 271 votes in the Electoral College, while the Gore-Lieberman ticket received 266 votes. Gore-Lieberman should have received 267 votes, but a Democratic elector from the District of Columbia abstained from casting a vote to protest the District's lack of voting representation in Congress (see Edwards 2005, 24). For the sake of this discussion we will assume that the Democratic ticket received 267 votes.

Had *any* state switched its electoral votes from George W. Bush to Al Gore in 2000, the Democratic ticket would have secured a majority of votes in the Electoral College. But even in the 2000 presidential election, the vice presidential candidates' home states had virtually no chance of serving as the pivotal state that would help a given ticket secure 270 or more electoral votes. Lieberman's home state of Connecticut – which had voted Democratic in the two previous presidential elections, and has voted Democratic in every presidential election since 2000 – predictably went for Gore-Lieberman. It was by no means a "swing" state at the time. Wyoming, for its part, had voted Republican in every presidential election since 1968, making it even less of a swing state, and it went for Bush-Cheney. While both Lieberman and Cheney hailed from small states – in each case, representing well below 1.5% of the national population[6] – and both candidates had significant experience representing their respective states, the presidential election in both Connecticut and Wyoming was not competitive enough for the vice presidential candidates to plausibly make a difference.

Discussion

These seven cases provide no clear evidence that a vice presidential HSA has ever decided a presidential election. Despite this lack of evidence, one should not assume that a vice presidential home state will never influence the outcome of a presidential election. First, it is possible that a vice presidential HSA could prove decisive in a future presidential election if the conditions detailed above are met. Second, it is quite possible that a decisive vice presidential HSA *could have* occurred in a past presidential election – that is, if a different running mate had been selected.

The second possibility is intriguing not just for purposes of historical curiosity; discovering a counterfactual example of a decisive vice presidential HSA would help to clarify the electoral significance of vice presidential candidates and the conditions under which a vice presidential HSA might prove decisive in a future presidential election. In the next section, then, we use state-level data to estimate counterfactual HSAs for vice presidential finalists in recent elections who were not ultimately chosen for their party's ticket, and who came from a state that was mathematically decisive in that year's election. In essence, we ask: did any recent presidential candidates miss the opportunity to win an election by *not* selecting a running mate who could have delivered his or her home state?

A counterfactual analysis of potentially decisive vice presidential HSAs

The likelihood that a vice presidential HSA will alter the outcome of a presidential election is – based upon the evidence and conditions detailed above – extremely small, *seemingly* almost irrelevant to consider. Indeed, election outcomes rarely hinge on the vote of a single state, let alone the vice presidential candidate's home state. For that matter, states with enough electoral votes to provide the margin of victory often are not competitive and they are often too populous to facilitate friends and neighbors voting. To credit a vice presidential candidate with delivering his or her home state, and with it the presidential election, requires that the presidential election be competitive enough to be decided by one state; that the home state have enough electoral votes to provide the decisive margin; and that the home state be highly competitive. The odds of all of these conditions being met are quite low. And even if they are met, a vice presidential HSA is unlikely to be decisive; vice presidential HSAs are not generally applicable but restricted to candidates with a great deal of elected experience in relatively less populous home states.

And yet, having administered a large dose of empirical skepticism, we must step back and concede the obvious: a decisive vice presidential HSA *is possible*, and that enormously consequential possibility makes it a consideration worthy of serious strategic and scholarly attention. That is why, in this section, we empirically evaluate the possibility that such a decisive advantage could have occurred in a modern presidential election.

Qualifying elections

Franklin Roosevelt became the first presidential candidate to select his running mate, rather than have one selected by the National Party Convention, when he chose Henry Wallace for the Democratic ticket in 1940. In doing so, he set a precedent that each presidential candidate, save Adlai Stevenson in 1956, has followed since. This period, then, provides an appropriate time frame for evaluating whether a presidential candidate has ever *missed* a strategic opportunity to select a running mate who would have delivered a decisive HSA – that is, an HSA that would have won an election that the ticket, in fact, lost.

As our previous analyses indicate, such opportunities are rare. Of the nineteen presidential elections held between 1940 and 2012, only four were decided in the Electoral College by the vote of a single state: 1968, 1976, 2000, and 2004. But could the outcome of these elections have been decided on the basis of friends and neighbors voting? First, in 1968, Hubert Humphrey could have deprived Richard Nixon of an Electoral College majority, and sent the election to the Democratically-controlled House of Representatives, had Humphrey won the state of California rather than losing it by 3.3% of the two-party vote share. But California was too populous a state to facilitate friends and neighbors voting for a vice presidential candidate, and it was already the home state of the Republican presidential candidate, Richard Nixon – which, given previous research, suggests that Nixon would have enjoyed the HSA over and above anything that a vice presidential candidate might have otherwise provided. Thus, it is unlikely that Humphrey could have won if he had selected a running mate from California. Moreover, no Californians were included among Humphrey's vice presidential finalists in 1968 (see Hiller and Kriner 2008).

The election of 1976 presents a similar circumstance. Gerald Ford could have won if he had carried New York, the second-most populous state in the union at the time. However, the fact that New York was such a populous state made it, once more, unlikely to yield a vice presidential HSA. Also, as with Humphrey, Ford included no New Yorkers on his list of vice presidential finalists.[7]

The most compelling examples are found in the 2000 and 2004 presidential elections. Both elections were competitive enough that a shift in one state's electoral votes could have resulted in a different Electoral College outcome. In 2000, if any state carried by Bush had switched its votes to Gore, Bush would have lost the presidential election. In 2004, John Kerry would have needed an additional 19 electoral votes to defeat the Bush-Cheney ticket. That meant that Kerry would have needed to win one of three states that he lost: Texas, Florida, or Ohio. Of these states, Ohio was the smallest and most competitive. However, at the time Ohio comprised 3.7% of the nation's population,[8] making it too large to facilitate friends and neighbors voting based on our analysis in Chapter 4. And, again, no candidates from that state were included among Kerry's vice presidential finalists.[9]

Jeanne Shaheen, 2000

The 2000 presidential election is – for this purpose, as for so many others – unique. Again, if *any* state – including the least populous ones, which are most likely to yield a vice presidential HSA – switched its support from Bush to Gore, that change in electoral votes would have resulted in a victory for the latter. But was it the case that Gore had a *genuine* opportunity to change the outcome of the election by selecting a running mate other than Joe Lieberman – one who could have delivered a decisive home state? To make this determination we must first identify potential Democratic vice presidential candidates for the

2000 election, and then determine if any of their home states met the criteria for friends and neighbors voting. In doing so, we adhere to the research methodology of Sigelman and Wahlbeck (1997), who – noting that "there is no definitive, 'official' source of such information" (p. 857) – draw upon contemporary media reports and historical accounts to compile a credible list of vice presidential finalists for elections occurring between 1940–1996 (see Chapter 3 for further discussion).

While historical accounts are limited for most recent presidential elections, media reports are typically abundant and in 2000 they were quite definitive. That year, the Gore campaign took the unusual step of leaking to the media its vice presidential "short list" just days before announcing Joe Lieberman's selection on August 7.[10] The six names on that list were Lieberman (senator, Connecticut); Evan Bayh (senator, Indiana); John Edwards (senator, North Carolina); Richard Gephardt (representative, Missouri); John Kerry (senator, Massachusetts); Jeanne Shaheen (governor, New Hampshire). Of the five potential candidates not chosen, only John Kerry hailed from a state that would ultimately vote for the Gore-Lieberman ticket. The remaining four vice presidential finalists came from states that would vote for Bush-Cheney. However, only one finalist's home state was small enough to be conducive to friends and neighbors voting: Jeanne Shaheen's New Hampshire.[11]

At the time, New Hampshire comprised 0.44% of the national population, thereby meeting the first condition of the friends and neighbors interactive effect explained in Chapter 4.[12] Shaheen also had nine years of elected experience in New Hampshire at that time, serving multiple terms as a state senator and governor, thereby meeting the second condition of the interactive effect. Considering the extraordinary circumstances of New Hampshire's role in the 2000 presidential election and Jeanne Shaheen's potential candidacy, it is only reasonable to ask: could Al Gore have won New Hampshire's electoral votes, and with them the 2000 presidential election, if he had selected Shaheen as his running mate?

To assess this possibility we impute HSA scores for the counterfactual Gore-Shaheen ticket in New Hampshire based on a regression model of HSA. Modeling *past* vice presidential HSA is the most reasonable starting point for imputing estimates of a counterfactual HSA. The process of imputing HSA values is not unlike forecasting models widely employed throughout the social sciences. This practice has been accepted in the scholarly literature for decades,[13] and within the political science literature forecasting has long been applied to presidential elections (see, for example, Rosenstone 1983). In addition, symposia comprising articles on presidential election forecasts have been featured in the journal *PS: Political Science & Politics*, published by the American Political Science Association, in 2004, 2008, and 2012, as well as for recent midterm Congressional elections. In short, imputing values based on past empirical relationships in order to project specific electoral outcomes is by no means a new, or an obscure, research practice in the social science literature.[14]

But before proceeding further with our analysis we must offer a few words of caution. Obviously it is impossible to say with absolute certainty that a counterfactual vice presidential candidate would have altered the outcome of presidential election. After all, the dynamics of a presidential election could change, perhaps even drastically, if a presidential candidate selected a different running mate. If a running mate committed a significant gaffe or was the subject of a scandal, this might alter the course of a presidential campaign, not only within a home state, but potentially on a national scale. However, these dynamics are impossible to estimate with precision and any effort to do so amounts to mere speculation. As with any forecasting model, we can only estimate changes within a given parameter based upon observable characteristics of past elections and specific candidacies. Thus, we assume – for purposes of empirical estimation – that a counterfactual running mate would not significantly alter the course of the presidential campaign.

To achieve our goal of estimating a credible, counterfactual HSA score for Jeanne Shaheen in 2000, simply relying on the regression models presented in Chapter 4 is not sufficient. The purpose of the models presented in Chapter 4 is to determine if, and to what extent, specific independent variables are associated with HSA scores. In that chapter our focus is on home state population, political experience, and the interaction of these two variables. The model that we use to impute a counterfactual HSA in this chapter must predict a large amount of variance in the dependent variable to ensure that the imputed values are a reasonable statistical approximation of what the counterfactual candidate might have received if selected as a running mate. As such, our new model of vice presidential HSA is informed by both the model we present in Chapter 4, and the scholarly literature on presidential election forecasting. Specifically, the new HSA model includes variables that account for the political party of the incumbent president and economic indicators measuring state- and national-level unemployment and changes in personal disposable income, in addition to state population, political experience, and the interaction of these two variables.

The variable *Incumbent Party* is coded as 1 if the candidate's political party controlled the White House at the time of the election, and 0 otherwise. To account for economic conditions, we include measures of the percentage change in personal disposable income at both the state and national level in relation to the preceding year (see Bartels and Zaller 2001; Klarner 2012, 2013),[15] and the average annual state and national unemployment rates (Berry and Bickers 2012; Jerôme and Jerôme-Speziari 2012, 2013).[16] While many forecasting models of presidential elections include quarterly measures of economic indicators, we are unable to do so in these models because state-level data are often limited to annual measures, particularly before 1976. As a result, we must utilize annual measures of unemployment and changes in personal disposable income. While these economic variables are important predictors of vote choice, it may be the case that their interaction with *Incumbent Party* would also be theoretically relevant. Specifically, an interactive effect may be expected if poor or favorable economic conditions are attributed to the failures/successes of the incumbent president's administration and political party. For this reason, all of the economic indicators are interacted with *Incumbent Party* in the full HSA model.

In Table 7.1, we present five ordinary least squares (OLS) models of vice presidential HSA using the five-election lag Lewis-Beck and Rice measure, for home state candidacy observations from 1960 through 2012. The purpose of presenting several different models in a stepwise fashion is to compare the predictive power of each, as measured by adjusted R^2 values. The model that explains the greatest amount of variance in the dependent variable will be used to impute an HSA value for Jeanne Shaheen.

The five models in Table 7.1 employ robust standard errors by clustering observations on the basis of election year. As we note in Chapter 4, the use of clustered standard errors is appropriate when, contrary to the assumptions of OLS regression, observations in the data are not independent and identically distributed (see Primo, Jacobsmeier, and Milyo 2007, 447–454). The first model is the "full" model, which includes all independent variables. The subsequent models eliminate, in a stepwise fashion, groups of variables that have the least explanatory power. Eliminating variables in this manner actually increases the adjusted R^2 value of each subsequent model estimation. The variables that measure political party incumbency, changes in national personal disposable income, changes in state personal disposable income, and state unemployment do not significantly add to our model's predictive power. The fifth model – which includes measures of state population, political experience, the interaction of population and political experience, and the national unemployment rate – yields the largest adjusted R^2 value, 0.614. Moreover, this model predicts the vice presidential HSA with greater precision, as measured by adjusted R^2, than any fixed effects model or model based on the Lewis-Beck and Rice equation in the HSA literature to date.[17]

In the fifth model (Column 5), the constituent term *Political Experience* attains statistical significance at the $p < 0.1$ level, while the variables measuring national unemployment rate, state population, and the interaction of state population and candidate experience are statistically significant at $p < 0.05$. The unemployment variable can be interpreted to mean that for every one percentage point increase in the unemployment rate, the HSA score of a candidate will decrease by 1.41 percentage points. To evaluate the substantive interactive effect of political experience and state population we employ the same method of analysis described in Chapter 4. The results of this analysis parallel those of Chapter 4 – candidates with significant political experience in less populous states are most likely to receive a statistically significant, positive HSA score.

To determine the estimated value of a counterfactual Jeanne Shaheen candidacy in the 2000 presidential election, we can substitute values unique to Shaheen and the 2000 presidential election for each of the three variables and the interaction term in Model 5, to derive an estimate of the dependent variable (HSA) with a confidence interval: Shaheen had nine years of elected political

Table 7.1: OLS regression of vice presidential home state advantage, 1960–2012

Variables	1	2	3	4	5
State population	1.04*	0.99*	0.91*	0.99*	0.99*
	(0.45)	(0.38)	(0.38)	(0.35)	(0.34)
Political experience	0.21	0.18	0.17+	0.17+	0.17+
	(0.11)	(0.1)	(0.09)	(0.09)	(0.08)
Population x experience	–0.19**	–0.18***	–0.18***	–0.18***	–0.18***
	(0.05)	(0.04)	(0.04)	(0.03)	(0.03)
Incumbent party	6.78	0.88	–	–	–
	(10.15)	(2.29)			
National unemployment	–1.86	–1.64	–1.67	–1.45+	–1.41**
	(2.03)	(1.11)	(1.11)	(0.73)	(0.45)
State unemployment	1.31	0.35	0.36	0.06	–
	(2.39)	(1.56)	(1.55)	(1.04)	
Change in national PDI	0.49	0.09	0.25	–	–
	(1.96)	(1)	(0.94)		
Change in state PDI	–0.32	0.02	–0.11	–	–
	(1.69)	(0.88)	(0.8)		
Incumbent party x national unemployment	0.07	–	–	–	–
	(3.09)				
Incumbent party x state unemployment	–1.52	–	–	–	–
	(3.26)				
Incumbent party x national PDI	–0.78	–	–	–	–
	(1.68)				
Incumbent party x state PDI	0.85	–	–	–	–
	(1.55)				
Constant	5.26	8.69	9.69	10.33*	10.4**
	(13.37)	(8.65)	(6.64)	(4.19)	(3.35)
N	24	24	24	24	24
Adjusted R^2	0.442	0.523	0.548	0.592	0.614

Robust standard errors clustered by year are included in parentheses.
+Denotes significant at $p < .01$; * denotes significant at $p < .05$; ** denotes significant at $p < .10$.

experience in New Hampshire at the time of the 2000 election; the state comprised 0.44% of the national population; and the average national unemployment at the time was 4%. These values result in an estimated HSA of 5.97, with a 95% confidence interval of 2.79 to 9.15. If we increase the confidence interval to 99%, the estimated value of HSA ranges from 1.79 to 10.15. While the confidence intervals are large, likely due to the model's small sample size, the estimated HSA score is nonetheless positive and statistically distinguishable from zero at conventional and even higher standards of significance.

Could Jeanne Shaheen's HSA have altered the outcome of New Hampshire's electoral votes? In 2000, the Bush-Cheney ticket won the state with 50.68% of the two-party vote share, resulting in a 1.36% margin of victory (in terms of two-party vote share) over the Gore-Lieberman ticket.[18] If we employ the most conservative estimate based on the imputed values for Jeanne Shaheen in New Hampshire in 2000 (HSA of 1.79 as determined by the lower bound of the 99% confidence interval), the counterfactual Gore-Shaheen ticket would be expected to carry the state of New Hampshire with 51.11% of the two-party vote.

Given that Shaheen's counterfactual candidacy meets the theoretical requirements of friends and neighbors voting, the finding of a statistically significant and positive HSA should not be surprising. Furthermore, there is circumstantial evidence that Shaheen's popularity might have benefited the Gore campaign had she been chosen as his vice presidential candidate. Although the Bush campaign won New Hampshire by 1.36% of the two-party vote share, in that same election Shaheen was reelected to her third term as governor with 52.69% of the two-party vote share in New Hampshire, for a 5.38% margin of victory.[19]

Discussion

While it is simply impossible to say with certainty that Shaheen would have given the Gore campaign an HSA large enough to attain a plurality of New Hampshire's vote, the estimates provided here, and the logic of friends and neighbors voting, provide strong empirical and theoretical bases for believing that Al Gore could have won New Hampshire's electoral votes if he had selected Shaheen as his running mate. And assuming that no other state's electoral votes would have changed as a result of the counterfactual Shaheen candidacy, the effects of this vice presidential HSA would have been momentous: Al Gore would have won the 2000 presidential election with 271 votes in the Electoral College, to George W. Bush's 267.

Conclusion

Widespread perceptions of a vice presidential HSA, documented earlier in this book, assume implicitly – if not explicitly – that a well-chosen running mate has the capacity to "deliver" a home state that may, in turn, "deliver" an Electoral College majority where otherwise one would not have existed. However, the probability of either outcome, let alone both outcomes, being "delivered" by a vice presidential candidate is extremely low. First, there are relatively few elections in which one state has a mathematical, much less a practical, opportunity to determine the election's outcome. Second, for the vice presidential HSA to be of consequence, the decisive state must be conducive to friends and neighbors voting – specifically, it must be a relatively less-populous state, which by definition means that it has a small number of electoral votes and is therefore even less likely than other states to change the outcome in the Electoral College. In short, it is so unlikely that the vice presidential HSA will make a substantive difference in the election that discussion of it, especially within a presidential campaign, may seem baseless.

Yet it would be going too far to argue that the vice presidential HSA is altogether irrelevant. While this chapter's analysis indicates that it is unlikely that any vice presidential candidate has "delivered" a decisive home state for his or her party's ticket in a presidential election, under narrow circumstances, like those present in the 2000 presidential election, it is *possible* that a running mate could help to secure the decisive electoral votes in his or her home state.

The empirical conclusions we draw from this analysis must, of course, be tempered by the recognition that we have estimated a counterfactual – an inherently imprecise endeavor, since there is no way to directly test an alternative historical reality. The most we can do, given this unavoidable limitation, is to take reasonable steps to maximize the credibility of our estimates. We have done so in this analysis by drawing upon the methodology of the election forecasting literature; developing an exceptionally predictive model of vice presidential HSA, for use in estimating a counterfactual advantage; and cautiously interpreting projected advantages based upon 99% confidence intervals.

We have identified only one election since 1960 in which: (1) a single state could have altered the outcome of the presidential election; and, (2) that same decisive state plausibly, based upon empirical analysis, could have changed its electoral vote due to the counterfactual selection of a known vice presidential finalist. Indeed, our empirical analysis, and the theoretical expectations of friends and neighbors voting, indicates that Jeanne Shaheen in 2000 would have provided a decisive HSA in that election.

Our findings should not be construed to suggest that the 2000 election was the only one in which a counterfactual running mate could have "flipped" a home state in the Electoral College. Rather, our HSA models in this chapter and in Chapter 4, each based upon the Lewis-Beck and Rice equation, indicate that such an outcome is possible only if the home state and candidate meet the criteria for friends and neighbors voting. Furthermore, flipping a state is not electorally consequential in and of itself; to truly make a difference, the state in question must provide a sufficient number of electoral votes to change the outcome in the Electoral College.[20] This, as we have shown, is unlikely given how few elections come down to the vote of a single state – and particularly unlikely if, as we find, HSAs are limited to states that are relatively less-populous and therefore have fewer votes in the Electoral College.

Based upon our current findings, we conclude that the vice presidential HSA *can* make the difference between winning and losing a presidential election. Although the probabilities of such an event are extremely low, our empirical analysis points toward a historical precedent for it: the Gore-Shaheen ticket that never was.

Notes

1 See: www.nytimes.com/2004/11/03/politics/campaign/03cnd-cheney-text.html. Accessed February 23, 2015.

2 These elections include 1796, 1800, 1812, 1844, 1848, 1876, 1880, 1884, 1888, 1916, 1976, 2000, and 2004. We do not include on this list elections that would have been decided by the House of Representatives if a decisive state switched its Electoral College votes to the runner up.

3 These elections include 1796, 1800, 1812, 1848, 1880, 1888, and 2000.

4 Certainly, one could make the argument that Aaron Burr provided a valuable electoral advantage for the Democratic-Republicans in 1800 by implementing modern campaign tactics in New York City to mobilize voters – after all, Jefferson lost New York in the election of 1796 and Burr's efforts seemed effective in securing New York's electoral votes (see Isenberg 2007, 196–200). While Burr was ahead of his time in terms of campaign strategy, this effect was not akin to friends and neighbors voting as discussed throughout this book. It is unlikely that voters supported the Democratic-Republicans because they felt a home state attachment to Burr; rather, Burr was able, with the help of local party machines, to identify voters who might support Democratic-Republican candidates for the New York legislature. And since the legislature controlled the state's electoral votes, Burr's success in stacking the legislature resulted in Adams losing New York's electoral votes.

5 See: www.presidency.ucsb.edu/showelection.php?year=1848. Accessed February 23, 2015.

6 See: www.census.gov/population/www/cen2000/briefs/phc-t2/tables/tab01.pdf. Accessed February 23, 2015.

7 A likely addition would have been incumbent Vice President and former New York Governor Nelson Rockefeller, who Ford had decided to leave off of the ticket in 1976.

8 See: www.census.gov/popest/data/state/totals/2012/tables/NST-EST2012-02.xls. Accessed February 23, 2015.

9 To demonstrate the unreliable nature of imputed HSA scores for candidates hailing from large states, later in this chapter we provide HSA estimates for Bob Graham and Bill Nelson, both Florida senators that Kerry considered selecting in 2004. See endnote 20 for more information.

10 See, for example, Chen (2000) and Bendavid and Davey (2000). Gore directly confirmed the number of finalists, telling reporters: "It's down to six with one wild card that I haven't completely eliminated."

11 As demonstrated in Figure 4.2, the marginal effect of political experience on the vice presidential HSA is statistically significant and positive only in states that contain 1.75% or less of the nation's population.

12 See: www.census.gov/population/www/cen2000/maps/files/tab02.pdf. Accessed February 23, 2015.

13 Perhaps the scholarly outlet of record for forecasting studies is the *Journal of Forecasting*, established in 1983. See http://onlinelibrary.wiley.com/journal/10.1002/(ISSN)1099-131X. Accessed February 23, 2015.

14 Furthermore, the use of predicted probabilities in binary outcome regression models, such as logit and probit, are examples of imputation used to predict a counterfactual outcome. Such models are commonly used, and quite reputable, in social science research.

15 All personal disposable income data were obtained from the Bureau of Economic Analysis through personal correspondence with the authors.

16 All unemployment data were obtained from the Bureau of Labor Statistics (BLS). Before 1976 the BLS did not measure state-level unemployment data. Instead, state-level unemployment rates between 1960 and 1975 were collected by individual states and reported in the *Manpower Report of the President* and *Economic Report of the President.*

17 For example, one of Kahane's fixed effects models produced an R^2 of 0.589, while Mixon and Tyrone (2004) estimated a model with a non-adjusted R^2 value of 0.55. Using the Lewis-Beck and Rice (1983) equations, Devine and Kopko (2011, see also 2013) produced an adjusted R^2 value of 0.152, and Dudley and Rapoport's (1989) model produced an R^2 value of 0.06.

18 See http://sos.nh.gov/WorkArea/DownloadAsset.aspx?id=3177. Accessed February 23, 2015. In terms of raw vote share, the Bush-Cheney ticket received 48.07% of the New Hampshire vote compared with 46.8% for the Gore-Lieberman ticket. This difference amounts to a 1.27% margin of victory for the Republican ticket.

19 See: www.sos.nh.gov/general2000/sumgov.html. Accessed February 23, 2015.

20 To illustrate the point, consider the 2004 presidential election and John Kerry's reported interest in selecting Iowa's then-governor, Tom Vilsack, as his running mate (see VandeHei and Balz, 2004). In that election, the Democratic ticket won 49.66% of the two-party vote share in Iowa (see http://sos.iowa.gov/elections/pdf/2004/general/CanvassSummary.pdf. Accessed February 23, 2015). If we impute a counterfactual HSA for Vilsack as we did for Shaheen, Vilsack would have received a 3.37 HSA, with a 99% confidence interval of 1.07–5.66. Iowa comprised approximately 1% of the country's population in 2004, and Vilsack had seventeen years of political experience at the time – thereby meeting both conditions necessary for friends and neighbors voting. It is statistically possible that a counterfactual Vilsack candidacy would have flipped Iowa in favor of the Democratic ticket. However, even if this were the case, the Bush-Cheney ticket would have received 279 electoral votes, and therefore a majority in the Electoral College. The counterfactual candidacy of Tom Vilsack and his home state of Iowa simply could not have provided the decisive electoral votes in 2004. The same applies to the counterfactual candidacies of the US senators from Florida in 2004: Democrats Bob Graham and Bill Nelson. Both of these individuals had extensive elected experience in their home state. However, as noted earlier in this chapter, Florida is a populous state that does not meet the first condition of friends and neighbors voting. When imputing estimates for Graham and Nelson, Model 5 reports a *negative* HSA score for each individual (–24.6 and –15.7, respectively), and each score results in a double-digit 99% confidence interval. It is simply implausible that these two seasoned public officials who served the citizens of Florida for multiple decades in elected office would have *cost* the Democratic ticket votes in their home state, let alone such a large percentage of the state vote. And, indeed, we make no such claim. Our evidence, instead, indicates that significant HSAs occur only in relatively less-populous states, and thus *no* advantage – or for that matter, disadvantage – occurs in relatively populous ones. Even so, why do our models return such large negative estimates and confidence intervals for the counterfactual Florida candidacies? The obvious culprits would seem to be the small sample size (N=24) of vice presidential candidacies in our data, and the small number of states therein that meet or exceed Florida's

population (N=5). In 2004, Florida comprised 5.91% of the nation's population, while 66.7% (N=16) of the states examined in Table 7.1 had populations that comprised less than 3% of the total US population. While we obtain reasonable estimates for most states in our data for the purpose of imputing counterfactual HSAs, this is not the case for Florida. Both theory and empirical evidence lead us to conclude that voting in that state was not susceptible to the influence of a home state candidacy.

8

Who votes for the running mate, anyway?

When the Democratic Party's nominee for president in 1956, Adlai Stevenson, allowed Convention delegates to choose Senator Estes Kefauver of Tennessee as his running mate, it marked the end of an era. This was the last time, to date and probably forever, that a major party presidential candidate declined the opportunity to select a vice presidential candidate for his ticket. In the time since, Convention delegates have merely served to ratify this selection – as they ratify the presidential nomination itself – in what can only be described as a symbolic exercise of parliamentary procedure. Barring the extraordinary spectacle of a brokered Convention, there will never be another Estes Kefauver. Instead, every presidential election is and will be marked by a process of intense strategic speculation about who one or both presidential nominees will choose for a running mate, and why – a process known popularly as the "veepstakes."

But why do so many Americans – or at least the political elites who shape public discourse – take such an obsessive interest in the veepstakes? After all, everyone knows that voters cast their presidential ballot for the *presidential* candidate and not his or her running mate – right? Actually, there are several reasons why those who participate in and study presidential politics *should* care about the selection of a running mate. For one, as we demonstrated in Chapter 2, there is a widespread perception that vice presidential candidates provide an electoral advantage in their home state, and this perception seems to influence campaign decisions regarding the selection process and the allocation of campaign resources (see Chapter 3). The home state advantage (HSA) is a common point of emphasis in veepstakes strategizing, but it is hardly the only one. Political observers often cite a wide range of assets (or liabilities) that various vice presidential contenders may "bring to the ticket," and in turn – so the story goes – enhance (or diminish) its chances of electoral success. Typically, these discussions involve speculating about a prospective running mate's potential to appeal to an important political or demographic constituency with whom the presidential candidate is insufficiently popular, or the potential to compensate for shortcomings in a presidential candidate's resumé that may affect his or her ability to govern effectively.

Consider a few recent examples. In the 2008 presidential election, Joe Biden's foreign policy credentials were frequently cited as a reason why Barack Obama should select him as a running mate (see Chait 2008; Rudin 2008), while Sarah Palin's candidacy was viewed as a way of reaching out to female and conservative voters who may not otherwise support John McCain (see Barbash 2008; MacGillis 2008; Schreiber 2008; Seelye 2008). In the 2004 presidential election, John Edwards was widely seen as an asset in helping John Kerry's campaign appeal to working-class and low-income voters, particularly in rural areas (see Fournier 2004; Nagourney 2004). And in the 2000 presidential election, Dick Cheney's extensive political experience in Washington, DC, helped to answer the criticism that George W. Bush lacked the federal and foreign policy experience necessary to serve effectively as president (see La Ganga and Barabak 2000; Mitchell 2000).

But, of course, there is an even more important consideration, perhaps the most important one of all, for taking the veepstakes seriously: if elected, and in the event of a presidential death or resignation, the winner of the veepstakes may one day take over as president. While the possibility of vice presidential succession is unlikely, it is more common than many people realize; indeed, the incumbent vice president has ascended to the presidency nine times in US history.[1]

Although the importance of selecting the "right" running mate may seem self-evident, there is a more nuanced reason why political observers should care about vice presidential selection: the choice of a running mate provides voters with potentially useful information about who the presidential candidate is and what he or she cares about. Recall our discussion of Karl Rove's (2012) *Wall Street Journal* op-ed in the preface of this book. As Rove noted, the selection of a running mate is a presidential candidate's "first presidential decision." That selection may, in fact, influence the tone and direction of the campaign's last months (e.g., Palin 2008), as well as the beginning of a new administration (e.g., Cheney 2000). Indeed, this decision provides valuable insight as to the presidential candidate's personal and political values, perceived strengths and weaknesses, quality of judgment, and the management style that will inform his or her governing if elected as president. Therefore, to the extent that voters gain such insights from the selection of a running mate, this decision might – and perhaps even should – influence their vote for president.

Until now our primary focus in this book has been on the electoral influence of vice presidential candidates *in their home state*. It is beyond the scope of this project to analyze with comparable rigor the influence of all significant running mate characteristics on voting behavior in presidential elections. However, to put our analysis of the vice presidential HSA in proper context requires that we provide at least some empirical basis for evaluating the running mate's effect on voting in a more general sense – that is, beyond the home state. Therefore, in this chapter we present the results of empirical models estimating the relationship between vote choice and vice presidential candidate evaluations, followed by an additional series of models testing potential predictors of vice presidential candidate evaluations. In essence, we seek to answer two questions: (1) Does a "VP advantage" – at the national, rather than state, level – typically occur in presidential elections?; and, (2) If so, then what dynamics shape that advantage?

We begin our analysis by reviewing existing scholarship on the electoral effect of vice presidential candidates. Then, based on previous research and our analysis of election-related behaviors and attitudes in Chapter 5, we estimate several models of vote choice and vice presidential candidate feeling thermometer ratings using American National Election Studies (ANES) data. These models allow us to estimate the electoral importance of vice presidential candidates relative to presidential candidates, at the individual level. Our analysis indicates that vice presidential candidates do, to some extent, influence voting behavior in presidential elections. However, vice presidential candidates' effect on presidential vote choice, not surprisingly, pales in comparison to the effect of the actual presidential candidates. Various voter and candidate characteristics significantly influence vice presidential evaluations, but jointly they explain a limited amount of variance in the predictive models and therefore offer little indication that running mates are evaluated in a consistent, systematic manner. To a specific point of interest, we find minimal evidence that the running mate's level of political experience – by itself or relative to that of the presidential candidate – affects evaluations of that candidate. These results provide insight into the value of vice presidential candidates, in general, and efforts to appeal to voters based on demographic factors and "ticket-balancing."

Literature review

"Once the [presidential] election is over, the vice president's usefulness is over," an aide to Vice President Hubert Humphrey once observed. "He's like the second stage of a rocket. He's … important going into orbit, but he's always thrown off to burn up in the atmosphere" (Light 1984, 11). While the vice president's role in governance has grown substantially over the course of recent administrations, as we explain in Chapter 1, the perception at the core of this observation – that candidates for vice president *matter* in a presidential election – remains as real as ever. But *why*, one must ask? Why – particularly with the days of Convention-inspired "ticket-balancing" behind us, and a four-decade run without a presidential death or resignation – do so many political operatives and observers believe that voters care who occupies the second slot on the presidential ticket? The reasons, of course, are many and they often depend upon the particular candidates and circumstances associated with a given presidential election.

Context

To begin, some vice presidential candidates are valued for their ability to serve as an "attack dog" during the campaign – that is, someone who can make negative or even inflammatory statements against the opposing presidential ticket and attract significant media attention in doing so, while allowing the presidential candidate to stay above the fray and avoid direct responsibility for those attacks (see Sigelman and Buell 2003). Richard Nixon most famously played this role as Dwight Eisenhower's running mate in 1952 and 1956, while Dick Cheney and Joe Biden have done so in more recent elections.

Additionally, vice presidential candidates may help to target subgroups within their political party who feel underappreciated by, or even at odds with, the presidential nominee (Court 2012). For example, as detailed in Chapter 6, many viewed Lyndon Johnson's candidacy in 1960 as a means of reaching out to southern Democrats unwilling to support John F. Kennedy – a liberal Catholic from the Northeast (although our empirical findings cast doubt on LBJ's success in doing so). In more recent years, presidential nominees distrusted by the base of their party – namely, John McCain in 2008 and Mitt Romney in 2012 – have chosen running mates closely identified with it – seemingly in order to reassure core supporters and mobilize them ahead of the election.

Next, presidential candidates might select their running mate with the intention of compensating for apparent weaknesses in their resumé – for example, George W. Bush's selection of Dick Cheney in 2000, and Barack Obama's selection of Joe Biden in 2008, both of which provided a young and relatively inexperienced presidential candidate with a much older and more experienced running mate – or to assuage concerns about their advanced age and questionable health, as was the case when Bob Dole in 1996 and John McCain in 2008 selected relatively young and energetic running mates in Jack Kemp and Sarah Palin, respectively.

Finally, presidential candidates might use vice presidential selection to reinforce a central campaign message. For example, Bill Clinton's selection of Al Gore in 1992 helped to reinforce his image as a young, moderate, southern "New Democrat," while John McCain's selection of Sarah Palin in 2008 was used in campaign ads and rhetoric to reinforce his image as an independent "maverick" willing to buck the Republican Party he shared with an unpopular incumbent president.[2]

These observations illustrate an obvious, but often-overlooked, fact about presidential elections. When voting for president of the United States, voters are casting a ballot for a slate of electors who support a presidential *ticket*, not just a single presidential candidate. Voters in a presidential election cast a ballot that includes two – sometimes quite different – individuals on a party's presidential ticket. These running mates may have different professional backgrounds, political career paths, and personalities – yet they are partners in their quest for the White House. While voters cast only one vote in a presidential election, they nonetheless have the ability to form opinions and judgments about each individual on the ticket. And given the fact that US presidential elections are dominated by two political parties – each with its own presidential and vice presidential candidates – this yields a total of four targets for voters to evaluate when deciding how to cast their ballot. If vice presidential candidates generally influence presidential vote choice, then that choice is a function of how the voter views each of the candidates on the major party presidential tickets, among other more obviously relevant factors. While there may be different reasons and strategies that presidential candidates draw upon when selecting a running mate, the consequences of that selection should have bearing on election-related attitudes and behaviors, perhaps including vote choice.

Evidence

Scholarly research on this subject, dating back more than thirty years, generally uses one of two methods to evaluate the relative electoral influence of presidential and vice presidential candidates, each involving measurements of the candidates' popularity. The first of these methods analyzes an individual's vote choice in relation to whether he or she "likes" or "dislikes" the presidential and vice presidential candidates, overall. This method is exemplified by Adkison's (1982) analysis of 1968–1976 ANES data. Adkison began his research by dividing ANES respondents into four categories, ranging from those who "like" both candidates on a given ticket, to those who "dislike" both candidates on a given ticket.[3] The middle categories – i.e., "like president/dislike vice president" and "dislike president/like vice president" – could be exploited to determine the relative influence of each candidate on vote choice, by comparing the percentage of respondents voting for a given ticket between these and the other two categories. Adkison found that disliking the vice presidential candidate did, in fact, influence vote choice; respondents who liked the presidential candidate but disliked his running mate were less likely to support that ticket than respondents who liked both members of the ticket – usually 30%–40% less likely, depending on the election year (Adkison 1982, 333). Not surprisingly, though, the top of the ticket seemed to have a more dramatic effect; respondents who liked a ticket's vice presidential candidate but disliked its presidential candidate were 60%–70% less likely to vote for it than respondents who liked both candidates. In summarizing his results, Adkison drew an important lesson about running mates' electoral significance:

> [There is a tendency] ...for the vice presidential candidate to hurt rather than help the ticket. The only times a vice presidential candidate could help a ticket are if the candidate is extremely popular or has a loyal following of his own. It is unlikely that a presidential candidate will find an extremely popular candidate that wishes to be vice president. The next best alternative would be for a presidential candidate to select a non-controversial, relatively unknown person for a running mate. This will minimize the negative feelings the voters might have for such a candidate. (Adkison 1982, 334)

Subsequent analyses, using data from different election years, reinforce Adkison's finding that evaluations of the vice presidential candidate influence vote choice, albeit less so than evaluations of the presidential candidate (see Grofman and Kline 2010; Kenski, Hardy, and Jamieson 2010, 149–174; Wattenberg 1984, 1995; Wattenberg and Grofman 1993). However, given the relatively limited number of individuals who have strong feelings about vice presidential candidates,[4] the likelihood of these candidates having a significant effect on the election is small. According to Grofman and Kline (2010, 308), "the net impact of vice presidential selection [on vote choice] is at most 1 percentage point."[5]

A second method commonly used to estimate the relative electoral influence of presidential and vice presidential candidates is multivariate logistic regression – specifically, testing models of vote choice that use evaluations of both candidates on a given ticket – alongside relevant covariates – as predictors. Multivariate regression models, like those presented in empirical analyses from the preceding chapters of this book, allow researchers to estimate independent variable effects on the dependent variable, with respect to statistical significance, direction, and magnitude. Using this approach, then, researchers can determine whether, and to what extent, presidential and vice presidential candidate evaluations influence vote choice.

The existing literature indicates that presidential and vice presidential candidate evaluations have a statistically significant effect on vote choice, but – not surprisingly – the effect of the former is much greater in magnitude than that of the latter.[6] In fact, when operationalizing candidate evaluations in terms of feeling thermometers,[7] the marginal effect on vote choice associated with a change in *presidential* candidate ratings is two to three times larger than the marginal effect of a change in *vice presidential* candidate ratings (Burmila and Ryan 2013; Ulbig 2010, 2013).[8]

Concerns about multicollinearity have led some scholars to operationalize presidential and vice presidential evaluations using net counts of candidate likes/dislikes or candidate image measures when estimating multivariate regression models (see Wattenberg 1995 and Knuckey 2012, respectively), rather than relying upon feeling thermometers ratings for both presidential *and* vice presidential candidates. These methods of operationalization generally yield similar conclusions to regression analyses using just feeling thermometers.

While the relationship between vice presidential candidate evaluations and vote choice is statistically significant in general, in some election years vice presidential candidates did not have a discernible effect on vote choice. For example, Ulbig's (2010, 2013) analysis of 1972–2008 ANES data indicates that feeling thermometer ratings of George H. W. Bush in 1984, Lloyd Bentsen in 1988, Jack Kemp and Al Gore in 1996, and Dick Cheney and John Edwards in 2004 had no effect on vote choice in those election years. With a few exceptions, Burmila and Ryan (2013) reported similar findings in their analysis of 1980–2008 ANES data.

These studies provide a reasonable basis for concluding that voters' feelings toward vice presidential candidates actually *matter* in presidential elections; indeed, a more positive evaluation of the vice presidential candidate is generally associated with an increased likelihood of voting for that candidate's ticket, while the inverse is true of a more negative evaluation. Building upon these findings, in the next section we test the relative effects of presidential and vice presidential evaluations on vote choice using the pooled, individual-level ANES data from Chapter 5. In addition, and distinct from previous studies of this topic, we investigate the *causes* of variation in vice presidential candidate evaluations. Specifically, we estimate a series of multivariate regression models that use characteristics of the survey respondents, the candidates, and the political environment, to predict vice presidential candidate feeling thermometer ratings. Our goal in doing is to understand not only whether, and to what extent, vice presidential candidates influence vote choice in presidential elections, but also the circumstances under which those candidates become more (un)popular and thereby increase their potential to shape the race's outcome.

Empirical analysis

To estimate the effect of vice presidential candidate evaluations on presidential vote choice, we once more make use of the ANES data from Chapter 5. Specifically, we use the ANES Cumulative Data File, but begin our analysis with the 1968 election since that year's survey was the first to include presidential and vice presidential candidate feeling thermometers. These feeling thermometers are the key independent variables in our initial analyses, and the latter set of thermometers are used to measure the dependent variable in subsequent analyses. Our objective is not to determine if *specific* vice presidential candidates have influenced individual vote choice, since other scholars have addressed that question for various election years (see Burmila and Ryan 2013; Knuckey 2012; Ulbig 2010, 2013; Wattenberg 1995). Rather, our objectives are to determine: (1) whether, and to what extent, vice presidential candidate evaluations *generally* influence vote choice; and, (2) which characteristics – of the respondents, the candidates, and the political environment – significantly influence vice presidential candidate evaluations.

Vote choice models

To address the first research objective, we replicate the vote choice models from Table 5.3 while adding presidential and vice presidential candidate feeling thermometers. For purposes of comparison, Model 1 of Table 8.1 reestimates the vote choice model of Chapter 5. Then, in Model 2, we add a feeling thermometer variable for each of the major party presidential and vice presidential candidates, consistent with past studies of individual elections.[9] In Models 3, 4,

Table 8.1: Models of presidential vote choice, 1968–2008

Parameter	1 Vote choice	2 Vote choice	3 Vote choice	4 Vote choice	5 Vote choice
VP thermometer Rating: Republican	–	–0.02*** (0.003)	–0.023*** (0.002)	–0.023*** (0.002)	–
VP thermometer rating: Democrat	–	0.021*** (0.003)	0.023*** (0.002)	0.023*** (0.002)	–
Pr. thermometer rating: Republican	–	–0.067*** (0.004)	–0.081*** (0.005)	–0.081*** (0.005)	–0.09*** (0.005)
Pr. thermometer rating: Democrat	–	0.073*** (0.006)	0.084*** (0.006)	0.083*** (0.006)	0.092*** (0.006)
VP home state: Republican	–0.108 (0.302)	–0.103 (0.206)	–0.16 (0.209)	–	–
VP home state: Democrat	–0.015 (0.170)	0.059 (0.202)	–0.066 (0.208)	–	–
Pr. home state: Republican	–0.405** (0.135)	–0.364* (0.166)	–0.103 (0.177)	–	–
Pr. home state: Democrat	0.179 (0.192)	0.235 (0.243)	0.089 (0.231)	–	–
Party identification	–0.876*** (0.037)	–0.46 (0.041)	–	–	–
Age	–0.003 (0.002)	–0.004 (0.002)	–	–	–
Gender	–0.064 (0.052)	0.019 (0.08)	–	–	–
Non-White	1.422*** (0.172)	0.93*** (0.133)	–	–	–
Education	0.083+ (0.044)	–0.03 (0.037)	–	–	–
Household income	–0.14*** (0.037)	–0.069+ (0.04)	–	–	–
South	–0.646*** (0.095)	–0.227* (0.097)	–	–	–
Change in PDI: State	0.017 (0.027)	0.139** (0.054)	–	–	–
Change in PDI: National	0.027 (0.244)	–0.412*** (0.088)	–	–	–
Incumbent party	–0.168 (0.891)	–0.378 (0.267)	–	–	–
Incumbent* state PDI	–0.025 (0.023)	–0.085** (0.031)	–	–	–
Incumbent *national PDI	–0.035 (0.125)	0.166** (0.055)	–	–	–

Table 8.1: (*cont.*)

Parameter	1 Vote choice	2 Vote choice	3 Vote choice	4 Vote choice	5 Vote choice
Constant	3.47*** (1.771)	3.35*** (0.488)	−0.148 (0.249)	−0.154 (0.249)	−0.044 (0.245)
Log-pseudolikelihood	−6,821.963	−2,444.062	−3,141.464	−3,142.184	−3,282.945
Reduction in error	66.34%	84.73%	82.51%	82.52%	81.79%
N	16,197	11,780	12,942	12,943	13,022

Robust standard errors clustered by year are included in parentheses.
***Denotes significant at $p<0.001$; ** denotes significant at $p<0.01$; * denotes significant at $p<0.05$; + denotes significant at $p<0.1$.
Dependent variable coding: Vote choice (Republican = 0, Democrat = 1, missing otherwise).

and 5, we eliminate other control variables to more directly estimate the effect of presidential and vice presidential candidate feeling thermometers on vote choice, and to compare their performance in terms of predictive power with those variables included in previous model iterations.

The empirical models presented in Table 8.1 predict vote choice quite well. Model 1 yields a reduction in error of 66.34% – meaning that we make 66.34% fewer incorrect predictions of vote choice when accounting for the independent variables, as opposed to predicting vote choice solely based on the dependent variable's modal value – and the reduction in error increases to 84.73% with the addition of the feeling thermometer ratings in Model 2. Even after controlling for a variety of respondent characteristics (including party identification, age, gender, race, education, household income, and region), candidate characteristics (including home state and incumbent party), and characteristics of the economic environment (including state and national changes in personal disposable income, as well as their interaction with incumbent party) we find that presidential and vice presidential feeling thermometer ratings have statistically significant effects on vote choice. As expected, when Democratic candidates are rated higher (i.e., more "warmly") on the feeling thermometer, respondents are more likely to vote for the Democratic ticket. Conversely, as feeling thermometer ratings of the Republican candidates increase (i.e., get "warmer"), respondents are less likely to vote for the Democratic ticket.[10] Across Models 2, 3, and 4, the effect of an increase in presidential candidate feeling thermometer ratings is more than three times larger in magnitude than that of an equal increase in the vice presidential candidate's thermometer rating. Such a relationship with the dependent variable makes intuitive sense given the more substantial constitutional and practical role of a president, versus a vice president, in governance (see Chapter 1).

Perhaps the most interesting empirical result to emerge from these models is the evident predictive power of the presidential and vice presidential candidate feeling thermometers, in and of themselves. Adding only the feeling thermometers to Model 2 increases the reduction in error over Model 1 by 18.39 percentage points. This is strong evidence that the thermometer ratings improve the fit of the logit model. But when eliminating all control variables in Model 3, except for home state controls, the reduction in error drops hardly at all – from 84.73% in Model 2 to 82.51% in Model 3. And when only including feeling thermometer ratings for each of the four candidates in Model 4, the reduction in error is virtually the same as in Model 3 (82.51% versus 82.52%, respectively). Finally, when dropping the vice presidential candidate feeling thermometers in Model 5, to predict vote choice solely based on presidential candidate thermometer ratings, the model yields an 81.79% reduction in error that falls only 2.94 percentage points short of Model 2, which includes the full range of respondent, candidate, and economic variables, and about 0.7 percentage points short of Models 3 and 4. Furthermore, the two presidential candidate feeling thermometers in Model 5 by far outperform the *sixteen variables and interactions* included in Model 1, as measured by a comparison of each model's reduction in error. These results underscore the importance of feelings toward presidential candidates in predicting vote choice; presidential evaluations do not capture the entire range of factors significantly influencing vote choice, but quite evidently they do most of the empirical work.

As a further means of comparison, we calculated the percentage of outcomes correctly predicted for Model 1 (83.78%), Model 4 (91.28%), and Model 5 (90.92%). While the vice presidential candidate feeling thermometer ratings increase predictive power – judging by these results – clearly the bulk of the model's predictive power is driven by evaluations of the presidential candidates.[11]

Are the results similar when estimating vote choice models only including individuals living in a vice presidential candidate's home state? It may be the case – if one adopts the logic of the vice presidential HSA – that evaluations of vice presidential candidates are more consequential in their home states, when compared to the electorate as a whole. To evaluate this possibility, in Table 8.2 we replicate Models 4 and 5 *among vice presidential home state respondents only*, while also testing models including only vice presidential candidate feeling thermometers.

The results of these analyses show no major differences from the models presented in Table 8.1. For both Democratic (Model 1) and Republican (Model 3) vice presidential home state respondents, between 1968 and 2008, the effect of presidential candidate feeling thermometer ratings on vote choice is statistically significant, and the magnitude of those variables' effects is greater than that of the vice presidential candidate thermometer ratings. It is worth noting that vice presidential candidate evaluations have an inconsistent effect on vote choice in these models; feeling thermometer ratings of Democratic running mates are statistically significant predictors in Models 1 and 3 – that is, among

Table 8.2: Models of vote choice within VP home states

Parameter	1 Democratic VP home state vote choice	2 Democratic VP home state vote choice	3 Republican VP home state vote choice	4 Republican VP home state vote choice
VP thermometer rating: Republican	−0.013	–	−0.016	–
	(0.018)		(0.01)	
VP thermometer rating: Democrat	0.031*	–	0.028*	–
	(0.015)		(0.014)	
Pr. thermometer rating: Republican	−0.07***	−0.076***	−0.067***	−0.071***
	(0.013)	(0.016)	(0.016)	(0.015)
Pr. thermometer rating: Democrat	0.068***	0.086***	0.071***	0.085***
	(0.017)	(0.014)	(0.013)	(0.013)
Constant	−1.148	−0.409	−1.089	−0.154
	(1.245)	(1.132)	(0.956)	(0.88)
Log-pseudolikelihood	−97.146	−104.163	−79.356	−81.745
Reduction in error	84.32%	82.26%	81.08%	80.41%
N	375	376	302	302

Robust standard errors clustered by year are included in parentheses.
*** Denotes significant at p<0.001; **denotes significant at p<0.01; * denotes significant at p<0.05; + denotes significant at p<0.1.
Dependent variable coding: Vote choice (Republican = 0, Democrat = 1, missing otherwise).

respondents in the Democratic *and* Republican vice presidential candidates' home states – while ratings of Republican running mates are not statistically significant predictors in either model. In short, while some might expect vice presidential candidate evaluations to be particularly consequential in the running mate's home state, in fact their empirical performance is less consistent when comparing the results of Table 8.1 and Table 8.2.

To make this analysis more intuitive, in Table 8.3 we present predicted probabilities estimating the effect of changes in candidate feeling thermometer ratings on presidential vote choice. Specifically, we use the results from Model 4 in Table 8.1 – predicting vote choice based upon only the four candidate thermometers, among *all* respondents to the 1968–2008 ANES – to estimate the change in a respondent's probability of voting for the Democratic presidential candidate as his or her rating of a given presidential or vice presidential candidate increases by five points. Model 4 is the most appropriate one for this analysis because, among the models from Table 8.1 that include each thermometer rating, it is the most parsimonious and its predictive power – in terms of

Table 8.3: Candidate feeling thermometer probability profiles

Probability profile	Probability of a Democratic vote	Change from baseline probability
Baseline: All thermometers at 50	0.497 (0.45–0.543)	–
Democratic VP thermometer rating = 55; All Others = 50	0.526 (0.48–0.571)	+0.029
Republican VP thermometer rating = 55; All Others = 50	0.468 (0.42–0.516)	−0.029
Democratic president thermometer rating = 55; All others = 50	0.6 (0.555–0.645)	+0.103
Republican president thermometer rating = 55; All others = 50	0.397 (0.353–0.442)	−0.10

95% confidence intervals reported in parentheses.

reduction in error and percentage of cases correctly predicted – is highly comparable to, if not better than, the other models.

When each candidate feeling thermometer rating is set at 50 (neutral), the probability of voting for the Democratic ticket is 0.497 (or, converting this proportion to a percentage, 49.7%). To estimate the effect of vice presidential candidate evaluations on vote choice, we begin by increasing the Democratic vice presidential candidate's feeling thermometer rating by five points, to 55, while holding all other thermometer ratings constant at 50. This increases the predicted probability of voting for the Democratic candidate by 0.029 (2.9 percentage points), from 0.497 to 0.526. The inverse is true of a five-point increase in the Republican vice presidential candidate's feeling thermometer rating; increasing the rating by five points, to 55, while holding the three other ratings at 50 decreases the probability of voting for the Democratic ticket by 0.029, from 0.497 to 0.468. Although these changes in probability are relatively small, the results indicate that vice presidential candidate evaluations *do* influence vote choice – even in response to modest changes in feeling thermometer ratings of that candidate.

Not surprisingly, a comparable uptick in presidential candidate evaluations has a more substantial effect on vote choice. When increasing the Democratic presidential candidate's thermometer rating by five points, to 55, while holding all other ratings constant at 50, the predicted probability of voting for the Democratic ticket increases by 0.103 (10.3 percentage points), from 0.497 to 0.6. A corresponding five-point increase in the Republican presidential candidate's thermometer rating, while holding all other ratings at 50, has essentially the same effect: the probability of voting for the Democratic ticket decreases by 0.1 (ten percentage points), from 0.497 to 0.397.

The totality of the preceding evidence clearly indicates, as expected, that presidential candidate evaluations influence vote choice much more than evaluations of their running mates. How much more, exactly? Consider this fact, based upon the last analysis: a respondent's feeling thermometer rating of the vice presidential candidate would have to increase by *eighteen points* to equal the change in predicted probability associated with a *five-point* increase in the presidential candidate's rating. The effect of presidential candidate evaluations on vote choice therefore is approximately three times greater than the effect of vice presidential candidate evaluations – essentially the same ratio found in previous studies of the candidates' relative effect on vote choice (Burmila and Ryan 2013; Ulbig 2010, 2013).

Candidate evaluation models

Given that candidate feeling thermometer ratings predict much of the variance in vote choice, and additional control variables add little to the predictive power of the model, this begs the question: what predicts an individual's rating of the vice presidential candidates? To put it another way, what factors might cause an individual to have particularly favorable or unfavorable feelings toward a running mate that could – as we see in the preceding analyses – influence his or her decision to vote for or against a presidential ticket? Obviously, a feeling thermometer rating is not randomly assigned to voters. Instead, there must be reasons why candidate evaluations vary – across people and election years – and we cannot understand the electoral significance of those evaluations unless we understand the dynamics underlying them. It stands to reason that the factors influencing candidate evaluation must include some combination of voter and candidate characteristics, as well as characteristics of the political environment in a given election year. These factors, to the extent that they influence candidate evaluations, may in turn influence vote choice. Figure 8.1 illustrates this process.

In the next step of our analysis, then, we estimate models of vice presidential candidate feeling thermometer ratings, using the variables from Model 2 of Table 8.1.

These variables measure characteristics particular to the survey respondents (party identification, age, gender, race, education, household income, and region), the candidates (home state and incumbent party), and the political environment in a given election year (state- and national-level changes in personal disposable income).

To the battery of variables from Model 2 of Table 8.1, we add two new variables measuring means of "ticket-balancing" that were referenced in our discussion at the beginning of this chapter. The first is political experience, which – as noted in that earlier discussion – presidential candidates might value as a means

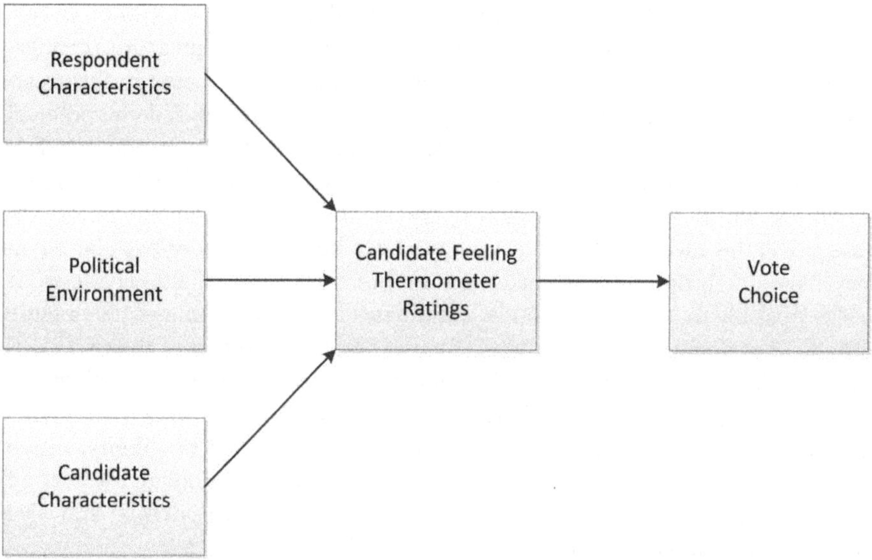

8.1 Hypothesized influences on candidate feeling thermometer ratings and vote choice

of signaling to voters that the running mate will serve as a competent and knowledgeable partner in governance once elected. Moreover, presidential candidates with relatively little experience in government, at the national level or in general, might seek to reassure voters who see this as a weakness by "balancing the ticket" with an experienced running mate. Both conceptions of experience are plausible influences on vice presidential candidate evaluations, and so we have constructed two experience variables for inclusion in our models.

The first experience variable measures the number of years that a vice presidential candidate served in a federal elected office (e.g., US House or Senate) and/or as a high-ranking federal appointee (e.g., cabinet secretary, White House chief of staff, federal agency director, etc.). This variable is intended to test the hypothesis that more experienced vice presidential candidates are, as a linear function, evaluated more positively. But it is also possible that the relationship between political experience and thermometer ratings is not linear. For example, voters might be unaffected by a one-unit increase in political experience for an already-seasoned candidate (e.g., thirty versus thirty-one years), as opposed to a one-unit increase in political experience for a relatively inexperienced candidate (e.g., three versus four years). If this is the case, the marginal effect of political experience on thermometer ratings may result in diminishing returns (i.e., a concave curve). For this reason, we also account for the squared value of political experience to test for a quadratic relationship between that variable and thermometer ratings.

Alternatively, it may be the case that political experience influences vice presidential candidate evaluations only when the running mate's level of experience differs substantially from that of the presidential candidate – in other words, when this factor helps to "balance the ticket." Our second measure of political experience therefore begins by calculating the difference between the presidential candidate and vice presidential candidate's years of federal political experience, subtracting the latter from the former. If its effect on the dependent variable is positive, this means that vice presidential candidates are more popular when they have much less experience than the presidential candidate; if negative, this means that vice presidential candidates are more popular when they have much more experience than the presidential candidate. However, it is also possible that vice presidential candidates are more popular when a large gap in either direction exists between their experience and that of the presidential candidate – essentially, ticket-balancing in either direction. If so, then the effect of a ticket's relative experience on vice presidential candidate evaluations is likely to be quadratic, rather than linear. Recognizing this possibility, which we consider more plausible than the linear alternative, we calculate the second experience variable as the squared difference between a presidential and vice presidential candidate's years of federal political experience.

Another way in which presidential candidates have attempted to balance their ticket is by making a "historic" selection – that is, by choosing a running mate from a demographic group that is historically underrepresented in presidential politics, or politics in general. An African-American or Latino candidate would certainly qualify as such, for example, but none was selected as a major-party vice presidential candidate in the period covered by our data. The two clearest examples of such running mates are the only females in our data: Geraldine Ferraro, who joined Walter Mondale's Democratic ticket in 1984; and Sarah Palin, who joined John McCain's Republican ticket in 2008. To capture the unique effect of such historic selections on vice presidential candidate evaluations, we include a "Female Vice Presidential Candidate" variable coded 1 for Ferraro or Palin, and 0 for all other running mates. To the extent that a historic vice presidential selection inspires enthusiasm from and for the underrepresented group while reflecting positively on the political courage of the presidential candidate – as those candidates seem to expect on both counts – we hypothesize that this variable will be associated with a statistically significant increase in vice presidential candidate feeling thermometer ratings.

Table 8.4 presents the results of eight Ordinary Least Squares (OLS) models predicting vice presidential candidate feeling thermometer ratings – for Democratic running mates in Models 1–4 and for Republican running mates in Models 5–8. We test four models for each candidate in order to compare results when using the four different measures of political experience. These models provide valuable insights as to what does – and does not – influence vice presidential candidate evaluations.

First, the political experience variables fail to attain statistical significance in seven of the eight models. The only exception is found in Model 8, where the squared measure of the presidential and vice presidential candidates' relative

Table 8.4: Models of vice presidential candidate feeling thermometer ratings

Parameter	1 Therm Dem. VP	2 Therm Dem. VP	3 Therm Dem. VP	4 Therm Dem. VP	5 Therm GOP VP	6 Therm GOP VP	7 Therm GOP VP	8 Therm GOP VP
Years of federal political experience	–0.056	0.167	–	–	–0.088	–0.97	–	–
	(0.053)	(0.349)			(0.239)	(0.807)		
Years of federal Political Experience²	–	–0.006	–	–	–	0.048	–	–
		(0.008)				(0.037)		
Pr./VP experience difference	–	–	–0.005	0.0353	–	–	0.033	0.006
			(0.038)	(0.062)			(0.08)	(0.065)
Pr./VP experience difference²	–	–	–	–0.003	–	–	–	0.03**
				(0.004)				(0.009)
Female VP candidate	6.945***	8.277*	7.063**	8.444**	6.163	4.689	8.062*	–7.582
	(1.503)	(2.863)	(1.852)	(2.329)	(4.252)	(4.478)	(3.388)	(5.548)
VP home state: Republican	–0.896	–1.073	–0.856	–1.109	6.019**	5.956**	5.947**	6.897**
	(1.839)	(1.991)	(1.867)	(1.723)	(1.693)	(1.725)	(1.828)	(1.828)
VP home state: Democrat	7.742^{+}	7.621^{+}	7.677^{+}	7.637^{+}	–1.143	–0.899	–1.177	–0.233
	(3.753)	(3.746)	(3.746)	(1.068)	(1.059)	(1.019)	(1.104)	(1.104)
Pr. home state: Republican	–0.039	–0.058	0.061	0.017	0.493	0.565	0.548	0.431
	(1.173)	(1.169)	(1.151)	(0.503)	(0.501)	(0.387)	(0.499)	(0.499)
Pr. home state: Democrat	3.421*	3.442*	3.471*	3.508*	–1.886	–1.997	–2.084	–2.296^{+}
	(1.446)	(1.422)	(1.415)	(1.38)	(1.318)	(1.296)	(1.185)	(1.185)
Party identification	–4.101***	–4.104***	–4.102***	–4.1***	4.629***	4.639***	4.617***	4.64***
	(0.373)	(0.372)	(0.37)	(0.5)	(0.499)	(0.495)	(0.493)	(0.493)
Age	0.054*	0.054*	0.053*	0.054*	0.087**	0.087**	0.084**	0.085*
	(0.02)	(0.02)	(0.02)	(0.026)	(0.027)	(0.026)	(0.027)	(0.027)
Gender	–1.439**	–1.444**	–1.433**	–1.438**	–0.711	–0.702^{+}	–0.727	–0.712^{+}
	(0.452)	(0.451)	(0.452)	(0.367)	(0.369)	(0.372)	(0.373)	(0.373)

Table 8.4: (*cont.*)

Parameter	1 Therm Dem. VP	2 Therm Dem. VP	3 Therm Dem. VP	4 Therm Dem. VP	5 Therm GOP VP	6 Therm GOP VP	7 Therm GOP VP	8 Therm GOP VP
Non-White	1.694	1.733	1.571	1.695	–1.44	–1.354	–1.661	–1.382
	(1.124)	(1.123)	(1.116)	(1.035)	(1.046)	(1.118)	(1.012)	(1.012)
Education	1.028***	1.029***	1.016***	1.034***	–0.732*	–0.697+	–0.831*	–0.767+
	(0.134)	(0.138)	(0.134)	(0.323)	(0.327)	(0.367)	(0.347)	(0.347)
Household income	–0.228	–0.23	–0.219	–0.234	0.77*	0.742+	0.814*	0.781*
	(0.32)	(0.321)	(0.325)	(0.34)	(0.341)	(0.334)	(0.331)	(0.331)
South	–1.722*	–1.708+	–1.754*	–1.72+	3.457***	3.491***	3.442***	3.462***
	(0.761)	(0.77)	(0.756)	(0.601)	(0.6)	(0.586)	(0.594)	(0.594)
Change in PDI: State	–0.328	–0.337	–0.345	–0.348	–0.16	–0.206	–0.154	–0.052
	(0.438)	(0.431)	(0.423)	(0.414)	(0.402)	(0.416)	(0.368)	(0.368)
Change in PDI: National	0.386	0.592	0.307	0.517	–2.471*	–0.473	–2.291*	–1.307
	(0.819)	(0.858)	(0.865)	(1.341)	(1.678)	(0.881)	(1.147)	(1.147)
Incumbent party	0.126	1.667	–0.681	0.982	–21.13*	–13.65+	–20.39**	–15.05*
	(2.75)	(3.637)	(2.93)	(6.73)	(7.181)	(5.89)	(5.041)	(5.041)
Incumbent* state PDI	0.083	0.089	0.097	0.092	0.206	0.223	0.214	0.135
	(0.228)	(0.224)	(0.221)	(0.259)	(0.252)	(0.275)	(0.223)	(0.223)
Incumbent* national PDI	–0.597	–0.792	–0.505	–0.73	2.029*	1.241	1.941*	1.507*
	(0.543)	(0.566)	(0.571)	(0.561)	(0.782)	(0.74)	(0.691)	(0.628)
Constant	70.33***	66.81***	70.37***	69.19***	58.26***	42.64*	56.21***	41.14**
	(5.069)	(8.086)	(5.2)	(11.97)	(14.21)	(8.173)	(10.56)	(10.56)
Adj. R^2	0.173	0.173	0.172	0.173	0.199	0.201	0.199	0.206
N	19,246	19,246	19,246	19,262	19,262	19,262	19,262	19,262

Robust standard errors clustered by year are included in parentheses.

*** Denotes significant at p<0.001; ** denotes significant at p<0.01; * denotes significant at p<0.05; + denotes significant at p<0.1.

Dependent variable coding: Feeling Thermometer Rating (0=Coldest; 50=Neutral; 100=Warmest, missing otherwise).

political experience is statistically significant at $p < 0.01$, and positively signed. For purposes of interpretation, this means that when members of a presidential ticket have widely discrepant levels of political experience, the result is a convex curve when compared with the fitted values of vice presidential candidate feeling thermometer ratings; in other words, the relationship is non-linear, or quadratic. This finding lends credibility to the importance of ticket-balancing – that is, selecting a "fresh face" as a running mate to complement an experienced presidential candidate; or selecting a seasoned running mate to complement a relatively inexperienced presidential candidate. As the discrepancy between presidential and vice presidential candidate political experience increases, so, too, does the thermometer rating of a vice presidential candidate. While this relationship makes intuitive sense, it is unclear why it only applies to Republican candidates. Future research may be helpful in explaining why these results vary between Democratic and Republican tickets.

Moving beyond political experience, we also find evidence that a historic vice presidential selection – specifically, a female running mate – may result in more positive feeling thermometer ratings for that candidate. In Models 1–4, the "Female Vice Presidential Candidate" variable is statistically significant and positively signed, indicating that Geraldine Ferraro was rated more positively on feeling thermometers than other Democratic vice presidential candidates in the 1968–2008 period, even when controlling for a variety of respondent, candidate, and environmental characteristics. However, there is limited evidence that Ferraro's popularity can be extrapolated to female running mates in general, since the same variable is statistically significant only once when applied to Sarah Palin in Models 5–8. Only in Model 7, when measuring experience using the raw difference score, does Palin emerge as uniquely popular among Republican vice presidential candidates when controlling for other variables. Given that Model 7 resulted in the lowest adjusted R^2 value of the four Republican models, this is a particularly weak model in which to find evidence of Palin's exceptional popularity. The most appropriate conclusion to draw from this range of evidence is that female running mates may enjoy greater popularity, but not automatically so.

Also, building upon our findings from Chapter 5, this evidence indicates that vice presidential candidates are more popular among respondents from their home state, in comparison to respondents in general. The Republican vice presidential home state variable is statistically significant, at $p < 0.05$, and positively signed, in each of the models predicting Republican vice presidential candidate thermometer ratings. Based upon the coefficients from Models 5–8, Republican running mates score 5.94–6.9 points higher on the feeling thermometer among home state respondents. The Democratic vice presidential home state variable, on the other hand, is marginally significant, at $p < 0.10$, in each of the models predicting Democratic vice presidential candidate thermometer ratings. Based upon the coefficients from Models 1–4, Democratic running mates score 7.62–7.74 points higher on the feeling thermometer among home state respondents. As indicated by the analyses in Chapter 5, however, this increase in home state popularity does not necessarily translate to an increase in home state votes for the running mate's presidential ticket.

Interestingly, we find limited evidence of economic indicators influencing vice presidential candidates' feeling thermometer ratings. In no case does the interaction of incumbent party and state- or national-level changes in personal disposable income significantly influence Democratic vice presidential candidates' ratings. However, in three of the models predicting Republican vice presidential candidates' thermometer ratings – Models 5, 7, and 8 – the interaction of incumbent party and national-level PDI is statistically significant and positively signed. To put this in substantive terms, when the incumbent president is a Republican and national PDI increases, we observe a corresponding increase in the feeling thermometer rating for the Republican vice presidential candidate. It is unclear why there would be a discrepancy between the effect of this interaction variable on Democratic (null) versus Republican (statistically significant, positive) vice presidential candidate evaluations. Once more, further research may be helpful in explaining these disparate results, particularly by making comparisons to models predicting feeling thermometer ratings for presidential candidates and political parties to see if this is a general party difference.

Although we estimate eight different models of vice presidential feeling thermometer ratings in Table 8.4, it is important to keep in mind that even with the inclusion of eighteen or nineteen independent variables (depending on the model), the highest adjusted R^2 value that the models produce is 0.206. In other words, approximately 80% of the variance in feeling thermometer ratings is left unexplained by each of these models. Given that candidate political experience, candidate gender, economic indicators, the incumbent president's political party, respondent partisan identification, and several other respondent demographic characteristics explain so little of the variance in the dependent variable, it is only reasonable to conclude that vice presidential candidate evaluations are influenced greatly by factors not represented in these models. It may be the case that voters are influenced by the running mate's personality traits, contributions to the tenor of the campaign, vice presidential debate performance, and a host of other factors particular to an individual candidacy and election year. Quite plausibly, the single-greatest influence on vice presidential candidate evaluations may be evaluations of the presidential candidate who selected him or her for the party ticket. Such an explanation would be consistent with our findings in this chapter and in previous chapters; vice presidential candidates can matter, but it is the presidential candidate who most defines and influences a presidential election.

Conclusion

Do vice presidential candidates influence vote choice at the national level? The evidence reviewed and presented in this chapter indicates that they do, but to a limited extent. Our analysis strongly supports the conventional wisdom that voters are most influenced by presidential candidates when voting in a presidential election. For every five points that a vice presidential candidate's feeling thermometer rating increases, holding all other candidate ratings at a constant level, a voter's probability of supporting the running mate's ticket increases by 0.029, or 2.9 percentage points. However, a five-point increase in a presidential candidate's feeling thermometer rating increases the probability of voting for that candidate by 0.1–0.103, or 10–10.3 percentage points. In general, evaluations of the presidential and vice presidential candidates (but mostly the former) explain a remarkable amount of variance when predicting presidential vote choice – far more than when thermometer ratings are excluded, and nearly to the same extent as models including a battery of respondent, candidate, and environmental characteristics alongside those thermometer ratings.

To better understand the dynamics shaping vice presidential candidate evaluations we tested a series of models in Table 8.4, including the same battery of characteristics, as well as home state variables and measures of ticket-balancing factors such as political experience and gender. While some of these variables significantly predict vice presidential candidates' feeling thermometer ratings – including many variables that we found to be significant in our analyses from Chapter 5 – the overall explanatory power of these models is rather limited. Indeed, it is difficult to identify factors other than party identification that consistently and substantially influence vice presidential evaluations. A distinct possibility is that vice presidential candidates are, for the most part, not judged independently, but primarily on the basis of their affiliation with the presidential candidate who selected them. Future research could address this possibility.

What does all of this mean in terms of electoral strategy? To say the least, a political party would be much better served in its quest for the White House by nominating a popular presidential candidate who, in turn, selects a competent prospective partner in governance as his or her running mate – rather than relying on a popular vice presidential candidate to compensate for weaknesses at the top of the ticket. As Adkison (1982) observed, the likelihood of selecting an exceptionally popular vice presidential candidate who, by implication, can "deliver" the presidential election is unlikely – and the potential to cause damage by choosing a suboptimal running mate for purposes of political expediency is great. More than thirty years later, we see no reason to doubt that claim. Given the relatively small effect that vice presidential candidates have on vote choice, presidential candidates should feel far less constrained by electoral considerations when choosing a running mate than by the obligation to choose an effective partner in governance who can lead the nation capably in the event of unforeseen tragedy. That is not to say that presidential candidates should feel free to pick a very unpopular or divisive running mate. Voters may view such a selection as evidence of poor judgment on the part of a presidential candidate, which in turn might lead to a decreased chance of electoral success. The prospects of such a selection are, of course, very unlikely, but possible given a misreading of our evidence.

In short, a presidential candidate should use his or her power to select a vice presidential candidate responsibly – not with the false hope of delivering an election, nor with a false sense of security from electoral consequences. This is not merely a normative recommendation; it is, first and foremost, a reflection of the empirical evidence, as presented in this chapter and throughout this book.

Notes

1 Also, the vice president may temporarily serve as acting president in the event of presidential incapacitation. George H. W. Bush did so in 1985 when President Ronald Reagan underwent a surgical procedure, as did Dick Cheney on two occasions – in 2002 and 2007, when President George W. Bush underwent a colonoscopy. For more information, see "List of Vice-Presidents Who Served as 'Acting' President Under the 25th Amendment," compiled by The American Presidency Project at the University of California, Santa Barbara (www.presidency.ucsb.edu/acting_presidents.php. Accessed February 23, 2015).

2 For an illustration of the Clinton-Gore message, see the campaign ad "Leaders 2" at www.livingroomcandidate.org/commercials/1992/leaders-2. And for an illustration of the McCain-Palin message, see the campaign ad "Original Mavericks" at www.livingroomcandidate.org/commercials/2008/original-mavericks. Accessed February 23, 2015.

3 Specifically, Adkison (1982, 336, endnote 14) coded respondents' feeling thermometer rating of a given candidate as a "like" if it was between 51 and 100, and a "dislike" if it was between 0 and 49, while excluding "neutral" feelings (scores of 50) from his analysis. See endnote 7 in this chapter for more on feeling thermometers.

4 Consider, for example, the evidence from our analysis of Lyndon Johnson's vice presidential candidacy in 1960. Despite the fact that Johnson was the majority leader of the US Senate and had been a leading candidate for the 1960 Democratic presidential nomination, 64.8% of respondents to the 1960 wave of the 1956 ANES panel data either reported having no strong feelings about him or said they did, but then failed to offer any.

5 Also see Frankovic (1985), who drew similar conclusions from CBS News/*New York Times* polling data in the 1984 presidential election.

6 A notable exception is Romero (2001). Romero analyzed ANES panel data to examine how feelings toward vice presidential candidates influenced the likelihood of voting for that party's ticket. He found that after accounting for "rationalization affects" – that is, opinions about the vice presidential candidate at a point prior to that election year – feeling thermometer ratings of the vice presidential candidates no longer predicted vote choice in the presidential election.

7 Feeling thermometers require respondents to rate a target along a scale ranging from 0 (very cold) to 100 (very warm), with a score of 50 indicating neutral feelings. See Chapter 5 for more details.

8 Most studies of these effects focus upon individual elections (i.e., cross-sectional analyses), however Ulbig (2013) includes a pooled analysis of elections from 1972–2008 in her empirical models.

9 As we have noted, some scholars – fearing that the inclusion of presidential and vice presidential candidate feeling thermometers in the same model will introduce multicollinearity – have preferred to use alternative candidate evaluation measures. For example, Wattenberg (1995, 511) found that thermometer ratings of presidential and vice presidential candidates were correlated at $r = 0.72$ in 1968–1992 ANES data, and Knuckey found similar correlations when examining 2008 ANES data. In our analysis of pooled data from the 1968–2008 ANES, we find that Republican candidate feeling thermometer ratings are correlated at $r = 0.59$, and Democratic candidate feeling thermometers are correlated at $r = 0.57$ ($p < 0.001$, in both cases). However, the variance inflation factor (VIF) for these four feeling thermometers is below 2.5 in each case, with a mean VIF of 2.12. Given that these values are well below the 2.5 VIF multicollinearity threshold recommended by Allison (1999), we find it appropriate to include all four feeling thermometer ratings in our empirical models. The average thermometer rating for each type of candidate in the pooled data is as follows: Democratic vice presidential candidate, 54.7; Democratic presidential candidate, 57.4; Republican vice presidential candidate, 51.1; Republican presidential candidate, 57.6.

10 Since vote choice is a dichotomous dependent variable, we use logistic regression models. As a result, the coefficients represent log odd ratios that do not allow for direct interpretation of the magnitude of the variables' effects, as would be the case if we were estimating linear regression models. The predicted probabilities, discussed below, provide a more intuitive means of interpretation.

11 For purposes of comparison, we also tested a model of vote choice only including vice presidential candidate feeling thermometer ratings. The model results in a reduction in error of 53.94%, and the percentage of outcomes correctly predicted is 77.02%. This is further evidence that vice presidential candidate evaluations, while empirically relevant, are far weaker predictors of vote choice than presidential candidate evaluations.

9

The VP advantage

The 2014 midterm elections dealt Congressional Democrats a stinging defeat. Republicans gained control of the US Senate for the first time since 2007, and the GOP added thirteen seats to its majority in the US House of Representatives. In the days that followed the election, political commentators and news outlets speculated as to what the results would mean for the immediate future of national politics. How would President Obama govern as he entered the final two years of his presidency? What policies would a Republican-controlled Congress prioritize? And what did the 2014 elections mean for the 2016 presidential election? Just five days after the midterms, the Associated Press published articles with headlines such as "GOP's midterm rout shapes 2016 presidential race"[1] and "For Hillary Clinton, the right time to get ready."[2] Already, the 2016 presidential election was high on the media's, if not the public's, agenda.

Presidential "buzz" grew over the next several weeks, as numerous candidates were reported to be actively exploring a run for the White House – including Jeb Bush, Chris Christie, Hillary Clinton, Ted Cruz, Mike Huckabee, Martin O'Malley, Rand Paul, Mitt Romney, Marco Rubio, Bernie Sanders, Scott Walker, and *many* others. And then, just twenty-four days after the midterm elections, came signs that another 2016 race was under way – the race for the vice presidency. On November 28, 2014, *Politico* published an article titled "Portman for (vice) president: Supporters think he's No. 1 for No. 2" (Everett and Palmer 2014). The article's authors, Burgess Everett and Anna Palmer, reported that US Senator Rob Portman's recently rumored exploration of a presidential run actually may have been designed to increase his national visibility and establish a base of support in hopes of becoming a frontrunner for the next *vice presidential* nomination. Certainly Portman had the credentials to serve at the highest levels of government. "His resumé goes on and on," the authors noted, "former House member, George W. Bush's US trade representative, director of the Office of Management" and, of course, "He's from the politically important state of Ohio." It was twenty-three months before the next presidential election, the field of *presidential* candidates was wide open – only long-shot James Webb had officially formed an exploratory committee – and yet the 2016 veepstakes had already started.

Given the fact that presidential campaigns begin earlier than they did in years past – due to the "frontloading" of many presidential primaries and the ever-increasing pressure to raise vast sums of campaign funds early in the "invisible primary" period – and the fact that vice presidents play a greater role in the governing process than they once did, perhaps it should not be surprising to see reports of vice presidential candidacies emerging much earlier in the election cycle. After all, we have demonstrated that there is a perception among presidential candidates, campaign officials, and journalists that running mates can substantially influence vote choice, particularly in the home state. Perceptions being what they are, our empirical findings offer only limited evidence to support this notion.

In our analysis of the 1884–2012 presidential elections, in Chapter 4, we find no evidence of a *general* vice presidential home state advantage (HSA); on average, a presidential ticket performs better in the running mate's home state by 0.58%–0.68% – using a four- or five-election lag to compare present to past state and national voting trends, respectively – but this effect is not statistically distinguishable from zero. This does not mean that vice presidential HSAs never occur, only that – according to regression analyses testing various predictors of home state advantages scores – the effect is conditional. Specifically, a running mate must come from a relatively less-populous state and have extensive elected experience in that state, in order to earn a significant HSA. All of this is in contrast to presidential candidates, who generally earn a statistically significant HSA.

The conclusions just described are based upon analyses that use the Lewis-Beck and Rice (1983) method of calculating HSA scores. This method is the one most commonly used in the HSA literature, and it has many strengths – but it is far from perfect. Indeed, an analysis that relies solely on this method, or for that matter any single method, is quite vulnerable to methodological critique. We do not rely solely on the Lewis-Beck and Rice method, however. Instead, we use a multi-method approach to analyze the vice presidential HSA. And the results of our diverse analyses are remarkably consistent.

The first alternative method that we use, in Chapter 4, is a fixed effects regression model predicting presidential vote choice based upon a variety of national- and state-level variables, including ones identifying the vice presidential home state. Due to variation in data availability, we test three models using different independent variables and election years, starting as early as 1884 and as late as 1972. Consistent with our initial findings, both the Democratic and Republican vice presidential home state variables are not statistically significant in any of the three models. Meanwhile, the Democratic presidential home state variable is statistically significant and correctly signed in each model, while the Republican presidential home state variable is at least marginally significant and correctly signed in two models.

Perhaps most persuasive is our analysis of American National Election Studies (ANES) data from the 1952–2008 presidential elections, in Chapter 5. To our knowledge, this is the first large-scale analysis of the HSA using individual-level data. This is significant because vote choice is an individual-level decision; therefore, any analysis of changes in vote choice based upon *aggregate*, i.e. state- and national-level, data – as is the case for our two previous methods of analysis, and the HSA literature, generally – risks drawing conclusions based upon an ecological fallacy. Rather than challenge our previous conclusions, though, the ANES analysis only confirms them; respondents from a vice presidential candidate's home state are no more likely to vote for that candidate's party ticket than respondents from other states, judging by t-tests or logistic regression models. In contrast, respondents from a presidential candidate's home state are more likely to vote for that candidate, at least in some analyses. Moreover, we find minimal evidence of a vice presidential HSA when using alternative indicators beyond vote choice, such as voter turnout, political participation, and candidate evaluations. While there is some evidence that running mates are evaluated more positively in their home state, there is no evidence that this popularity translates into changes in actual electoral behavior.

The claim that vice presidential candidates typically receive a HSA therefore runs up against a reinforced wall of empirical evidence. Moreover, those who emphasize the electoral significance of the vice presidential HSA must confront this fact: even if a running mate "delivers" his or her home state, the likelihood of any one state proving decisive in the Electoral College is extremely small. Worse yet, our analysis indicates that such an advantage would occur only in relatively less-populous states which are even less likely to flip an election result.

Our case study of Lyndon Johnson's 1960 vice presidential candidacy, in Chapter 6, helps to illustrate the limitations of the vice presidential HSA. As we describe in Chapter 1, even individuals who express doubts about the relevance of the vice presidential HSA today typically credit LBJ with "delivering" his home state (Texas) and region (the South), and in turn the presidential election, to the Democratic ticket that year. What's more, the historical record clearly indicates that then-Senator John F. Kennedy chose Johnson as his running mate with the expectation of such a home state and region advantage, and as president described that advantage as electorally decisive. However, our analysis of 1960 survey data – including that year's ANES and internal campaign polling – provides no direct evidence to justify rejecting the null hypothesis that Johnson did not provide an electoral advantage in Texas and the South. In fact, evaluations of Johnson were surprisingly weak in his home state and region in terms of the relative number and recorded content of respondent likes and dislikes. More directly, the interaction of those evaluations with home state or region variables fails to significantly predict vote choice in logistic regression models. Based upon the available individual-level data from 1960, then, we simply cannot affirm as an empirical reality the perception that Johnson provided a decisive advantage in that election. This null finding, it must be noted, is entirely in keeping with our characterization of the vice presidential HSA as conditioned by state population and political experience; Texas was one of the most-populous states in 1960, and thus unlikely to be heavily influenced by "friends and neighbors" voting.

Is it *possible*, then, for a vice presidential HSA to determine the outcome of a presidential election? Yes, we conclude, but only under extremely narrow conditions: in addition to those already stated – that the running mate must come from a relatively less-populous state and have extensive elected experience within that state – the election must be close enough to be decided by the home state in the Electoral College. The likelihood of all of these factors being met is extremely low, but not impossible. In fact, our analysis in Chapter 7 identifies one case in which the selection of a different running mate on the presidential candidate's list of finalists plausibly could have delivered the election: Jeanne Shaheen, of New Hampshire, in 2000. Based upon linear regression models predicting determinants of the vice presidential HSA in the 1960–2012 presidential elections, and imputing values associated with Shaheen's counterfactual candidacy, we estimate that her selection would have delivered New Hampshire's four electoral votes and, assuming the same Electoral College tally across other states, in turn would have delivered the 2000 election to Democrat Al Gore.

To provide further perspective on the electoral significance of vice presidential candidates, beyond home state factors, in Chapter 8 we analyze the relative effect of presidential versus vice presidential candidate evaluations on vote choice, as well as the determinants of the latter evaluations, among respondents to the 1968–2008 ANES. Our analysis indicates that feeling thermometer ratings of vice presidential candidates generally have a statistically significant and positive effect on vote choice, although a much smaller one than the statistically significant and positive effect of presidential candidate ratings. Specifically, a five-point increase in vice presidential candidate feeling thermometer ratings leads to a 0.029 change in the predicted probability of Democratic vote choice; while a five-point increase in presidential candidate ratings leads to a 0.1–0.103 change in the predicted probability of Democratic vote choice. Furthermore, feelings toward presidential candidates alone account for most of the variance in our vote choice models; variables measuring feelings toward vice presidential candidates add very little to the models' predictive power, as is the case for an extensive battery of variables measuring characteristics of the respondents, the candidates, and the political environment. In short, vice presidential candidates do influence vote choice among a nationally representative sample of respondents but only to a limited extent, and much less so than the presidential candidates who selected them.

While vice presidential candidates may be relevant to presidential voting, there is little evidence to indicate that they are *particularly* relevant to home state voters. Nonetheless, as we document in Chapters 1–3, there is a widespread and enduring perception that running mates can provide a substantial electoral advantage in their home state in a given election – even among those journalists, campaign strategists, and presidential candidates who dismiss such a notion in the abstract. The perception of a vice presidential HSA is deeply ingrained in the historical practice and analysis of vice presidential selection, and its influence is evident today among journalists who – as demonstrated by our empirical analysis in Chapter 2 – reference home state or region considerations approximately half the time that they substantively evaluate a prospective vice presidential candidate. Presidential candidates and their top campaign officials often seem to share this perception, according to our analysis in Chapter 3. This is indicated by their public comments made outside of an immediate electoral context, as well as our case studies of specific campaign responses to recent vice presidential selections. In terms of systematic evidence, we find that vice presidential contenders from electorally competitive states are disproportionately likely to make a presidential candidate's shortlist. Perhaps most significantly, we find that in 2012 the Obama and Romney campaigns devoted their most precious resources – time (i.e., campaign visits) and money (i.e., spending on campaign advertisements) – disproportionately toward contesting Wisconsin after the selection of Paul Ryan as running mate on the Republican ticket.

While this research is intended to provide an authoritative analysis of the vice presidential HSA – both in terms of perceptions and empirical realities – it also raises questions ripe for additional research. First, in Chapter 3 we hypothesize that presidential campaign activity will increase in a particular state following the selection of a native candidate whose party does not hold the advantage in that state prior to his or her selection. The evidence from Wisconsin in 2012 supports that hypothesis, but a more robust analysis would require studying multiple elections across varying election years and conditions. Is the effect general? Does activity decrease following the selection of a running mate whose party *does* hold the advantage in his or her home state? How large does the advantage or disadvantage have to be in order to trigger such effects? Is the response proportional across both campaigns? These are questions best left to future research.

Second, and on a related point, how exactly do home state candidates go about capitalizing on their perceived HSA? Specifically, how – if at all – do they tailor their campaign communications, including public rhetoric and campaign advertising content, to appeal to home state voters? Are these communications modified primarily in symbolic ways, to emphasize shared roots and identity, or in substantive ways, to demonstrate appreciation of localized issues and values? Do native candidates, and their campaigns, consistently cite home state identity in these communications, or only infrequently? Do strategies vary by campaigns, and if so on what bases?

Finally, to the extent that vice presidential HSAs are limited to less-populous states and running mates who have extensive elected experience within their state – as we find – further research would be helpful in understanding what factors shape and dramatize that process. For instance, which of the four criteria of friends and neighbors voting, as defined by Key (1949), are most effective in convincing voters to support a home state running mate's ticket, when otherwise they would not have done so – is it familiarity with the candidate's record? Personal contact? Perceived knowledge of local concerns? A shared sense of identity? For that matter, researchers might focus on more indirect effects on vote choice, such as a running mate's ability to capitalize on home state political networks by mobilizing political actors including state and/or local politicians, party organizations, and interest groups. Each of these actors might be better persuaded to actively support the campaign, or to increase their support, by a home state running mate who knows them personally – as opposed to an out-of-state candidate with no local political connections. Presumably, mobilizing these political actors should be easiest in a small state where these networks are most compact. If so, this increased activity may, in turn, have a direct effect on vote choice in the state.

While we hope our research will be of interest to scholars studying the presidency, campaigns and elections, and American politics in general, we also hope it will provide clarity to candidates, campaign officials, and political commentators regarding the significance of vice presidential candidates in presidential elections, in the home state and beyond. Again, while it is possible that vice presidential candidates could, under narrow circumstances, provide a significant HSA, the probability of that advantage actually deciding a presidential election is very low. The probability of a vice presidential candidate having a meaningful effect on presidential vote choice at the national level also is rather low, given that evaluations of the presidential candidate are most relevant to – and most influential for – choosing a president.

The mechanism by which presidents are chosen in the United States – the Electoral College – also is an important factor to consider. It is not enough for a vice presidential candidate to persuade a substantial portion of the American electorate to change its vote on the basis of his or her candidacy, as would be the case if presidents were chosen by national popular vote; rather, that candidate must be able to persuade a substantial portion of the electorate in a given state, or set of states, that is/are sufficiently competitive, to cast its/their electoral votes differently on the basis of his or her candidacy. A home state candidacy is the typical means by which campaigns have strategically targeted electoral votes through vice presidential selection, but as we have shown here this strategy generally does not succeed, and when it does the targeted state typically has relatively few electoral votes and therefore is even less likely to determine the outcome in the Electoral College. That is why, while plausible in theory, the prospect of an electorally decisive vice presidential selection is more akin to the "holy grail" than the "game changer" at a presidential candidate's fingertips, as electoral strategists often presume it to be.

What does all of this mean for presidential candidates and campaign officials? Ultimately, we think that Karl Rove's observations are right. Presidential candidates should, in Rove's words, select the "best partner in the White House and a person the country would have confidence in if something terrible happened" to the president (Rove 2012). A vice presidential candidate should not be solely, or primarily, viewed as a means to gain an electoral advantage. After all, what does it say about a presidential candidate who places primary emphasis on electoral considerations rather than policy expertise or leadership potential in this process, given that a running mate could become president? In the heat of a campaign, undoubtedly a candidate and his or her staff will consider a running mate's influence on the electorate. But that's to be expected. The purpose of a campaign is to win an election. However, presidential candidates are unwise to emphasize electoral considerations when selecting a running mate. Once more, this is not simply a normative statement but a reflection of the empirical evidence. In general, and particularly in the home state, a vice presidential candidate's influence on the outcome of a presidential election is minimal. What is not minimal, however, is the effect of a vice president on national governance, especially in the event of an unforeseen tragedy that elevates him or her to the highest office in the land. As a matter of electoral strategy and good governance, then, our conclusion is simple: when choosing his or her running mate, a presidential candidate ought to select the person best qualified to serve as vice president and to advance their common agenda for the nation.

Our research also ought to inform the contributions of journalists and other political actors as they comment upon, and potentially influence, the vice presidential selection process. Instead of debating which veepstakes contender will provide the best strategic advantage in a presidential election, these political actors would be better-served – and would better serve the public – to ask a different set of questions: which running mate will best complement the presidential candidate, in terms of his or her ability to develop and communicate a common policy agenda? If elected, which running mate would most effectively and responsibly serve as vice president? What skills or experiences does this person add that the presidential candidate lacks? Everett and Palmer (2014) were right in their *Politico* article to focus on Rob Portman's extensive political resumé – with the exception of a brief reference to his home state – when analyzing Portman's potential as a running mate in the 2016 election. That is exactly the type of discussion candidates, campaign officials, and political commentators should engage in when playing the veepstakes; it holds our presidential candidates to a higher standard. As the vice president continues to assume a greater role in the governing process, voters should expect – and they deserve – that the occupant of that office hold what power he or she has on the basis of being more than just a relic of campaign strategy whose usefulness is outlived. Vice presidential candidates should be selected to deliver competent service to the nation, not to "deliver" an election.

Notes

1 See www.nytimes.com/aponline/2014/11/09/us/politics/ap-us-election-2016.html. Accessed February 23, 2015.

2 See www.nytimes.com/2014/11/10/us/politics/for-hillary-clinton-the-right-time-to-get-ready.html. Accessed February 23, 2015.

Appendix A

Documentation of media "veepstakes" coverage

2012 Republican veepstakes articles

Media source	Date	Author(s)	Title
ABC News	Apr. 18, 2012	Jonathan Karl	"The list of top republican VP candidates"
http://abcnews.go.com/blogs/politics/2012/04/the-list-of-top-republican-vp-candidates/			
CNN	Aug. 7, 2012	N/A	"Rating Romney's possible running mates"
www.cnn.com/interactive/2012/04/politics/interactive.vp.candidates/index.html			
Daily Beast	Jan. 11, 2012	Howard Kurtz	"Mitt Romney's dilemma"
www.thedailybeast.com/articles/2012/01/11/mitt-romney-s-dilemma-picking-a-running-mate-if-he-s-the-gop-nominee.html			
Huffington Post	Apr. 19, 2012	Jon Ward	"Mitt Romney's vice presidential pick: Signs point to risk avoidance"
www.huffingtonpost.com/2012/04/19/mitt-romneys-vice-president_n_1439122.html			
National Journal	Feb. 1, 2012	Hotline staff	"Your favorite vice: Hotline's veepstakes power rankings"
www.nationaljournal.com/politics/your-favorite-vice-hotline-s-veepstakes-power-rankings-20120201			
New Republic	Jan. 12, 2012	Eliza Gray	"Vice squad"
www.newrepublic.com/article/politics/magazine/99515/vice-president-republican-2012?page=0,0			
New York Times	N/A	N/A	"Romney's potential running mates"
http://elections.nytimes.com/2012/romney-potential-running-mates			

2012 Republican veepstakes articles

Media source	Date	Author(s)	Title
Time	N/A	Mark Halperin	"The Romney veepstakes"
www.time.com/time/interactive/0,31813,2114492,00.html			
Wall Street Journal	N/A	N/A	"Who might be a Romney running mate?"
http://online.wsj.com/article/SB10001424052702303299604577326173506475792.html			
Washington Post ("The Fix" blog)	Mar. 23, 2012	Chris Cillizza	"Veepstakes 2012: The inaugural edition"
www.washingtonpost.com/blogs/the-fix/post/veepstakes-2012-the-inaugural-edition/2012/03/22/gIQAAAbKUS_blog.html			

2008 veepstakes articles

Media source	Date	Author(s)	Title
ABC News (Dem.)	Aug. 1, 2008	Rick Klein	"Who's in the Democratic veepstakes?"
http://abcnews.go.com/Politics/Vote2008/story?id=5210851&page=1			
ABC News (Rep.)	Aug. 28, 2008	N/A	"Who's in the Republican veepstakes?"
http://abcnews.go.com/Politics/Vote2008/story?id=4710917&page=1			
American Prospect	Feb. 22, 2008	The editors	"The 2008 veepstakes"
http://prospect.org/article/2008-veepstakes			
CBS News	N/A	Vaughn Ververs	"Potential VP bios: Republicans"
www.cbsnews.com/stories/2008/06/16/politics/main4184046.shtml			
CNN	Jul. 30, 2008	Suzanne Malveaux *et al.*	"CNN analysis: Who'll win the Obama veepstakes?"
www.cnn.com/2008/POLITICS/07/30/dem.veepstakes/			
Human Events	Jul. 9, 2008	Tim Carney	"ENPR: Ranking vice presidential contenders"
www.humanevents.com/2008/07/09/enpr-ranking-vice-presidential-contenders/			
Los Angeles Times	Jul. 21, 2008	Jonah Goldberg	"John McCain's veepstakes"
www.latimes.com/news/opinion/commentary/la-oe-goldberg21-2008jul21-b,0,172602.htmlstory			

2008 veepstakes articles

Media source	Date	Author(s)	Title
New York Magazine (Dem.)	Jun. 30, 2008	Peter Keating	"Obama's potential running mates: A who's who"
http://nymag.com/daily/intelligencer/2008/06/obamas_potential_running_mates.html			
New York Magazine (Rep.)	Jun. 30, 2008	Peter Keating	"McCain's potential running mates: A who's who"
http://nymag.com/daily/intelligencer/2008/06/mccains_potential_running_mate.html			
New York Times	NA	Adam Nagourney/ Jeff Zeleny	"Potential running mates"
http://politics.nytimes.com/election-guide/2008/candidates/vp/index.html			
Newsweek	Oct. 3, 2007	Howard Fineman	"The Hillary veepstakes"
www.newsweek.com/fineman-inside-hillary-veepstakes-102851			
NPR	Aug. 19, 2008	Ken Rudin	"Who's up, who's down In the veepstakes"
www.npr.org/news/graphics/2008/july/veepstakes/veepstakes.html			
RealClearPolitics	Jul. 25, 2008	Reid Wilson	"Laying odds on McCain's veep"
www.realclearpolitics.com/politics_nation/2008/07/laying_odds_on_mccains_veep.html			
Time	N/A	Massimo Calabresi	"Playing the veepstakes"
www.time.com/time/specials/2007/article/0,28804,1813163_1813157_1813124,00.html			
Washington Post ("The Fix" blog)	May 9, 2008	Chris Cillizza	"The Friday line: veepstakes!"
http://voices.washingtonpost.com/thefix/the-line/the-friday-line-veepstakes-1.html			

2004 veepstakes articles

Media Source	**Date**	**Author(s)**	**Title**
Bloomberg Businessweek	Mar. 14, 2004	N/A	"The strategy behind Kerry's veepstakes"
www.businessweek.com/stories/2004-03-14/the-strategy-behind-kerrys-veepstakes			
CBS News	N/A	Dotty Lynch	"Fantasy veepstakes"
www.cbsnews.com/2100-500157_162-618130.html			
Chicago Tribune	Mar. 17, 2004	Alison Neumer	"Running mate game"
http://articles.chicagotribune.com/2004-03-17/news/0403180040_1_vp-candidate-north-carolina-senator-evan-bayh			
CNN	N/A	Keating Holland	"Who will John Kerry pick as his running mate?"
www.cnn.com/ELECTION/2004/veepstakes/misc/story1.html			

2004 veepstakes articles

Media Source	Date	Author(s)	Title
National Review	Feb. 12, 2004	John J. Miller	"Kerry's veep: A short list in the making"
http://old.nationalreview.com/miller/miller200402120825.asp			
NBC News	Mar. 2, 2004	Jonathan Alter	"With Kerry in, let the veepstakes begin"
www.nbcnews.com/id/4433232/ns/politics/t/kerry-let-veepstakes-begin/			
New York Daily News	Jul. 6, 2004	N/A	"Handicapping the veepstakes"
www.nydailynews.com/archives/news/handicapping-veepstakes-article-1.577329			
NPR	N/A	Ken Rudin	"Who will be Kerry's VP?"
www.npr.org/politics/vp/			
Slate	May 28, 2004	Michael Crowley	"John Kerry's long shortlist"
www.slate.com/articles/news_and_politics/assessment/2004/05/john_kerrys_long_shortlist.html			
Washington Post	N/A	N/A	"Who will it be?"
www.washingtonpost.com/wp-srv/politics/elections/2004/veepomatic_bios.htm			

2000 veepstakes articles

Media source	Date	Author(s)	Title
ABC News	Jul. 21, 2000	Mark Halperin *et al.*	"Gov. Bush says he will choose VP soon"
http://abcnews.go.com/US/storynew?id=96428&page=1			
Associated Press	Jul. 26, 2000	Mike Glover	"Gore has 'short list' of VP possibilities"
http://amarillo.com/stories/2000/07/26/usn_LA0748.shtml			
Bloomberg Businessweek	May 21, 2000	N/A	"Despite all the name dropping, the veep short list is short indeed"
www.businessweek.com/stories/2000-05-21/despite-all-the-name-dropping-the-veep-short-list-is-short-indeed			
CBS News	N/A	N/A	"Veepstakes 2000"
www.cbsnews.com/2100-250_162-172481.html			
CNN (Crossfire)	Jul. 18, 2000	N/A	"Who would make the best running mates for Al Gore and George W. Bush?"
http://transcripts.cnn.com/TRANSCRIPTS/0007/18/cf.00.html			

2000 veepstakes articles

Media source	Date	Author(s)	Title
Los Angeles Times	Jul. 17, 2000	Ronald Brownstein	"In veepstakes, candidates look for partners who are already winners"
http://articles.latimes.com/2000/jul/17/news/mn-54370			
National Journal (Dem.)	Jun. 14, 2000	Chuck Todd	"Crystal ball veep-gazing"
www3.nationaljournal.com/members/buzz/2000/trail/061400.htm			
National Journal (Rep.)	Jun. 7, 2000	Chuck Todd	"Raising the (veep) stakes"
www3.nationaljournal.com/members/buzz/2000/trail/060700.htm			
New York Daily News	Jul. 16, 2000	Thomas M. DeFrank	"On picking No. 2: Don't make waves"
www.nydailynews.com/archives/news/picking-2-don-waves-article-1.893271			
New York Times	Jun. 19, 2000	Frank Bruni	"Bush's list of possible running mates getting shorter, but not clearer"
www.nytimes.com/2000/06/19/us/2000-campaign-search-bush-s-list-possible-running-mates-getting-shorter-but-not.html			
USA Today	Aug. 3, 2000	Kathy McCabe	"Democratic VP contenders"
http://usatoday30.usatoday.com/news/e98/vp.htm			
Time	Jul. 23, 2000	Frank Pelligrini	"Yee-haw! In GOP veepstakes, it's the last roundup"
www.time.com/time/nation/article/0,8599,50629,00.html			
Washington Monthly	Jul/Aug 1999	Alexandra Starr	"Running mates: Who will be on the ticket in 2000?"
www.washingtonmonthly.com/features/1999/9907.starr.campaign.html			
Weekly Standard	Mar. 20, 2000	Matthew Rees	"The veep's veep"
www.weeklystandard.com/Content/Protected/Articles/000/000/011/199cdolc.asp			

Appendix B

Fixed effects model of Democratic vote share with interaction terms, 1884–2012

Variables		Variables (continued)	
Dem. VP home state	1.69	Rep. VP home state x state population	0.63
	(4.21)		(0.78)
GOP VP home state	–5.56	Rep. VP home state x Rep. VP political experience	0.13
	(4.86)		(0.27)
Dem. presidential home state	3.99*	State population x Rep. VP political experience	–0.02*
	(1.61)		(0.01)
GOP presidential home state	–1.8	Rep. VP home state x State pop. x Rep. VP political experience	–0.001
	(1.65)		(0.05)
Incumbent president's party	–0.23	Dem. VP home state x state population	–1.09
	(0.51)		(0.99)
Congressional midterm ideology	–15.89***	Dem. VP home state x Dem. VP political experience	–0.1
	(1.16)		(0.2)
Dem. two-party vote share, previous election	0.5***	State population x Dem. VP political experience	0.009
	(0.02)		(0.009)
State population	0.11	Dem. VP home state x state pop. x Dem. VP political experience	0.11+
	(0.21)		(0.06)
Rep. VP political experience	0.31***	Constant	19.47***
	(0.03)		(1.61)
Dem. VP political experience	0.14***		
	(0.03)		
	N	1,565	
	Adj. R^2	0.6257	

Model accounts for fixed effects of states (estimates omitted). *** denotes p < .001; ** denotes p < .01; * denotes p < .05; + denotes p < .10.

References

Abadie, Alberto, Alexis Diamond, and Jens Hainmueller. 2010. "Synthetic control methods for comparative case studies: Estimating the effect of California's tobacco control program." *Journal of the American Statistical Association* 105(490): 493–505.

Adkison, Daniel M. 1982. "The electoral significance of the vice presidency." *Presidential Studies Quarterly* 12(3): 303–336.

Allison, Paul D. 1999. *Multiple Regression: A Primer*. Thousand Oaks, CA: Pine Forge Press.

Alvarez, R. Michael, and Jason L. Saving. 1997. "Deficits, Democrats, and distributive benefits: Congressional elections and the pork barrel in the 1980s." *Political Research Quarterly* 50(4): 809–831.

Arzheimer, Kai, and Jocelyn Evans. 2014. "Candidate geolocation and voter choice in the 2013 English county council elections." *Research and Politics* 1(2): 1–9.

Aspin, Larry T., and William K. Hall. 1987. "The friends and neighbors effect in judicial retention elections." *The Western Political Quarterly* 40(4): 703–715.

Aspin, Larry T., and William K. Hall. 1989. "Friends and neighbors voting in judicial retention elections: A research note comparing trial and appellate court elections." *The Western Political Quarterly* 42(4): 587–596.

Baker, Peter. 2013. *Days of Fire: Bush and Cheney in the White House*. New York: Knopf Doubleday.

Barbash, Fred. 2008. "What's behind Palin's appeal to women?" *Politico*, September 10. Accessed February 24, 2015. www.politico.com/news/stories/0908/13358.html.

Bartels, Larry M. 2006. "What's the matter with *What's the Matter with Kansas?*" *Quarterly Journal of Political Science* 1(2): 201–226.

Bartels, Larry M., and John Zaller. 2001. "Presidential vote models: A recount." *PS: Political Science and Politics* 34(1): 9–20.

Baumgartner, Jody C. 2008. "The veepstakes: Forecasting vice presidential selection in 2008." *PS: Political Science and Politics* 41(4): 765–772.

Bazinet, Kenneth R., and Michael McAuliff. 2008. "Evan Bayh, Joe Biden and Tim Kaine on short list to run with Barack Obama." *New York Daily News*, August 19. Accessed February 23, 2015. www.nydailynews.com/news/politics/evan-bayh-joe-biden-tim-kaine-short-list-run-barack-obama-article-1.314302.

Bendavid, Naftali, and Monica Davey. 2000. "Gore's list of potential running mates narrows." *Seattle Times*, August 4. Accessed February 23, 2015. http://community.seattletimes.nwsource.com/archive/?date=20000804&slug=4035135.

Berry, Michael J., and Kenneth N. Bickers. 2012. "Forecasting the 2012 presidential election with state-level economic indicators." *PS: Political Science and Politics* 45(4): 669–674.

Black, Earl and Merle Black. 1973. "The Wallace vote in Alabama: A multiple regression analysis." *The Journal of Politics* 35(3): 730–736.

Borneman, Walter R. 2009. *Polk: The Man Who Transformed the Presidency and America*. New York: Random House.

Bourne, Peter G. 1997. *Jimmy Carter: A Comprehensive Biography from Plains to Post-Presidency*. New York: Scribner.

Bowler, Shaun, Todd Donovan, and Joseph Snipp. 1993. "Local sources of information and voter choice in state elections: Microlevel foundations of the 'friends and neighbors' effect." *American Politics Research* 21(4): 473–489.

Brambor, Thomas, William Roberts Clark, and Matt Golder. 2006. "Understanding interaction models: Improving empirical analyses." *Political Analysis* 14(1): 63–82.

Braumoeller, Bear F. 2004. "Hypothesis testing and multiplicative interaction terms." *International Organization* 58(4): 807–20.

Brodsky, Alyn. 2000. *Grover Cleveland: A Study in Character*. New York: St. Martin's Press.

Brogan, Dennis William. 1954. *Politics in America*. New York: Harper.

Bryan, Frank. 1981. *Politics in Rural States: People, Parties, and Processes*. Boulder: Westview.

Burmila, Edward M., and Josh M. Ryan. 2013. "Reconsidering the 'Palin effect' in the 2008 US presidential election." *Political Research Quarterly* 66(4): 952–959.

Burns, James MacGregor. 1970. *Roosevelt: The Soldier of Freedom*. New York: Harcourt Brace Jovanovich.

Bush, George W. 2010. *Decision Points*. New York: Crown.

Calabresi, Massimo. 2008. "Playing the Veepstakes." *Time*, n.d. Accessed July 15, 2014. www.time.com/time/specials/2007/article/0,28804,1813163_1813157_1813124,00.html.

Campbell, Angus, Philip E. Converse, Warren E. Miller, and Donald E. Stokes. 1960. *The American Voter*. New York: John Wiley and Sons, Inc.

Campbell, James E. 1992. "Forecasting the presidential vote in the states." *American Journal of Political Science* 36(2): 386–407.

Campbell, James E., Syed Ali, and Farida Jalalzai. 2006. "Forecasting the presidential vote in the states, 1948–2004: An update, revision, and extension of a state-level presidential forecasting model." In Wayne Steger, Sean Kelly, and Mark Wrighton (eds), *Campaigns and Political Marketing*. New York: Routledge.

Caro, Robert A. 2012. *The Years of Lyndon Johnson: The Passage of Power*. New York: Alfred A. Knopf.

Chait, Jonathan. 2008. "Obama's veepstakes." *Los Angeles Times*, July 7. Accessed February 23, 2015. http://articles.latimes.com/2008/jul/07/news/OE-CHAIT7.

Chen, Edwin. 2000. "Gore in final stages of choosing running mate." *Los Angeles Times*, August 7. Accessed February 23, 2015. http://articles.latimes.com/2000/aug/07/news/mn-130.

Chernow, Ron. 2010. *Washington: A Life*. New York: The Penguin Press.

Clinton, Bill. 2004. *My Life*. New York: Alfred A. Knopf.

Cockerham, Sean. 2008. "Obama targets Alaska as battleground state, aide says." *Anchorage Daily News*, July 18, p. A8.

Cole, Donald B. 2004. *Martin Van Buren and the American Political System*. Fort Washington, PA: Eastern National.

Court, Whitney Lauraine. 2012. "The risks and rewards of selecting vice presidential nominees." PhD dissertation, University of Kansas. Accessed February 23, 2015. http://libprddspap.lib.ku.edu/bitstream/handle/1808/10431/Court_ku_0099D_12001_DATA_1.pdf?sequence=1&isAllowed=y.

Cuba, Lee, and David M. Hummon. 1993. "A place to call home: Identification with dwelling, community, and region." *The Sociological Quarterly* 34(1): 111–131.

Dallek, Robert. 2003. *An Unfinished Life: John F. Kennedy, 1917–1963*. Boston: Little, Brown.

DeFrank, Thomas M. 2000. "On Picking No. 2: Don't Make Waves." *New York Daily News*, July 16. Accessed July 15, 2014. www.nydailynews.com/archives/news/picking-no-2-don-waves-article-1.893271.

Devine, Christopher J., and Kyle C. Kopko. 2011. "The vice presidential home state advantage reconsidered: Analyzing the interactive effect of home state population and political experience, 1884–2008." *Presidential Studies Quarterly* 41(1): 1–17.

Devine, Christopher J., and Kyle C. Kopko. 2013. "Presidential versus vice presidential home state advantage: A comparative analysis of electoral significance, causes, and processes, 1884–2008." *Presidential Studies Quarterly* 43(4): 814–838.

DiSarro, Brian, Jillian Barber, and Tom W. Rice. 2007. "The home state effect in presidential elections: Advances in the study of localism." *Presidential Studies Quarterly* 37(3): 558–566.

Dudley, Robert L., and Ronald B. Rapoport. 1989. "Vice-presidential candidates and the home state advantage: Playing second banana at home and on the road." *American Journal of Political Science* 33(2): 537–540.

Edwards, George C. III. 2005. *Why the Electoral College is Bad for America*. New Haven: Yale University Press.

Evans, Diana. 2004. *Greasing the Wheels: Using Pork Barrel Projects to Build Majority Coalitions in Congress*. Cambridge: Cambridge University Press.

Everett, Burgess, and Anna Palmer. 2014. "Portman for (vice) president: Supporters think he's No.1 for No. 2." *Politico*, November 28. Accessed February 23, 2015. www.politico.com/story/2014/11/rob-portman-2016-vice-president-113202.html.

Fenno, Richard F., Jr. 1978. *Home Style: House Members in their Districts*. Boston: Little, Brown, and Co.

Ferejohn, John A. 1974. *Pork Barrel Politics: Rivers and Harbors Legislation, 1947–1968*. Stanford: Stanford University Press.

Fineman, Howard. 2007. "Inside the Hillary Veepstakes." *Newsweek*, October 3. Accessed July 15, 2014. www.newsweek.com/fineman-inside-hillary-veepstakes-102851.

Fiorina, Morris P. 1981. *Retrospective Voting in American National Elections*. New Haven: Yale University Press.

Fournier, Ron. 2004. "AP poll: Bush gains slight lead over Kerry – Bush 49 Kerry 45." Associated Press, July 8. Accessed February 23, 2015. www.freerepublic.com/focus/news/1167776/posts.

Frank, Thomas. 2004. *What's the Matter with Kansas? How Conservatives Won the Heart of America*. New York: Henry Holt & Company.

Frankovic, Kathleen A. 1985. "The 1984 election: The irrelevance of the campaign." *PS: Political Science & Politics* 18(1): 39–47.

Gallup, George. 1960. "Highest 'enthusiasm quotient' rating goes to Lodge; Nixon, Kennedy about equal on scale." *The Morning Herald* (Hagerstown, MD), August 19: 21.

Garand, James C. 1988. "Localism and regionalism in presidential elections: Is there a home state or regional advantage?" *The Western Political Quarterly* 41(1): 85–103.

Gelman, Andrew, Boris Shor, Joseph Bafumi, and David Park. 2007. "Rich state, poor state, red state, blue state: What's the matter with Connecticut?" *Quarterly Journal of Political Science* 2(4): 345–367.

Gillon, Steven M. 1992. *The Democrats' Dilemma: Walter F. Mondale and the Liberal Legacy*. New York: Columbia University Press.

Gimpel, James G., Kimberly A. Karnes, John McTague, and Shanna Pearson-Merkowitz. 2008. "Distance-decay in the political geography of friends-and-neighbors voting." *Political Geography* 27(2): 231–252.

Goldstein, Joel K. 1982. *The Modern American Vice Presidency: The Transformation of a Political Institution*. Princeton, NJ: Princeton University Press.

Gould, Lewis. 2003. *Grand Old Party: A History of the Republicans*. New York: Random House.

Gourevitch, Philip. 2008. "Palin on Obama." *New Yorker*, September 8: 20–21.

Green, Donald P., Bradley Palmquist, and Eric Schickler. 2002. *Partisan Hearts and Minds: Political Parties and the Social Identities of Voters*. New Haven: Yale University Press.

Greene, Steven. 2004. "Social identity theory and party identification." *Social Science Quarterly* 85(1): 136–153.

Grofman, Bernard, and Reuben Kline. 2010. "Evaluating the impact of vice presidential selection on voter choice." *Presidential Studies Quarterly* 40(2): 303–309.

Heersink, Boris, and Brenton D. Peterson. 2014. "Strategic choices in election campaigns: Measuring the vice-presidential home state advantage with synthetic controls." Working paper. Available from Social Science Research Network. Accessed February 23, 2015. http://ssrn.com/abstract=2464979.

Hiller, Mark, and Douglas Kriner. 2008. "Institutional change and the dynamics of vice presidential selection." *Presidential Studies Quarterly* 38(3): 401–421.

Holbrook, Thomas M. 1991. "Presidential elections in space and time." *American Journal of Political Science* 35(1): 91–109.

Holland, Keating. 2004. "Who Will John Kerry Pick as His Running Mate?" CNN, n.d. Accessed July 15, 2014. www.cnn.com/ELECTION/2004/veepstakes/misc/story1.html.

Holt, Michael F. 1999. *The Rise and Fall of the American Whig Party: Jacksonian Politics and the Onset of the Civil War*. New York: Oxford University Press.

Hoogenboom, Ari. 1995. *Rutherford B. Hayes: Warrior & President*. Lawrence, KS: Kansas University Press.

Huber, Peter J. 1967. "The behavior of maximum likelihood estimates under nonstandard conditions." In *Proceedings of the Fifth Berkeley Symposium on Mathematical Statistics and Probability*. Berkeley, CA: University of California Press: 221–233.

Isenberg, Nancy. 2007. *Aaron Burr: Fallen Founder*. New York: Penguin Books.

Jerôme, Bruno, and Véronique Jerôme-Speziari. 2012. "Forecasting the 2012 US presidential election: Lessons from a state-by-state political economy model." *PS: Political Science and Politics* 45(4): 663–668.

Jerôme, Bruno, and Véronique Jerôme-Speziari. 2013. "Why the state-by-state political economy model did it right." *PS: Political Science & Politics* 46(1): 45–46.

Johnston, R.J. 1974. "Local effects in voting at local election." *Annals of the Association of American Geographers* 64(3): 418–429.

Kahane, Leo H. 2009. "It's the economy, and then some: Modeling the presidential vote with state panel data." *Public Choice* 139 (3–4): 343–356.

Kenny, Christopher, and Michael McBurnett. 1997. "Up close and personal: Campaign contact and candidate spending in US House Elections." *Political Research Quarterly* 50(1): 75–96.

Kenski, Kate, Bruce W. Hardy, and Kathleen Hall Jamieson. 2010. *The Obama Victory: How Media, Money, and Message Shaped the 2008 Election*. Oxford: Oxford University Press.

Ketcham, Ralph. 2000. *James Madison: A Biography*. Charlottesville: University Press of Virginia.

Key, V.O., Jr. 1949. *Southern Politics in State and Nation*. New York: Random House.

Key, V.O., Jr. 1956. *American State Politics: An Introduction*. New York: Alfred A. Knopf.

Kjar, Scott A., and David N. Laband. 2002. "On 'home grown-ness' in politics: Evidence from the 1998 election for Alabama's third Congressional district." *Public Choice* 112 (1–2): 143–150.

Klarner, Carl E. 2012. "State-level forecasts of the 2012 federal and gubernatorial elections." *PS: Political Science and Politics* 45(4): 655–662.

Klarner, Carl E. 2013. "2012 presidential, US House, and US Senate forecasts." *PS: Political Science and Politics* 46(1): 44–45.

Knuckey, Jonathan. 2012. "The 'Palin effect' in the 2008 US presidential election." *Political Research Quarterly* 65(2): 275–289.

Kohler, Ulrich, and Frauke Kreuter. 2005. *Data Analysis Using Stata*. College Station, TX: Stata Press.

Kopko, Kyle C. 2012. "Religious identity and political participation in the Mennonite Church USA." *Politics and Religion* 5(2): 367–393.

Kopko, Kyle C., Sarah McKinnon Bryner, Jeffrey Budziak, Christopher J. Devine, and Steven P. Nawara. 2011. "In the eye of the beholder? Motivated reasoning in disputed elections." *Political Behavior* 33(2): 271–290.

La Ganga, Maria L., and Mark Barabak. 2000. "Bush chooses his running mate; all signs point to Cheney for job." *Los Angeles Times*, July 25. Accessed February 23, 2015. http://articles.latimes.com/2000/jul/25/news/mn-58518.

Lee, Frances E. 2003. "Geographic politics in the US House of Representatives: Coalition building and distribution of benefits." *American Journal of Political Science* 47(4): 714–728.

Leech, Margaret. 1959. *In the Days of McKinley*. New York: Harper & Brothers.

Lewis-Beck, Michael S., and Tom W. Rice. 1983. "Localism in presidential elections: The home state advantage." *American Journal of Political Science* 27(3): 548–556.

Lewis-Beck, Michael S., William G. Jacoby, Helmut Norpoth, and Herbert F. Weisberg. 2008. *The American Voter Revisited*. Ann Arbor: The Michigan University Press.

Light, Paul C. 1984. *Vice Presidential Power: Advice and Influence in the White House*. Baltimore: Johns Hopkins University Press.

MacGillis, Alec. 2008. "For the Republican base, Palin pick is energizing." *Washington Post*, September 8. Accessed February 23, 2015. www.washingtonpost.com/wp-dyn/content/article/2008/09/07/AR2008090702747.html.

Malcová, Karolína. 2012. "The local aspect of electoral support for candidates to the Senate of the Czech Republic." *Czech Sociological Review* 48(2): 283–313.

Malveaux, Suzanne, Bill Schneider, Robert Yoon, Alan Silverleib, and Ed Homick. 2008. "CNN Analysis: Who'll Win the Obama Veepstakes?" CNN, July 30. Accessed July 15, 2014. www.cnn.com/2008/POLITICS/07/30/dem.veepstakes.

Martin, John Bartlow. 1977. *Adlai Stevenson of Illinois*. Garden City: Doubleday.

McCullough, David. 1992. *Truman*. New York: Simon & Schuster.

McCullough, David. 2001. *John Adams*. New York: Simon & Schuster.

Milkis, Sidney M., and Michael Nelson. 2011. *The American Presidency: Origins & Development, 1776–2011*, 6th edition. Washington, DC: CQ Press.

Mitchell, Alison. 2000. "The 2000 campaign: The running mate; Bush is reported set to name Cheney as partner on ticket." *New York Times*, July 25. Accessed February 23, 2015. www.nytimes.com/2000/07/25/us/2000-campaign-running-mate-bush-reported-set-name-cheney-partner-ticket.html.

Mixon, Franklin G., Jr. 2013. "Warm Springs ran deep: Friends-and-neighbors voting in the US presidential elections of 1940 and 1944." *Journal of Politics and Law* 6(2): 105–115.

Mixon, Franklin G., Jr., and Matthew Tyrone. 2004. "The 'home grown' presidency: Empirical evidence on localism in presidential voting, 1972–2000." *Applied Economics* 36(16): 1745–1749.

Moulton, Brent R. 1990. "An illustration of a pitfall in estimating the effects of aggregate variables in micro units." *Review of Economics and Statistics* 72(2): 334–338.

Nagourney, Adam. 2004. "Kerry camp sees Edwards helping with rural vote." *New York Times*, July 9. Accessed February 23, 2015. www.nytimes.com/2004/07/09/politics/campaign/09battle.html.

Nagourney, Adam, and Zeleny, Jeff. 2008. "Potential running mates. Election Guide 2008." *New York Times*. Accessed July 15, 2015. http://politics.nytimes.com/election-guide/2008/candidates/vp/index.html.

Neal, Steve. 1984. "And now, the race for second place." *Chicago Tribune*, June 10. Accessed February 23, 2015. http://archives.chicagotribune.com/1984/06/10/page/73/article/and-now-the-race-for-second-place.

Nixon, Richard. 1978. *RN: The Memoirs of Richard Nixon*. New York: Grosset & Dunlap.

Paasi, Anssi. 1986. "The institutionalization of regions: A theoretical framework for the understanding of the emergence of regions and the constitutions of regional identity." *Fennia* 164(1): 105–146.

Paasi, Anssi. 2003. "Region and place: Regional identity in question." *Progress in Human Geography* 27(4): 475–485.

Paasi, Anssi. 2009. "The resurgence of the 'region' and 'regional identity': Theoretical perspectives and empirical observations on regional dynamics in Europe." *Review of International Studies* 35 (Supplement S1): 121–146.

Pika, Joseph A., and John Anthony Maltese. 2013. *The Politics of the Presidency*, 8th edition. Los Angeles: Sage.

Potter, Philip. 1964. "How LBJ got the nomination." *Reporter*, June 18.

Powell, Richard J. 2004. "The strategic importance of state-level factors in presidential elections." *Publius* 34(3): 115–130.

Primo, David M., Matthew L. Jacobsmeier, and Jeffrey Milyo. 2007. "Estimating the impact of state policies and institutions with mixed-level data." *State Politics and Policy Quarterly* 7(4): 446–549.

Quinn, Steve. 2008. "Obama camp quiet since Palin picked." *Anchorage Daily News*, September 24: A3.

Reeves, Thomas C. 1975. *Gentleman Boss: The Life of Chester Alan Arthur*. New York: Alfred A. Knopf.

Remler, Dahlia K., and Gregg G. Van Ryzin. 2015. *Research Methods in Practice: Strategies for Description and Causation*, 2nd edition. Thousand Oaks, CA: Sage Publications, Inc.

Rice, Tom W., and Alisa Macht. 1987a. "Friends and neighbors voting in statewide general elections." *American Journal of Political Science* 31(2): 448–452.

Rice, Tom W., and Alisa Macht. 1987b. "The hometown advantage: Mobilization or conversion?" *Political Behavior* 9(3): 257–262.

Richards, David. 2012. *Once Upon a Time in Texas: A Liberal in the Lone Star State.* Austin, TX: University of Texas Press.

Rogers, William. 1993. "sg17: Regression standard errors in clustered samples." *Stata Technical Bulletin* 13: 19–23.

Romero, David W. 2001. "Requiem for a lightweight: Vice presidential candidate evaluations and the presidential vote." *Presidential Studies Quarterly* 31(3): 454–463.

Rosenstone, Steven J. 1983. *Forecasting Presidential Elections.* New Haven, CT: Yale University Press.

Rove, Karl. 2012. "I was wrong about Dick Cheney … and other lessons I learned from vetting vice-presidential candidates." *Wall Street Journal*, April 25. Accessed February 23, 2015. www.wsj.com/articles/SB10001424052702304811304577365870484193362.

Rudin Ken. 2004. "Who Will Be Kerry's VP?" National Public Radio, n.d. Accessed July 15, 2014. www.npr.org/politics/vp/.

Rudin, Ken. 2008. "Who's up, who's down in the veepstakes." National Public Radio, August 19. Accessed February 23, 2015. www.npr.org/news/graphics/2008/july/veepstakes/veepstakes.html.

Schreiber, Ronnee. 2008. "Commentary: Don't underestimate Palin's appeal to women." CNN.com, September 9. Accessed February 23, 2015. www.cnn.com/2008/POLITICS/09/09/schreiber.palin/index.html?iref=24hours.

Seelye, Katharine Q. 2008. "Palin and the women's vote." *New York Times*, August 29. Accessed February 23, 2015. http://thecaucus.blogs.nytimes.com/2008/08/29/palin-and-the-womens-vote/.

Serra, George, and David Moon. 1994. "Casework, issue positions, and voting in Congressional elections: A district analysis." *The Journal of Politics* 56(1): 200–213.

Shapiro, Ian, Peter A. Swenson, and Daniela Donno (eds). 2008. *Divide and Deal: The Politics of Distribution in Democracies.* New York: New York University Press.

Shepsle, Kenneth A., and Barry R. Weingast. 1981. "Political preferences for the pork barrel: A generalization." *American Journal of Political Science* 25(1): 96–111.

Shesol, Jeff. 1997. *Mutual Contempt: Lyndon Johnson, Robert Kennedy, and the Feud That Shaped a Decade.* New York: W. W. Norton.

Sigelman, Lee, and Emmett H. Buell, Jr. 2003. "You take the high road and I'll take the low road? The interplay of attack strategies and tactics in presidential campaigns." *Journal of Politics* 65(2): 518–531.

Sigelman, Lee, and Paul J. Wahlbeck. 1997. "The 'veepstakes': Strategic choice in presidential running mate selection." *American Political Science Review* 91(4): 855–864.

Smith, Jean Edward. 2008. *FDR.* New York: Random House.

Smith, Richard Norton. 1982. *Thomas Dewey and His Times.* New York: Simon and Schuster.

Tajfel, Henri. 1981. *Human Groups and Social Categories: Studies in Social Psychology.* Cambridge, UK: Cambridge University Press.

Tajfel, Henri, and John C. Turner. 1979. "An integrative theory of intergroup conflict." In Austin, William G., and Stephen Worchel (eds), *The Social Psychology of Intergroup Relations.* Monterey, CA: Brooks/Cole.

Tatalovich, Raymond. 1975. "'Friends and neighbors' voting: Mississippi, 1943–1973." *The Journal of Politics* 37(3): 807–814.

Thielemann, Gregory S. 1993. "Local advantage in campaign financing: Friends, neighbors, and their money in Texas Supreme Court elections." *The Journal of Politics* 55(2): 472–478.

Todd, Chuck. 2000. "Crystal Ball Veep-Gazing." *National Journal*, June 14. Accessed July 15, 2014. www3.nationaljournal.com/members/buzz/2000/trail/061400.htm.

Tubbesing, Carl D. 1973. "Vice presidential candidates and the home state advantage: Or, 'Tom who?' was Tom Eagleton in Missouri." *The Western Political Quarterly* 26(4): 702–716.

Turner, John C., Michael A. Hogg, Penelope J. Oakes, Stephen D. Reicher, and Margaret S. Wetherell. 1987. *Rediscovering the Social Group: A Social Categorization Theory*. Oxford: Blackwell.

Ulbig, Stacy G. 2010. "The appeal of second bananas: The impact of vice presidential candidates on presidential vote choice, yesterday and today." *American Politics Research* 38(2): 330–355.

Ulbig, Stacy G. 2013. *Vice Presidents, Presidential Elections, and the Media: Second Fiddles in the Spotlight*. Boulder, CO: First Forum Press.

Unger, Irwin, and Debi Unger. 1999. *LBJ: A Life*. New York: Wiley & Sons.

Van Wingen, John R., and Joseph B. Parker. 1979. "Measuring friends-and-neighbors voting." *American Politics Quarterly* 7(3): 367–383.

VandeHei, Jim, and Dan Balz. 2004. "Kerry picks Edwards as running mate." *Washington Post*, July 7. Accessed February 23, 2015. www.washingtonpost.com/wp-dyn/articles/A30354-2004Jul6.html.

Wattenberg, Martin P. 1984. "And Tyler, too." *Public Opinion* 7: 52–54.

Wattenberg, Martin P. 1995. "The role of vice-presidential candidate ratings in presidential voting behavior." *American Politics Quarterly* 23(4): 504–514.

Wattenberg, Martin P., and Bernard Grofman. 1993. "A rational choice model of the president and vice-president as a package deal." In Bernard Grofman (ed.), *Information, Participation, and Choice: An Economic Theory of Democracy in Perspective*. Ann Arbor: University of Michigan Press: 173–177.

Waugh, John C. 2001. *Reelecting Lincoln: The Battle for the 1864 Presidency*. Cambridge, MA: De Capo.

Weingast, Barry R., Kenneth A. Shepsle, and Christopher Johnsen. 1981. "The political economy of benefits and costs: A neoclassical approach to distributive politics." *The Journal of Political Economy* 89(4): 642–664.

Weisberg, Herbert F., Eric S. Heberlig, and Lisa M. Campoli. 1999. *Classics in Congressional Politics*. New York: Longman.

White, Ronald C, Jr. 2009. *A. Lincoln: A Biography*. New York: Random House.

Witcover, Jules. 1992. *Crapshoot: Rolling the Dice on the Vice Presidency: From Adams and Jefferson to Truman and Quayle*. New York: Crown.

Woodward, Bob. 1996. *The Choice*. New York: Simon & Schuster.

Woodward, Bob. 2010. *Obama's Wars*. New York: Simon & Schuster.

Woodward, Bob. 2012. *The Price of Politics*. New York: Simon & Schuster.

Yiannakis, Diana Evans. 1981. "The grateful electorate: Casework and Congressional elections." *American Journal of Political Science* 25(3): 568–580.

Index

Note: page numbers in *italic* refer to tables or figures.

'n.' after a page reference indicates the number of a note on that page.